WITHDRAWN

NABOKOV

NABOKOV

The Mystery of Literary Structures

LEONA TOKER

Cornell University Press

Ithaca and London

First published 1989 by Cornell University Press.

International Standard Book Number 0-8014-2211-6
Library of Congress Catalog Card Number 88-47927
Printed in the United States of America
*Librarians: Library of Congress cataloging information
appears on the last page of the book.*

The paper in this book is acid-free and meets the guidelines for permanence and durability of the Committee on Production Guidelines for Book Longevity of the Council on Library Resources.

To my parents,
Nedda and Aba Strazhas

The eye was placed where one ray should fall,
that it might testify of that particular ray.

Ralph Waldo Emerson, "Self-Reliance"

Contents

Preface

Several years ago, while reading, without interruption, all the books on "the Nabokov shelf," I ceased to deplore the penalties one pays for having turned one's love of literature into a profession. A return to the same shelf became, time and again, an effective antidote for sundry vexations of the spirit. The magic lay in the earnestly playful eschatology that transpires through these books, as well as in the limpid sense of freedom that suffuses their style, a sense not divorced from an awareness of whatever threatens to curb freedom of action, sensation, and thought.

Because the "aesthetic bliss" of a literary critic seldom remains unpragmatic for long, I am fortunate that it is within my professional purview to discharge the debt I owe to Nabokov—although, paradoxically, the relatively sober study that follows does not entirely reflect what charmed me in Nabokov's style. The approach I have taken here is, largely, a response to an imbalance in the critical literature devoted to Nabokov. Much of this literature either discusses his breathtakingly subtle techniques or explores his humanistic themes (the latter a rather recent reaction to the previously unjust treatment of Nabokov as a cold virtuoso). In the best studies of technique, the humanism of Nabokov's content is taken for granted; in the best studies of his thematic content, the technical refinements are tacitly assumed. Only a few, most of them of limited scope, deal with the combination of formal refinement and poignant humanism in Nabokov's fiction. Precisely how this combination works is the subject of my inquiry.

I first treat Nabokov's *Pnin*, a novel that provides useful insights into the tendencies manifest throughout his fiction. Then, in chronological order, I discuss nine of his other novels, starting with his first, *Mary* (1926), through *King, Queen, Knave* (1928), *The Defense* (1930), *Glory* (1932), *Laughter in the Dark* (1933/1938), *Invitation to a Beheading* (completed 1935, published 1938), *The Gift* (first serialized in 1937–38), and *Bend Sinister* (1947), ending with *Lolita* (1955), part of which he wrote during roughly the same period as *Pnin*. The quasi-circular structure of my book is not merely a reflection of Nabokov's preference for quasi-circular forms. It is meant to suggest that the relationship between the features of his various works is a matter of evolvement rather than of development: each novel explores a potentiality that has always been present in the moral/aesthetic phenomenon called Vladimir Nabokov. Such a retrospective look at his literary career is, of course, related to the Schopenhauerian view of character that he seems to have held.

I analyze Nabokov's early works in their revised English versions, taking into account the significance of the changes that occurred during their linguistic transubstantiation. The ten novels chosen display variations on those formal issues (perspective, recurrent motifs, self-referentiality) to which I wished to limit the scope of the structuralist aspect of my analysis. In other words, these are the novels to which my somewhat eclectic model approximation is most conveniently applicable. The selection does not imply value judgments.

The relative space given to the theme and the structure of each of the ten has, to a large extent, been determined by the state of Nabokov criticism. For example, I devote much more space to the structure than to the main theme of *Invitation to a Beheading* because my basic interpretive approach to this novel is similar to that of several earlier studies. I give more attention to thematic analysis when a formerly neglected aspect of the novel's theme has to be brought into relief or when my reading is at variance with most existing interpretations. The book is deliberately nonpolemical, however, despite a few sore temptations. I refer to the critical literature either to acknowledge my indebtedness or to explain why I do not discuss certain issues.

Portions of this book have appeared elsewhere in earlier versions, and I thank the publishers for permission to use the following material. Chapter 2 is based on my article "*Pnin*: A Story of Creative Imagination," *Delta* (the Paul Valéry University of Montpellier, France), 17 (October 1983), 61–74. Chapter 3 is a revision of "Ganin in *Mary*land: A Retrospect on Nabokov's First Novel," published in *Canadian-*

American Slavic Studies, 19 (1985), 306–13. Chapter 6, "Nabokov's *Glory* 'Good Example of How Metaphysics Can Fool You,'" appeared in *Russian Literature*, 21 (1987), 293–312. Part of Chapter 8 is reproduced from "Ambiguity in Vladimir Nabokov's *Invitation to a Beheading*" in Hans Braendlin, ed., *Ambiguities in Literature and Film: Selected Papers from the Seventh Florida State University Conference on Literature and Film*, with the permission of the publisher, The Florida State University Press, Tallahassee.

I am grateful to the U.S.–Israel Educational Foundation for a research grant that financed a three-month stay in the United States in 1984 and to the 1985 School of Criticism and Theory (held at Northwestern University) for a fellowship that allowed me to broaden my critical perspective.

A number of people have read chapters of the manuscript, and I thank them for their suggestions and constructive criticism. In particular, I thank Mrs. Vera Nabokov (for comments on the essay that eventually became Chapter 2), Helena Goscilo of the University of Pittsburgh, Gerald Bruns of the University of Notre Dame, and my Hebrew University Colleagues Shuli Barzilai, Lawrence Besserman, Baruch Hochman, Shlomith Rimmon-Kenan, and H. M. Daleski. Discussions with Professor Daleski have been of major importance to me from the start and have had an effect both on my critical strategies and on the texture of the book.

The help of my research assistants, Ilana Rosberger and Barbara Hall, considerably speeded up my work. I am grateful to Patricia Sterling, copy editor for Cornell University Press, for her careful critical attention to the manuscript.

Special thanks to my husband, Gregory Toker, for (among other things) smoothing my way into the wonderful world of word processors.

LEONA TOKER

Jerusalem

Abbreviations

The following abbreviations are used for the editions of Nabokov's works cited in this book.

A   *Ada, or Ardor: A Family Chronicle* (New York: McGraw-Hill, 1981).

BS   *Bend Sinister* (New York: McGraw-Hill, 1974).

D   *The Defense*, trans. Michael Scammell in collaboration with the author (New York: G. P. Putnam's Sons, 1980).

Dar   *Dar* (Ann Arbor, Mich.: Ardis, 1975).

DS   *Details of a Sunset and Other Stories* (New York: McGraw-Hill, 1981).

Dp   *Despair* (New York: G. P. Putnam's Sons, 1979).

E   *The Eye*, trans. Dmitri Nabokov in collaboration with the author (New York: Phaedra, 1965).

En   *The Enchanter*, trans. Dmitri Nabokov (New York: G. P. Putnam's Sons, 1986).

EO   *Eugene Onegin: A Novel in Verse* by Aleksandr Pushkin, Translated from the Russian, with a Commentary by Vladimir Nabokov (Princeton: Princeton University Press, 1981).

G   *The Gift*, trans. Michael Scammell with the collaboration of the author (New York: G. P. Putnam's Sons, 1979).

Gl   *Glory*, trans. Dmitri Nabokov in collaboration with the author (New York: McGraw-Hill, 1981).

IB   *Invitation to a Beheading*, trans. Dmitri Nabokov in collaboration with the author (New York: G. P. Putnam's Sons, 1979).

KQK *King, Queen, Knave*, trans. Dmitri Nabokov in collaboration with the author (New York: McGraw-Hill, 1981).

Kdv *Korol', dama, valet* (Ann Arbor, Mich.: Ardis, 1979).

L   *The Annotated Lolita*, ed. Alfred Appel (New York: McGraw-Hill, 1970).

LATH *Look at the Harlequins!* (New York: McGraw-Hill, 1981).

LD   *Laughter in the Dark* (London: Weidenfeld & Nicolson, 1961).

LDQ   *Lectures on Don Quixote* (New York: Harcourt Brace Jovanovich, 1983).

LL   *Lectures on Literature* (New York: Harcourt Brace Jovanovich 1980).

LRL   *Lectures on Russian Literature* (New York: Harcourt Brace Jovanovich, 1981).

LS   *Lolita: A Screenplay* (New York: McGraw-Hill, 1983).

M   *Mary*, trans. Michael Glenny in collaboration with the author (New York: McGraw-Hill, 1981).

Ma   *Mashen'ka* (Ann Arbor, Mich.: Ardis; New York: McGraw-Hill, 1974).

MUSSR   *The Man from the USSR and Other Plays*, trans. Dmitri Nabokov (New York: Harcourt Brace Jovanovich, 1984)

ND   *Nabokov's Dozen: Thirteen Stories* (London: Heinemann, 1959).

NG   *Nikolai Gogol* (New York: New Directions, 1961).

P   *Pnin* (London: Heinemann, 1957).

Pd   *Podvig* (Ann Arbor, Mich.: Ardis; New York: McGraw-Hill, 1974).

PF   *Pale Fire* (London: Weidenfeld & Nicolson, 1962).

PP   *Poems and Problems* (New York: McGraw-Hill, 1981).

Pr   *Priglashenie na kazn'* (Ann Arbor, Mich.: Ardis, 1979).

PS   *Perepiska s sestroi* (Correspondence with the sister) (Ann Arbor, Mich.: Ardis 1985).

RB   *A Russian Beauty and Other Stories* (New York: McGraw-Hill, 1974).

RLSK   *The Real Life of Sebastian Knight* (New York: New Directions, 1977).

S   *Stikhi* (Ann Arbor, Mich.: Ardis, 1979).

SM   *Speak, Memory: An Autobiography Revisited* (New York: G. P. Putnam's Sons, 1966).

SO   *Strong Opinions* (New York: McGraw-Hill, 1981).

TD   *Tyrants Destroyed and Other Stories* (New York: McGraw-Hill, 1981).

TT   *Transparent Things* (New York: McGraw-Hill, 1981).

ZL   *Zashchita Luzhina* (Ann Arbor, Mich.: Ardis, 1979).

NABOKOV

I

Introduction

Another thing we are not supposed to do is to explain the
inexplicable.

Vladimir Nabokov, *Transparent Things*

I

Vladimir Nabokov belongs among those writers who are continually exposed to distrust during their lives, whose first steps encounter inauspicious predictions, who must struggle against the
prejudices of the audience yet have admirers as ardent as the general
public is unjust. When such writers die, there often follows a reversal:
their works almost instantly become part of the classical canon.

The recognition of V. Sirin (Nabokov's prewar pseudonym) by the
Russian émigré readers of the twenties and thirties was slow and frequently reluctant. In the forties, having moved to the United States
and adopted English as the language of his prose (and partly of his
poetry), he found himself in relative obscurity once again. With the
publication of *Lolita* in 1955, Nabokov became one of the rich and
famous and then had to spend a considerable amount of energy fighting such side effects of glory as irresponsible misrepresentations of
both his art and his life. The sexual thematics of *Lolita*, combined with
its best-seller/cover-story popularity, placed him in a sort of literary
demimonde, among the beautiful and damned. To this day some readers
are surprised to learn about the serenely old-fashioned happiness of his
monogamous private life.

The need to vindicate Nabokov, however, no longer exists. The
quantity of literature about him published in recent years testifies to

the growing recognition of his stature.[1] An increasing number of scholars believe that he is our century's foremost writer of fiction, that his works demand and reward multiple readings, and that his art is an aesthetic puzzle requiring a great deal of solving. His novels, with their countless discoveries on the way toward constantly receding bottom lines, with their moments of mirth and those other moments—of what can only be called "aesthetic bliss" (*L*, 316)—give one the feeling of basking in an intelligence vastly superior to one's own. Yet the appeal of these novels is not purely cerebral: they also contain a deeply touching human reality—not a demonstrative human interest but a "personal truth" (*ND*, 14) protected from wear and tear by layers of exquisite wrapping made up of lexical and acoustic games ("contextual shades of color" and "nuances of noise": *LATH*, 118), complex allusions, triplefold reticences and circumlocutions, defamiliarizing reversals, and subtly subversive wit.

Because at least part of this wrapping must be lifted before one can approach the real thing, some of the most valuable Nabokov criticism includes a strong element of extended annotation. The work of Donald Barton Johnson, for instance, reveals astonishing subtleties of the texture and structure of Nabokov's narrative and then cautiously ("handle with care") relates them to themes; Dabney Stuart shows the connection between the texture and the generic features of the novels; and Brian Boyd demonstrates the links of narrative details to the central features of both the novel in which they appear and of Nabokov's work in general.[2] Much of the earlier criticism annotated just for the fun of the game; it was often uneasy about this self-indulgence and presented Nabokov as a cold virtuoso aesthetician whose artistic feats would, or would not, allow a grudging forgiveness of what seemed to be his doubtful ethos. Page Stegner's *Escape into Aesthetics*[3] is destined to be considered a prime example of this trend, even though its bias is largely redeemed by its numerous insights.

[1]The range has been sketched in Stephen Jan Parker, "Nabokov Studies: The State of the Art," in George Gibian and Stephen Jan Parker, eds., *The Achievements of Vladimir Nabokov* (Ithaca, 1984), pp. 81–97.

[2]See esp. Donald B. Johnson, *Worlds in Regression: Some Novels of Vladimir Nabokov* (Ann Arbor, Mich., 1985), and "Nabokov as a Man-of-Letters: The Alphabetic Motif in His Work," *Modern Fiction Studies*, 25 (1979–80), 397–412; Dabney Stuart, *Nabokov: The Dimensions of Parody* (Baton Rouge: 1978); and Brian Boyd, *Nabokov's "Ada": The Place of Consciousness* (Ann Arbor, Mich., 1985), which focuses on one novel yet contains valuable commentary on Nabokov's fiction in general.

[3]Page Stegner, *Escape into Aesthetics: The Art of Vladimir Nabokov* (New York, 1966).

Nabokov remained undaunted. "I believe that one day a reappraiser will come," he remarked in a 1971 interview, "and declare that, far from having been a frivolous firebird, I was a rigid moralist kicking sin, cuffing stupidity, ridiculing the vulgar and cruel—and assigning sovereign power to tenderness, talent, and pride" (*SO*, 193). That day dawned earlier than Nabokov had expected. It was already heralded by the work of Andrew Field[4] and Alfred Appel,[5] whose analysis of Nabokov's themes and intricate texture proceeded from the assumption that the author's heart was, so to say, always in the right place; however, their personal ties to Nabokov partly discredited their positions in the eyes of the their (somewhat envious) colleagues. Of greater persuasiveness, therefore, were the articles of, for instance, Robert Alter and Stanley Edgar Hyman,[6] who revealed the seriousness of Nabokov's moral and political concerns in *Invitation to a Beheading* and *Bend Sinister*; and the books of Donald Morton, Julian Moynahan, and Ellen Pifer,[7] who emphasized the humanistic, ideological contents of Nabokov's fiction. Pifer's book, in particular, successfully accomplishes its avowed aim of redressing the injustice that Nabokov's literary reputation suffered as a result of criticism's earlier preoccupation with the form of his novels at the expense of their content.

The purpose of this book is not only to reinforce the camp of the readers who believe in the humanistic value of Nabokov's work but also to reconcile the two camps by demonstrating the close connection between its moral attitudes and virtuoso techniques, the mutual adjustment of the major thematic concerns and the structure of his novels.

Nabokov characterized his college lectures on literature as, among other things, "a kind of detective investigation of the mystery of literary structures" (*LL*, epigraph). The word "mystery" here is polysemous. Each great work has a structure of its own, to be investigated

[4]Andrew Field, *Nabokov: His Life in Art* (Boston, 1967); unfortunately, the attitude apparent in Field's subsequent books is rather disappointing.

[5]See, esp. Alfred Appel, Jr., "Nabokov's Puppet Show," in Jerome Charyn, ed., *The Single Voice* (London, 1969), pp. 87–93, as well as Appel's preface, introduction, and notes in *The Annotated Lolita* (*L*).

[6]Robert Alter, "*Invitation to a Beheading*: Nabokov and the Art of Politics," in Alfred Appel, Jr., and Charles Newman, eds., *Nabokov: Criticism, Reminiscences, Translations, and Tributes* (London, 1971), pp. 41–59; Stanley Edgar Hyman, "The Handle: *Invitation to a Beheading* and *Bend Sinister*," in Appel and Newman, *Nabokov*, pp. 60–71.

[7]Donald Morton, *Vladimir Nabokov* (New York, 1974); Julian Moynahan, *Vladimir Nabokov* (Minneapolis, Minn., 1971); Ellen Pifer, *Nabokov and the Novel* (Cambridge, Mass., 1980).

by a minute Sherlock-Holmesian attention to detail until its mystery—that is, its specific relation to specific dreams, desires, and limitations of human life—begins to emerge. Yet the mystery of a literary structure can be approximated rather than solved. It lies in the quaint appropriateness of the structure to an attitude; the "aesthetic bliss" produced by this harmony retains mysteriousness even after the approaches to it have been mapped. An attempt to unravel the *enigmas* of Nabokov's structure ultimately confronts one with a *Mystery*: "a fictional technique," if Jean-Paul Sartre is to be believed, "always relates back to the novelist's metaphysics."[8]

But what was Nabokov's metaphysics? "Total rejection of all religions ever dreamt up by man and total composure in the face of total death," writes a dying fictional writer in *Transparent Things*. "If I could explain this triple totality in one big book, that book would become no doubt a new bible and its author the founder of a new creed. Fortunately for my self-esteem that book will not be written . . . because [it] would never express in one flash what can only be understood *immediately*" (*TT*, 84). The uncertainty of the latter idea is, of course, matched by the uncertainty with which the character's position can be ascribed to the author. Nabokov's own voice is more mild and modest: "I know more than I can express in words, and the little I can express would not have been expressed, had I not known more" (*SO*, 45). Elusive as this statement may be, it leaves no doubt of the tinge of mysticism in Nabokov's view of the world. His mysticism was a matter of feeling, of relationship with the world, rather than of definable hypostasis: Nabokov "knew" what he could not express the way one "knows" love, or hope, or suffering. Only a few aspects of his world view can be formulated as beliefs.

II

Nabokov seems to have "liked" these beliefs rather than to have really "held" them: in his life he would have had the courage to face their crumbling, yet in his fiction he was free to create a universe controlled by the cosmogony of his choice. His favorite brand of mysticism seems to have been the gnostical belief in a transcendent reality that can occasionally be glimpsed through the chinks in our material

---

[8]Jean-Paul Sartre, *Literary and Philosophical Essays*, trans. Annette Michelson (New York, 1962), p. 84.

existence and which is fully attained at death.[9] Among the precious times when one feels contact with what he would call the "Beyond" are not only mystical moments (the peak experience of the protagonists of *Invitation to a Beheading* and *The Gift*) but also moments of genuine emotion, of madness, and of a disinterested aesthetic contemplation that silences suffering and desire. The value attached to these moments of "aesthetic bliss" is an overlap between Nabokov's views and the philosophy of Arthur Schopenhauer, who is respectfully mentioned in chapter 4 of *The Gift*: under Schopenhauer's "critical fingernail" the pragmatic Chernyshevski's "saltatory thinking would not have survived for a second" (*G*, 258).

I single out Schopenhauer from all the philosophers referred to in *The Gift* because he is somewhat erroneously considered to have preached that "escape into aesthetics" of which Nabokov was often accused. The egoistic connotation of the slogan is largely a misreading of both Schopenhauer's and Nabokov's hostility to the pragmatic view of art. Schopenhauer did not really advocate an artist's selfish retreat to an ivory tower; in his system, it is for the audience rather than for the artist that the beautiful provides a temporary haven. Aesthetic experience is not sensuous gratification; it does not *satisfy* desires but *silences* them and thereby suspends the ominous will that they manifest. The pleasure derived from the beautiful is "the momentary silencing of all willing, which comes about whenever as pure will-less subject of knowing, the correlative of the Idea, we are devoted to aesthetic contemplation."[10] These are the moments when the individual gains freedom from the bondage of will; they are steps toward the self-suppression through which he or she breaks away from the grim chain of apparent causality and gains knowledge at the expense of the fulfillment of desires (another way to the same goal is the *via negativa* of ascetic self-discipline). The ultimate goal that Schopenhauer sets for mankind is the achievement of a state in which the cosmic will comes to know itself and is completely abolished—the state that man imagines as complete nothingness, the opposite of Being. Yet according to Schopenhauer, the negation of the world is not what we imagine as void or darkness. It is a vantage point for an opposite vision: "To those

[9]Imprints of gnostic beliefs in Nabokov's work are discussed in detail in Julian Moynahan, "A Russian Preface for Nabokov's *Beheading*," *Novel*, 1 (1967), 12–18; and Sergei Davydov, *Teksty-Matreshki Vladimira Nabokova* (Munich, 1982), pp. 100–82.

[10]Arthur Schopenhauer, *The World as Will and Representation*, trans. E. F. J. Payne (New York, 1969), 1:363.

in whom the will has turned and denied itself, this very real world of ours with all its suns and galaxies, is—nothing."[11]

This coda of *The World as Will and Representation* can be read as a commentary on the ending of Nabokov's *Invitation to a Beheading*, in which the world of the "converted" protagonist is destroyed in the brief course of what looks like a filming-site disaster (all the world is a filming site). However, though *unichtozhenie* (the Russian for "destruction") is dramatized in the last paragraph of *Invitation*, the word itself is avoided; Nabokov would not have failed to hear in it the ominous ghost word *nichto*, the Russian for Schopenhauer's "nothing." The Russian title of Nabokov's story "Tyrants Destroyed" is "Istrebleniye tiranov," or "tyrants exterminated"—*nichto* is eschewed again (though the choice of *istrebleniye* may have been determined by the roughly trochaic pattern that it creates in combination with *tiranov*).

Despite Schopenhauer's paradoxical optimism about the positive nature of ultimate nothingness, Nabokov was reluctant to imagine his "Beyond" as "nothing." The execution of a young man in his early poem "Rasstrel" (1928) is followed by "merciless darkness" (*neumolimaya t'ma: S*, 209), but this poem is kept out (as unsafe?) from the later collection *Poems and Problems*. The protagonist of his last novel wonders whether "the brook and the boughs and the beauty of the Beyond all [begin] with the initial of Being" (*LATH*, 16). The Mystery is sometimes imagined in the metaphorical shape of a "formula" that connects the Being and the Beyond. In Nabokov's story "Ultima Thule," the mad mathematician Falter, whose name is German for "butterfly," an emblem of the soul (Psyche, the "myth behind the moth": *A*, 437), claims to have discovered that eschatological formula but will not impart it to others because the knowledge would lead to madness or death.[12] In Nabokov's other works the characters' quest for the "solution of the Universe" is likewise safely sabotaged by the intrusions of "reality." The transcendent reality is a sort of a coexisting "parallel world" (*LATH*, 74) to which the obsolete rule that parallel lines never meet does not apply. Let us note also that metaphor, madness, and mathematics all begin with the initial of Mystery.

Nabokov seems to imagine the contact with the Beyond not as negation but as incipient merger, a carnivalistic removal of partitions.

[11] *Ibid.*, 1:412.
[12] See the discussion of Nabokov's "Ultima Thule" theme in Johnson, *Worlds in Regression*, pp. 206–19.

The individual world loses its hermetic separateness, and the individual identity moves not toward nothingness but toward a dissolution in something infinitely greater than itself. Such moments of divestment are the essence of mystical experience, yet the loss of identity is also associated with death. It is with an elaborate defense mechanism, the stylistic equivalent of "a grain of salt," that the menace is presented in *Pnin*: "I do not know if it has ever been noted before that one of the main characteristics of life is discreteness. Unless a film of flesh envelops us, we die. Man exists only insofar as he is separated from his surroundings. The cranium is the space-traveler's helmet. Stay inside or you perish. Death is divestment, death is communion. It may be wonderful to mix with the landscape, but to do so is the end of the tender ego" (*P*, 20).

The facetious tone of this paragraph is the armor for its very serious anxiety. The last sentence suggests that Nabokov was well aware of the danger involved in the Romantic quests for the infinite and yearnings for a merger of subject and object. The passage deals not only with physical death, the "waltwhitmanesque" (*BS*, 95) semisocial "mixing" with the grasses of the landscape ("the dead are good mixers, that's quite certain, at least": *TT*, 93), but also with the loss of spiritual identity through divestment and communion. Even if death is not a total negation of consciousness but, according to the hypothesis of *Bend Sinister*, the attainment of "infinite consciousness" (*BS*, 192), of "perfect knowledge" in which a point in space and time can "identify itself with every other point" (*BS*, 175), it still involves the dissolution of "the tender ego," the loss of the individual identity no matter how "painstakingly" it has been "fashioned" (*IB*, 21).

Not all of Schopenhauer's ideas, then, were acceptable to Nabokov. Although a detailed line of demarcation is beyond the scope of this discussion, it has to be noted that Nabokov would not have sympathized, for instance, with the element of dismissiveness in Schopenhauer's attitude to the individual. I cannot, moreover, determine at what point in his life Nabokov first read *The World as Will and Representation*; therefore, I refer to Schopenhauer's major work not as Nabokov's "source" but as a text that can improve our understanding of his fiction. Nor has this text been chosen arbitrarily. Schopenhauer and Nietzsche were widely read by Russian writers of the turn of the century, and the disillusionments caused by the political events of the early twentieth century led to a Schopenhauer revival between the two world wars. Nabokov, of course, would never follow fashions; in his works one does not find such Schopenhauerian catchwords as "subject of knowing" or "will-to-live" (especially since the latter eventually came to be associated with Freud's life drive), yet he seems to have been impressed by the poetic element in Schopenhauer's writings, by his psychological insights and his extended metaphors. It is noteworthy that in *Strong Opinions*, Henri Bergson—a philosopher whose attitudes were very close to Nabokov's way of thinking—is mentioned not separately but among the poets and novelists whom Nabokov read during his stay in Germany (see *SO*, 43). A philosopher is thus denied privilege; his authority does not exceed that of an artist.

Bergson did suggest something of a formula for connecting the physical and the spiritual. His bridge between the two was memory. Nabokov seems to have enjoyed Bergson's discussion of memory as highly poetic but not necessarily as definitive. In addition, Nabokov must have appreciated the insights into the nature of the comic presented in Bergson's *Le rire*—insights put to the test by some of the techniques used in *King, Queen, Knave* and *Laughter in the Dark*.

III

Laughter. . . The mixture of humor and earnestness in Nabokov's work suggests that his cautious metaphysics was characterized by a sort of a tongue-in-cheek eschatological alertness. He loved cryptographic patterns, quaint coincidences, life's combinatorial quirks; they encouraged a half-serious, half-playful half-expectation that things might suddenly fall together into a solution of the Mystery. The more earnest aspect of this attitude accounts for the structure of his autobiographical *Speak, Memory*, which traces the development of thematic lines rather than a sequence of events.

Nabokov recollects, for instance, how in 1904 General Kuropatkin showed him tricks with matches just before being ordered to assume supreme command of the Russian army in the Far East (Russia eventually suffered a defeat in that war with Japan). During his flight from St. Petersburg after the Bolshevik coup, Nabokov's father was accosted "by an old man who looked like a gray-bearded peasant in his sheepskin coat." That was Kuropatkin in disguise; he wanted a light, a match. "I hope old Kuropatkin . . . managed to evade Soviet imprisonment," adds Nabokov, "but that is not the point. What pleases me is the evolution of the match theme: those magic ones he had shown me had been trifled with and mislaid, and his armies had also van-

ished, and everything had fallen through, like my toy trains that . . .
I had tried to run over the frozen puddles in the grounds of the Hotel
Oranien. The following of such thematic designs through one's life
should be, I think, the true purpose of autobiography" (*SM*, 27).
Revolutionary Russia likewise "trifled with and mislaid" great numbers of its liberal intellectuals—did she later miss them as badly as
Kuropatkin missed the matches? Did émigré intellectuals likewise
come to miss what they had once taken for granted? Similar designs
are followed through the life of Chernyshevski in chapter 4 of *The
Gift*, not without a touch of admiration for the witty vengefulness of
fate. Yet the train of symbolic associations never becomes explicit or
ponderous in Nabokov's texts because as soon as it stops being a mere
ghost of a thought, it may "fall through" like the toy trains.

Incidentally, Nabokov probably never found out that General Kuropatkin did escape imprisonment. After the revolution he stayed on his
estate of Sheshurino, in the province of Pskov, where he taught sec-
ondary school and eventually established an agricultural school. Unknown to Nabokov, Kuropatkin's peasant disguise thus belongs to a
"thematic design" of its own.

On the more playful side, Nabokov is sympathetic to his characters'
private creeds. The charm of Cynthia Vane in his story "The Vane
Sisters" (written in 1951) is associated with her belief that "recur-
rently, in an irregular series," anything that happened to her "after a
given person had died, would be . . . in the manner and mood of that
person. The event might be extraordinary, changing the course of
one's life; or it might be a string of minute incidents just sufficiently
clear to stand out in relief against one's usual day and then shading off
into still vaguer trivia as the aura gradually faded" (*TD*, 228).
Cynthia—according to the morose narrator, who is not Nabokov's
spokesman—is also

> on friendly terms with an eccentric librarian called Porlock who in the last
> years of his dusty life had been engaged in examining old books for
> miraculous misprints such as the substitution of "l" for the second "h"
> in the word "hither." Contrary to Cynthia, he cared nothing for the thrill
> of obscure predictions; all he sought was the freak itself, the chance that
> mimics choice, the flaw that looks like a flower; and Cynthia, a much
> more perverse amateur of misshapen or illicitly connected words, puns,
> logogriphs, and so on, had helped the poor crank to pursue a quest that
> in the light of the example she cited struck me as statistically insane.
> [*TD*, 230]

It is known that the frequency of queer phenomena that can be ascribed to chance tends to surpass the statistical probability of coincidence, but this, again, is not the point. The histrionic tune that often accompanies Nabokov's eschatological alertness is, or should be, contagious. That is why I frequently attempt to reduce my inevitable overstatement on the side of high seriousness by somewhat illicit surmises, by fictionalizing hypotheses based on incipient or residual patterns of motifs, and by a preference for explaining each pattern as a signal of meaning rather than as "a chance crease in the texture of time" (A, 34).

The thin ice through which Nabokov's toy trains fell into the puddles near the Hotel Oranien will, of course, be taken as a warning. Cynthia Vane of icicle fame went too far when it dawned on her, upon reading a quotation from Coleridge's "Kubla Khan," that " 'Alph' was a prophetic sequence of the initial letters of Anna Livia Plurabelle (another sacred river running through, or rather around, yet another fake dream), while the additional 'h' modestly stood, as a private signpost, for the word that had so hypnotized Mr. Porlock" (TD, 230). The patterns that Nabokov observes sometimes lead to dead ends symbolized by ends of sections; the patterns that he creates are usually imperfect: geometrical completeness is not allowed to conflict with verisimilitude. His restraint in the handling of patterns is probably also motivated by the same proud humility that keeps the narrator of Jorge Luis Borges's "Tlön, Uqbar, Orbis Tertius" from succumbing to the attraction of the artificial world of Tlön, the involute design that has gained dominion over the other intellects in his private dystopia: "Ten years ago any symmetry with a semblance of order—dialectical materialism, anti-Semitism, Nazism—was sufficient to entrance the minds of men. How could one do other than submit to Tlön, to the minute and vast evidence of an orderly planet? It is useless to answer that reality is also orderly. Perhaps it is, but in accordance with divine laws—I translate: inhuman laws—which we never quite grasp. Tlön is surely a labyrinth, but it is a labyrinth devised by men, a labyrinth destined to be deciphered by men".[13]

The suspicion that certain patterns are traps and fakes rather than cryptic signals from the transcendent realm is a recurrent motif of Nabokov's novels. His texts, as is well known, set many traps for the

[13]Jorge Luis Borges, "Tlön, Uqbar, Orbis Tertius," in *Labyrinths* (New York, 1964), pp. 17–18.

reader, who is thus made to reenact the experience of those characters who confuse ideals with idols, the aesthetic with the sensual, the metaphysical with the carnal. This, in general terms, is one of the ways in which Nabokov's rhetoric relates back to his metaphysics.

IV

An ethical consequence of Nabokov's tentative metaphysics is a reservation about the Romantic quest for the infinite. This quest is beautiful and ennobling so long as it does not lead to the neglect of the finite. Nabokov favors self-discipline but not the Schopenhauerian virtue of an ascetic retreat from the world. Nor does he preach the gnostical rejection of the material world; his claim to be "an indivisible monist" (*SO*, 85) denies the very belief in the existence of the purely material. The outside world demands appreciation: when a railway passenger turns the page of an absorbing book, the world darts up to him with the "bright bound" of a "playful dog" that has been "waiting for that moment" (*KQK*, 10). The least one owes it is an authentic, deliberate, actively reciprocal relationship.

In the absence of such a relationship the world is doomed. This is not a paraphrase of the dependence of an object on a subject. In Borges's Tlön, things "become effaced and lose their details when they are forgotten," yet at times "some birds, a horse, have saved the ruins of an amphitheatre."[14] For Nabokov, however, birds and horses would not suffice, because the act of perception retains its efficacy only if it is deliberate and creative. "Average reality," he says to an interviewer, "begins to rot and stink as soon as the act of individual creation ceases to animate a subjectively perceived texture" (*SO*, 118). An authentic creative act—V. Sirin's writing of a novel, Rainer Maria Rilke's dreamy waxing of chairs,[15] or Thoreau's hoeing of a bean field—is

[14]Ibid., p. 14.

[15]See Gaston Bachelard's comment on the letter in which Rilke describes himself waxing furniture: "When a poet rubs a piece of furniture—even vicariously—when he puts a little fragrant wax on his table with the woolen cloth that lends warmth to everything it touches, he creates a new object; he increases the object's human dignity; he registers this object as a member of the human household. . . . Objects that are cherished in this way really are born of an intimate light, and they attain to a higher degree of reality than indifferent objects, or those that are defined by geometric reality. For they produce a new reality of being, and they take their place not only in an order

spiritualized and redemptive. Genuine love, creative perception, authentic culture—all the things that make up what in a secular context is called spiritual life—are equivalent to such an act.

The bracing spirit of this position is reminiscent of the crisp optimism of Emerson and Thoreau, the major philosophical self-expression of the country whose citizen Nabokov became after having for long years carried the Nansen passport through dusky Germany and France. In biographical terms, a direct influence of Emerson or other American writers on Nabokov is unlikely; what he seems to have been eventually affected by is a recognition of the affinities between his own work and the writings of a few quaint persons who had at different times haunted the environs of Concord, Massachusetts. [16] Taken out of the biographical context, Nabokov's ethical principles may be considered a swerve from Emerson and Thoreau, just as his metaphysics is a swerve from Schopenhauer. [17]

With Thoreau, Nabokov shared a love of nature over and above the transcendentalist glorification of the natural world as the language of the spirit. He also shared Thoreau's sense of the importance of any individual's creative relationship to the world. If, as some believe, Nabokov devotes his novels to different aspects of artistic creativity, [18] this is because a professional artist is but the most obvious exponent of human creativity; any individual's activities and attention are, or should be, creative. Thoreau's view of the writer's vocation, as explained by Stanley Cavell, is also Nabokov's:

> Each calling—what the writer means (and what anyone means, more or less) by a "field" of action or labor—is isomorphic with every other. This is why building a house and hoeing and writing and reading. . . are allegories and measures of one another. All and only true building is

---

but in a community of order" (*The Poetics of Space*, trans. Maria Jolas [Boston, 1969], pp. 67–68).

[16]More about this in my essay "Nabokov and the Hawthorne Tradition," *Scripta Hierosolymitana*, 32 (1987), 323–49.

[17]The word "swerve" is here used in more or less the same sense as in Harold Bloom, *The Anxiety of Influence* (New York, 1973), p. 14: "A poet swerves away from his precursor, by so reading his precursor's poem as to execute a *clinamen* in relation to it. This appears as a corrective movement in his own poem, which implies that the precursor poem went accurately up to a certain point, but then should have swerved, precisely in the direction that the new poem moves."

[18]See, e. g., the treatment of the theme of art in Julia Bader, *Crystal Land: Artifice in Nabokov's English Novels* (Berkeley, Calif., 1972).

edifying. All and only edifying actions are fit for human habitation. Otherwise they do not earn life. If your action, in its field, cannot stand such measurement, it is a sign that the field is not yours. This is the writer's assurance that his writing is not a substitute for his life, but his way of prosecuting it. He writes because he is a writer. This is why we can have the sense, at once, that he is attaching absolute value to his words, and that they do not matter. What matters is that he show in the way he writes his faithfulness to the specific conditions and acts of writing as such.[19]

Nabokov was frequently accused of not responding to the problems of the age; Thoreau was notorious for his indifference to politics and to the daily deluge of media information. From "the angle of a leaden wall, into whose composition was poured a little alloy of bell metal" (his version of the ivory tower), Thoreau would hear the "confused *tintinnabulum*" of his contemporaries. He was as bored with it as with "The Daily Times"; what one should read and write are things that reveal essences and not garments: "A goose is a goose still, dress it as you will." What we call the issues of the day are but "transient and fleeting phenomena."[20]

This is not, however, a Romantic dressing of another ornithological metaphor, that of the proverbial ostrich. Nabokov's constantly changing dwellings (angles rather than nooks) had considerably more bell metal in their composition than Thoreau's leaden wall. Contrary to widespread opinion, his fiction did resonate with the times; it did explore contemporary issues. These were issues not of the outer but of the inner agenda of the culture:[21] not the surge of Nazism but its psychological grounds; not the dawn of the sexual revolution but the vulnerability of norms; not religious revivals but impatience with rationalism; not the patching of socioeconomic wounds but the survival of conscience in the postcataclysmic world.

Lest all this sound too much like the "general ideas" that Nabokov recommended abandoning for the sake of detail, let us examine another metaphor related to the Romantic cliché about art presenting essences rather than garments. Schopenhauer emphasizes this idea by

[19]Stanley Cavell, *The Senses of "Walden"* (San Francisco, 1981), pp. 61–62.
[20]Henry David Thoreau, *Walden, or Life in the Woods* (New York, 1950), pp. 274–75.
[21]For the distinction between the inner and the outer agenda of culture I am indebted to Stanley Cavell, *Pursuits of Happiness: The Hollywood Comedy of Remarriage* (Cambridge, Mass., 1981), pp. 16–17.

alluding to an early photographic device already in use by the time a late edition of his book came out: "If the whole world as representation is only the visibility of the will, then art is the elucidation of this visibility, the *camera obscura* which shows the objects more purely, and enables us to survey and comprehend them better."[22] Indeed, Daguerre's *camera obscura* recorded only objects that did not move, since in the absence of lenses it required a very long exposure to light; hence, it ignored all incidental—that is, "transient and fleeting"—phenomena and presented objects "more purely" than they appeared to the eye. Within a few years this metaphor was realized in the image of the daguerreotypist Holgrave in Hawthorne's *House of the Seven Gables*.

It also underlies the title of Nabokov's 1933 Russian novel *Kamera obscura*. In a subsequent revision this book was renamed *Laughter in the Dark*, perhaps because its pervasive modern film imagery was felt to conflict with the reference to a gadget from a museum shelf. Moreover, in his description of nature and individual emotion, Nabokov, unlike Thoreau, would attempt to arrest the fleeting moments that Daguerre's camera was powerless to capture. It was as if for him these fleeting moments, the halftones of mirages and the ghosts of motion, were in fact the "real" essence of experience.[23] "The pleasure of a drink of cold water on a hot day, the pain of a hard blow on the head, the irritation from a tight-fitting shoe, and many other human sensations . . . are similarly peculiar to every mortal," Nabokov wrote in an early article in *Rul'*, a daily paper.[24] The sensations rendered in his narratives possess such a common denominator but also, superimposed on it, a touch that makes them individual and unique. Their artistic reality lies in their difference. The combination of the typical with the unique is also a feature of Nabokov's character portrayal. While pointing to the bond between the characters and the readers, Nabokov also reminds us that his characters are more than mirror images in which we recognize ourselves. In Schopenhauer's terms, we are made to see in them the same will of which we too are phenomena,

---

[22]Schopenhauer, *The World as Will and Representation*, 1:266–67.

[23]Cf. Borges, *Labyrinths*, p. 12n: "Today, one of the churches of Tlön Platonically maintains that a certain pain, a certain greenish tint of yellow, a certain temperature, a certain sound, are the only reality. All men, in the vertiginous moment of coitus, are the same man. All men who repeat a line from Shakespeare *are* William Shakespeare."

[24]Quoted in David Rampton, *Vladimir Nabokov: A Critical Study of the Novels* (London, 1984) pp. 6–7.

but at the same time we are made to recognize and accept their "otherness" and uniqueness.

The problem of the balance between the universal and the unique, the general and the individual, characterizes both the form and the content of Nabokov's work. Needless to say, it is a problem of great social and cultural relevance. Things have to be worked out between the "chips fly when trees are cut" spirit of the Bolshevik Revolution and the bourgeois definition of individual happiness as the gratification of all fundamental needs. More specifically, in everyday life we wonder not just how much money can be spared from the rehabilitation of disadvantaged neighborhoods for, say, space projects (or vice versa) but, mainly, how well we have divided our time between our jobs and our families, between keeping up with current books and visiting that boring lonely aunt, between the proportion of lead and bell metal in the walls of our homes. A Nabokovian text reflects these and other modern dilemmas by staging a tug-of-war between self-immolating metaphysical or aesthetic pursuits and the daily meticulous reclamation of "average reality."

Nabokov once noted that he liked Emerson's poetry (*SO*, 64); the ideas of Emerson's essays he left without comment. Emerson goes so far as to reject the claims of human commitment during moments of vision: "The name of the nearest friend sounds then foreign and accidental: to be brothers, to be acquaintances, master or servant, is then a trifle and a disturbance."[25] It is from this element of Romantic individualism that Nabokov swerves. A human commitment does interfere with one's work or vision; it is a disturbance—but not a trifle. "What if those tears / cost more than our redemption?" thinks the apostle John, on hearing Mary's sobs after Golgotha, in Nabokov's 1925 poem "The Mother" (*PP*, 33).

The imperative need for reconciling human commitment with aesthetic or metaphysical pursuit is a major theme that binds Nabokov's work into a unified *oeuvre*: each novel presents this theme from a different angle, thus complementing the others. His first novel, *Mary* (1926), demonstrates the need for a balance between sympathy and detachment; the conflict between the two tendencies is reflected in the clash of the different levels of interpretation (for example, the moral versus the symbolic) that the book invites. *King, Queen, Knave* (1928)

[25]Ralph Waldo Emerson, "Nature," in *The Complete Works* (New York, 1968), 1:10.

examines the consequences of rejecting authentic spiritual life; its comic approach to the theme controls the potentially horrifying effect of the "average reality" of conformism and convention. *The Defense* (1930), on the contrary, shows the tragedy of a chess genius whom recondite art too thoroughly diverts from the "average reality."

Glory (1932) is the first of a series in which the protagonist devotes himself to the pursuit of the transcendent reality but misjudges the nature of his quest. Martin Edelweiss mistakes a prophetic awareness of mystery for nostalgia; having conquered fear, he embarks on an illegal and (as he subconsciously knows) suicidal trip to Russia. The line between his version of heroic knight-errantry and egotistic self-emulation is obliterated by his placing his duty to himself above his duty to the people who love him. *Laughter in the Dark* (1933/1938) forms a sequel to the motif of mistake: here it is the pursuit of a sexual eidolon that takes the place of the transcendental quest, stifles the protagonists' sympathy, and makes him betray his commitments. The worst possible mistake, however, is committed by the protagonist of *Despair* (1934), who confuses artistic creativity with its polar opposite, murder.

The protagonist of Nabokov's first dystopia, *Invitation to a Beheading* (written in 1934–35, first published in 1938), makes no metaphysical mistake. Cincinnatus C. is aware of being different from the others and of knowing more: this is the crime for which his environment condemns him to death. What he fails to understand for a long time is that his tormentors exist only so long as his imagination evokes them and his thoughts grant them life. On finding himself betrayed by all he cared for in his world, Cincinnatus becomes free from any commitment and can make his way, undeterred, to the mysterious "other dimension."

In *The Gift*, Nabokov's last novel written in Russian (serialized, with an important omission, in 1937–38), the young writer Fyodor Godunov-Cherdynstev shares Cincinnatus's wish to live authentically, to love genuinely, to create his own "fiction" and remain true to it; but he also draws support from his awareness of the transcendent dimension lying somewhere beyond his vibrant life. Fyodor is the only Nabokovian character who manages to find a balance between his somewhat mystical art and his relationships with the people around him.

The protagonist of *The Real Life of Sebastian Knight* (published in 1941, written two years previously) seems to have the makings of

Fyodor and Cincinnatus but commits the mistake of Albinus of *Laughter in the Dark*; he too allows an obsessive passion for an undeserving woman to usurp that place in his life which should have been devoted to a tentative eschatological quest. This, in my opinion, is a flaw in the plot formula. For all its dazzling brilliance, *Sebastian Knight*—the first of Nabokov's novels written directly in English—seems to have been something of a false start.

Adam Krug in *Bend Sinister* (1947), Nabokov's first "American" novel and second major dystopia, is caught between his wish to retain intellectual independence and his love for his child, who is threatened by a bloodthirsty regime. His plight is more realistic than the ecstasy with which Cincinnatus's freedom is asserted at the end of *Invitation*.

In *Lolita* (1955) Nabokov returns to the theme of a metaphysical mistake. Like Albinus of *Laughter*, Humbert Humbert pursues his perverted sexual passion with all the energy of a misdirected metaphysical quest and ruins the life of the object of this passion, a very young girl who does not identify with the role of sexual eidolon. One of the central dramas of the novel is the conflict over what the two central characters regard as normal; the reader's own values are likewise questioned by the rhetoric of the narrative.

Pnin (1957) portrays a complex character whose scholarly research keeps diverting him from the "average reality" but who comes back to this reality and makes pathetic efforts to cope with it, who is constantly left in the lurch by his loved ones but returns kindness for callousness, who combines a survivor's guilt with resilence and love of life, who suffers pain but tries not to share it with others—in at least two meanings of the word "share." It is as though Nabokov needed his mild Pnin—no believer in an individual's constitutional right to fulfillment—as a counterbalance for the predatory, hedonistic Humbert.

In *Pale Fire* (1962) John Shade, like the protagonist of *The Gift*, has found a happy balance between his work and his love for his wife Sybil (and grief for their daughter), but he has no more psychic energy left for humoring Charles Kinbote (Botkin), whom he sincerely respects and pities, despite Sybil's energetic dislike of this intrusive neighbor. Shade's kindness to Kinbote, combined with his wish to keep his privacy, and Kinbote's pain at not being granted a closer friendship are among the most touching motifs of the novel.

In *Ada, or Ardor* (1969)—which is set on the planet "Antiterra"—the memoirist Van Veen attempts to deemphasize the callousness and cruelty that he has displayed throughout his life, but he cannot conceal that the force of his love for his sister Ada has increased his insensitivity to the other people around him.[26] As they grow up, the *Wunderkinder* retain both their striking, if sterile, intellectual prowess and their attitude of superiority to almost everyone else; they exclude the rest of humanity from their intensely passionate conversation, and inflict fatal wounds on people who come too close—unless their strength and egotism match the lovers' own.

Transparent Things (1972) approaches the conflict from a totally new angle: it shows the tragedy of a man who wastes a great talent on humdrum tasks and whose psychic energy, not expended on any courageously painstaking creative endeavor, erupts all too violently when his consciousness is at rest: he strangles his beloved wife in his sleep, confusing nightmare with reality.

Finally, *Look at the Harlequins!* (1974) is the story of a writer so completely absorbed by his work and by his attempts to satisfy his desires that he becomes blatantly insensitive to his daughter's needs and fails to prevent "average reality" from wrecking the lives of the weaker ones among the women he loves.

The structure of each novel is based on a specific manner of combining the perspective (the "point of view," variations of the camera eye's trajectory, the presence or absence of an illusion of spatial depth) with recurrent imagery and self-referential games. No combination is repeated unchanged from one narrative to another, because each is appropriate to the specific thematic features of the work. The central object of my analysis is the unique relationship between the theme and the structure in ten of Nabokov's seventeen novels. "All hangs together—shape and sound, / heather and honey, vessel and content," says Nabokov in his 1945 poem "An Evening of Russian Poetry" (*PP*, 158). I place particular emphasis on the handling of recurrent images and motifs because this is a sphere in which the distinction between "vessel and content" is practically annihilated.

V

The discussion of the ten works begins and ends with Nabokov's novels of the fifties. *Pnin*, published in 1957, is a convenient

---

[26]Boyd, *Nabokov's "Ada,"* expresses a similar view. A valuable earlier extended study is Bobbie Ann Mason, *Nabokov's Garden: A Guide to "Ada"* (Ann Arbor, Mich., 1974).

introduction to some of his major methods. Following the reading of a number of his earlier novels in the order of their composition, the circle closes with the chapter on *Lolita*, which was written at approximately the same time as *Pnin*. The ten texts chosen provide the best examples of the mutual adjustment of Nabokov's virtuouso techniques and humanistic concerns. The model that I use to demonstrate this adjustment is less central (though not inapplicable) to *The Eye* (a very short work), *Despair*, and *The Real Life of Sebastian Knight*; therefore, these three novels are not discussed in detail, even though they belong to the relevant period. [27]

The treatment of Nabokov's novels as parts of an *oeuvre* involves regarding his various texts—novels, poems, short stories, interviews, lectures—as indirect commentary on one another. I frequently use Nabokov's own expressions, from other works or from different parts of the novel under discussion, in lieu of blander critical language. This method of out-of-context quotation is a partial compensation for not dwelling at greater length on Nabokov's brilliant, witty, synaesthetic style. It also implies a monolithic character of Nabokov's views. His philosophy, however, should not be imagined as preexisting his writing: it evolved in the process of continuous discovery, revealing new aspects and realizing new potentialities with every work.

The dates of composition, rather than of publication, are the landmarks of this process; and though I frequently juxtapose Nabokov's works for the sake of a synchronic comment, I also take into account the biographical links between, say, a novel and some poems and short stories written at the same period. The shorter works may be preparatory sketches for the novel, or channels for material that would disrupt it, or repositories for matters left over from the novel, or a development of its latent technical feats. In any case, the complex of the production of a certain period testifies to that period's dominant concerns.

---

[27]For the most valuable studies of these three novels, see Donald B. Johnson, "Eyeing Nabokov's *Eye*," *Canadian-American Slavic Studies*, 19 (1985), 328–50; Shlomith Rimmon, "Problems of Voice in Nabokov's *The Real Life of Sebastian Knight*," in Phyllis A. Roth, ed., *Critical Essays on Vladimir Nabokov* (Boston, 1984), pp. 109–29; Charles Nicol, "The Mirrors of Sebastian Knight," in L. S. Dembo, ed., *Nabokov: The Man and His Work* (Madison, Wis., 1967), pp. 85–94; Catherine Tiernan O'Connor, "Nabokov's *The Real Life of Sebastian Knight*: In Pursuit of a Biography," in Joachim T. Baer and Norman W. Ingham, eds., *Mnemozina: Studia literaria russica in honorem Vsevolod Setchkarev* (Munich, 1974), pp. 281–93; Stuart, *Nabokov*, pp. 1–53; Johnson, *Worlds in Regression*, pp. 30–31; and the studies of *Despair* cited in Chapter 7, n. 2.

It is now common knowledge that Nabokov made a considerable number of revisions in most of his Russian novels when he was preparing them for publication in America because, in retrospect, he had a clearer view of his artistic goals. These revisions, to which I frequently refer, are a boon to the literary scholar because they present clear evidence of the writer's development. In Nabokov's terms, the true shape of the book was more clearly perceptible for him in the mature years when the revisions were made. "I am afraid to get mixed up with Plato, whom I do not care for," he observed in an interview with Alfred Appel, "but I do think that in my case it is true that the entire book, before it is written, seems to be ready ideally in some other, now transparent, now dimming, dimension, and my job is to take down as much of it as I can make out and as precisely as I am humanly able to" (SO, 69).

The statement is metaphorical rather than metaphysical. *The Gift* contains a similar observation about the composition of chess problems (G, 183) and expresses the need for the artist to believe in his power. The "other dimension" is, here, a metaphor for an aesthetic potentiality. As records of a clearer vision of the right book (in what Borges calls "the Library of Babel"),[28] the changes made in the translated novels are more reliable indications of Nabokov's positions than some of his on-record programmatic remarks. Indeed, his habitual disparagement of meat-and-potatoes human appeal or social relevance in fiction is a rhetorical overstatement in response to the journalistic high-handedness of standard misreadings.

Nabokov no longer needs to be defended, but we are still a long way from solving the aesthetical problem that his work represents, and there are still many discoveries to be made on the journey. One day, farther down this road, philosophical inquiry may find that his work truthfully reflects the slow processes of a vertiginously dynamic age.

[28]Borges, *Labyrinths*, p. 51.

2

Pnin: The Quest That Overrides the Goal

We came into the world like brother and brother,
And now let's go hand in hand, not one before another.
William Shakespeare, *The Comedy of Errors* 5.1

Around 1950–51, with *Lolita* still unfinished, Nabokov started intermittently working on *Pnin*. Separate chapters first appeared in the *New Yorker*, and the book came out in 1957, four years after the completion and two years after the publication of *Lolita*.

Lolita deliberately excludes explicit Russian references, the only exception being the Paris taxi driver Maximovich.[1] The symbolic element in its story (see Chapter 11), is not estranged from the Russian connection, yet the "Russian" material—that is, such issues as the predicament of Russian intellectuals in America, and Nabokov's own status as a Russian-born author of a would-be all-American novel—had no place in the world of Humbert Humbert. It had to be channeled elsewhere. The story of Professor Timofey Pnin became, to some extent, a contrasting companion piece to *Lolita*.

Pnin is largely the debt that Nabokov pays to Russian emigration. Not surprisingly, a number of its motifs—for example, Pnin's

---

[1] Priscilla Meyer, "Nabokov's *Lolita* and Pushkin's *Onegin*: McAdam, McEve, and McFate," in Gibian and Parker, *Achievements,* pp. 179–211, points to what Meyer regards as connections between *Eugene Onegin* and *Lolita* in order to prove that *"Lolita* represents a translation through space and time of a Russian literary monument of the 1820s into an American one of the 1950s, a parody of 'paraphrastic' translation at its most extreme, which Nabokov wrote concomitantly with his literal one" (p. 180). I do not agree with this thesis. What Meyer presents as analogies between the two works may be symptoms of Pushkin's blood diffusely running in the arteries of Nabokov's imagination; they are not a "trail of colored pebbles" (p. 192n) intentionally dropped by Nabokov. Moreover, the impulse to allude to Puskin was channeled into *Pnin,* the

"Russian-intelligentski" way of getting into his overcoat (*P*, 65), or a character who imitates somebody else so frequently that he actually becomes like him—are echoes of the material of *The Gift*, the last novel that Nabokov wrote in Russian. Remnants of the émigré intellectual circles that seem to have reached an impasse in the pre-apocalyptic world of *The Gift* are transplanted to America and almost miraculously revived in the world of *Pnin*. This novel, however, is much more than a comic account of one ethnosocial group. The present century is the age of the greatest Migration of the Peoples: in Nabokov's hands, the portrayal of a Russian immigrant in America becomes an inquiry into the art of exile,[2] into the secret of any expatriate's resilience, into the morality of his resilience, into the conflict between his qualms of conscience and love of life. The inquiry takes the shape of a quest for the real life of Timofey Pnin, a quest that "overrides the goal" (*P*, 143), so that both its subject and its object eventually dissolve—yet not without leaving behind an account of the experience that may be true for "you, and me, and him over there" (*IB*, 25), a generalized version of "personal truth" (*ND*, 14). In most of Nabokov's fiction an Everyman is a seeker of the Grail; as such, he is also an Exile.

I

As a structural principle, the quest that "overrides the goal" roughly follows the scheme of Nabokov's 1935 short story "Recruiting," which begins with a seemingly omniscient account of a poor sick old émigré, one of a long series of Nabokovian émigré Russians who have learned to live without hope in prewar Europe. The old man is on his way home from a funeral; he sits down to rest in a small park and is overcome by an unaccountable feeling of happiness. At that moment the narrator steps in and admits that he has just invented a whole life story for a fat shabby stranger on the bench beside him. The narrator's imagination has been triggered by a sudden wave of joy, which he also attributes to the old man. Yet though the pro-

other work that Nabokov was engaged in while preparing his volumes on *Eugene Onegin*; see Gene Barabtarlo, "Pushkin Embedded," *Vladimir Nabokov Research Newsletter*, 8 (1982), 28–31.

   [2]For an interesting discussion of the theme of exile in *Pnin*, see David Cowart, "Art and Exile: Nabokov's *Pnin*," *Studies in American Fiction*, 10 (1982), 197–207.

tagonist's biography thus turns out to be spurious, he seems to share the narrator's mood. This mood is a secret bond between the two, a bond more important than their fictional identities.[3]

Like the first half of "Recruiting," the first six of the seven chapters of *Pnin* seem to be presented by an omniscient narrator. This impression is not destroyed even by the narrator's intrusions into the fictional universe: for example, by his claim to have visited the Cooks before Pnin did, or to have helped him write a letter to a newspaper.[4] In the seventh chapter, however, the narrator turns out to be a flesh-and-ink inhabitant of the fictional world, the "littérateur" (*P*, 45) who is responsible for Liza Bogolepov's suicide attempt and marriage to Pnin, the "fascinating lecturer" (*P*, 169) who supersedes Pnin at Waindell College, the owner of the "private collection" (*P*, 45) in which Pnin's love letter is preserved. As a first-person narrator, the "I" of *Pnin* has little authority over the protagonist's thoughts or the scenes that he did not witness: he was not there to see the events of chapters 1–6; hence, these events turn out to be largely a product of his imagination.[5]

The narrative may thus seem to fall into two parts: (a) *biographie romancée*, where the skeleton of the historical facts is coated with imaginary scenes and dialogue (a genre supremely scorned by the narrator of *The Real Life of Sebastian Knight*), and (b) firsthand evidence that reveals the narrator's "sources" (compare *Roots III*, in which Alex Haley describes his search for the information out of which he has spun the first two volumes in the *Roots* sequence).[6] A disconcerting

[3]The relationship between the short story and the novel is discussed in greater detail in my essay "Self-Conscious Paralepsis in Vladimir Nabokov's 'Recruiting' and *Pnin*," *Poetics Today*, 7 (1986), 459–69.

[4]These intrusions illustrate the narrative convention of *metalepsis*, a "transgressional" movement from one narrative level to another, a movement not based on a definite embedding of narrative levels; see Gérard Genette, *Narrative Discourse: An Essay in Method*, trans. Jane E. Lewin (Ithaca, 1980), pp. 234–36. Genette's is among the modern literary systems for which Nabokov's work has proved a vast though perhaps not entirely safe playground. An extensive discussion of Nabokov's work in terms of modern critical conversation can be found in Maurice Couturier, *Nabokov* (Lausanne, 1979); and David Packman, *Vladimir Nabokov: The Structure of Literary Desire* (Columbia, Mo., 1982).

[5]According to Genette's nomenclature, the material of chapters 1–6 is paraleptic. *Paralepsis* is the presentation of more information than is authorized by focalization: i.e., more information than the focal character (in our case, the narrator) can possibly possess; see *Narrative Discourse*, p. 195.

[6]Different aspects of the point of view in *Pnin* have been discussed in, e. g., Paul Grams, "*Pnin*: The Biographer as Meddler," in Carl R. Proffer, ed., *A Book of Things*

detail, however, undermines this division of the material: on two occasions the protagonist denies the veracity of the narrator's eyewitness reports. First, Pnin rebels against some statements for whose accuracy the narrator is prepared to vouch:

> I tried not only to remind Pnin of former meetings, but also to amuse him and other people around us with the unusual lucidity and strength of my memory. However, he denied everything. He said he vaguely recalled my grandaunt but had never met me. He said that his marks in algebra had always been poor and that, anyway, his father never displayed him to his patients; he said that in *Zabava (Liebelei)* he had only acted the part of Christine's father. He repeated that we had never seen each other before. Our little discussion was nothing more than good-natured banter, and everybody laughed; and noticing how reluctant he was to recognize his own past, I switched to another, less personal topic. [*P,* 179–80]

Second, Pnin accuses the narrator of having told false stories about him: "Now, don't believe a word he says, Georgiy Aramovich. He makes up everything. He once invented that we were schoolmates in Russia and cribbed at examinations. He is a dreadful inventor (*on uzhasnïy vïdumshchik)"* (*P,* 185).

The narrator never records having mentioned that Pnin was his schoolmate. On the contrary, he talks about having attended a more liberal school than Pnin's (see *P,* 176). It is, therefore, not clear whether Pnin is mistaken or whether the narrator is indeed a "dreadful inventor"—that is, a liar.[7] What are the implications of these mutually exclusive yet co-present possibilities?

If the narrator has withheld from us some shameful jokes that he permitted himself at Pnin's expense, his surprise at Pnin's sally (see *P,* 185) is likewise a lie. In such a case the material not only of the first six chapters but also of the seventh (the so-called eyewitness information) is no more reliable than the news brought by the boy who cried "Wolf!" once too often. We cannot be sure that anything in the narrator's story "really happened," and this reminds us of what we have

about Vladimir Nabokov (Ann Arbor, Mich., 1974). pp. 193–202; Fred Moody, "At *Pnin's* Center," *Russian Literature Triquarterly,* 14 (1976), 73–77; G. M. Hyde, *Vladimir Nabokov: America's Russian Novelist* (London, 1977), p. 163.

[7] This element of "the liar's paradox" in *Pnin* is also discussed in Grams, "*Pnin*: The Biographer as Meddler," p. 194.

known all along but did not like to keep in mind. Pnin is, after all, a fictional character, and no statement about him can be true or false. The narrator's cognitive unreliability amounts to the novel's self-conscious admission that the protagonist, no matter how vivid and legible, is nonexistent.

Yet what if Pnin himself is unreliable? What if he is confusing the narrator with someone else? He is presented as liable to such confusion. In chapter 6, for instance, he is unable to distinguish between professors Wynn and Thomas at Waindell: "For recalling certain other duplications in the past—disconcerting likenesses he alone had seen—bothered Pnin told himself it would be useless to ask anybody's assistance in unraveling the T. Wynns" (*P*, 150).

Since Nabokov belonged to those writers who were perfectly capable of "remembering"their future work, among the "disconcerting likenesses" that Pnin alone had seen there may have been the resemblance between Nabokov and the protagonist of his 1974 novel, *Look at the Harlequins!*: the Anglo-Russian writer Vadim Vadimich, whose name and patronymic sound like "Vladimir Vladimirovich" when pronounced with familiarity and speed, whose appearance mimics Nabokov's portrait, whose career is modeled on that of Nabokov, and whose books seem to be Antiterran transformations of Nabokov's fiction. Vadim Vadimich is frequently confused with someone else, and on two occasions it is the authorship of Nabokov's books that is mistakenly ascribed to him. Moreover he is haunted by a troubling fantasy of being someone's inferior double: "I now confess that I was bothered that night, and the next and some time before, by a dream feeling that my life was the nonidentical twin, a parody, an inferior variant of another man's life, somewhere on this or another earth. A demon, I felt, was forcing me to impersonate that other man, that other writer who was and would always be incomparably greater, healthier, and crueler than your obedient servant" (*LATH*, 89).

In *Pnin*, Vadim Vadimich is mentioned as an old acquaintance of the protagonist: "In reviewing his Russian friends throughout Europe and the United States, Timofey Pahlch could easily count at least sixty dear people whom he had intimately known since, say, 1920, and whom he never called anything but Vadim Vadimich, Ivan Hristoforovich, or Samuil Izrailevich, as the case might be" (*P*, 105). The lepidopterist Vladimir Vladimirovich is also mentioned—by Pnin's friend Professor Chateau, who is fascinated by a butterfly:

"Pity Vladimir Vladimirovich is not here," remarked Chateau. "He would have told us all about these enchanting insects."

"I have always had the impression that his entomology was merely a pose."

"Oh, no," said Chateau. [P, 128]

The cryptographic butterfly (which, unknown to Chateau, is supposed to be *Lycaeides samuelis* Nabokov)[8] evokes the motif of doubling: Pnin is acquainted with both the twins, the man and the shadow. He is the only person to be aware of the likeness, just as the narrator is the only person to know the depth of Pnin's feeling for Liza. When Professor Thomas wonders why Pnin calls him Wynn (a Nabokovian variation on the "Tim and Win are twins" theme), the grumpy philosopher Clements wryly observes: "He probably mistook you for somebody else. . . . And for all I know you *may* be somebody else" (P, 165). These words apply to the narrator rather than to the baffled anthropologist. Indeed, the narrator's name is never mentioned, and for all we know he may be not Vladimir Vladimirovich, the fictional extension of the novelist, but Vadim Vadimich, the "I" of *Look at the Harlequins!* This additional ambiguity reminds us that, in effect, the narrator is also a fictional character, that like Pnin he is legible but nonexistent. The story of creative imagination told in *Pnin* is likewise fictional and not to be identified with the actual genesis of the novel.

Thus, both the protagonist and the narrator are canceled out: each dissolves in the image of the nonexistent other, leaving us with a subtle record of human experience and of its transformation into a work of art.

II

On repeated reading, aware of the narrator's cognitive unreliability, we have to treat the narrative of chapters 1–6 as recording not the random flow of plausible events but the workings of the narrator's imagination. We are challenged to seek a specific *raison d'être* for the salient narrative details and thus to reconstruct the story that the narrative pretends to tell us about itself. The main clues lie in the recurrent

[8]See Simon Karlinsky, ed., *The Nabokov-Wilson Letters, 1940–1971* (New York, 1980), p. 307.

imagery and in the relationship between the images presented in chapters 1–6 on the one hand and in chapter 7 (*Roots III*) on the other.

"Were I a writer," says the protagonist-narrator of Nabokov's "Spring in Fialta," "I should allow only my heart to have imagination, and for the rest rely upon memory, that long-drawn sunset shadow of one's personal truth" (*ND*, 13–14). Relying upon memory for narrative details, the narrator composes six chapters out of images drawn from the would-be "hard facts" of the seventh. One of the most striking of these images is that of the squirrel.[9] The "shadow-tailed" little animals that abundantly populate Pnin's world turn out to be the progeny of the stuffed squirrel that in chapter 7 the narrator recollects having glimpsed through the open door of young Pnin's St. Petersburg schoolroom: "I could see a map of Russia on the wall, books on a shelf, a stuffed squirrel, and a toy monoplane with linen wings and a rubber motor. I had a similar one but twice bigger, bought in Biarritz. After one had wound up the propeller for some time, the rubber would change its manner of twist and develop fascinating thick whorls which predicted the end of its tether" (*P*, 177).

In a first reading the stuffed squirrel is eclipsed by the toy monoplane and gets lost among the homogeneous parts of the sentence[10]—it is, indeed, natural for a teenaged observer to focus on a mechanical contrivance rather than on a routine zoological item (the St. Petersburg home of young Luzhin in Nabokov's *Defense* also contains a stuffed squirrel). With repeated reading, however, one begins to suspect that the narrator was moved to attach a cryptographic significance to the stuffed squirrel several years later, on seeing Pnin in the company of Mira Belochkin (*belochka* is the Russian diminutive for "squirrel"). The strong impression that Mira produced on the narrator is conveyed by his cutting the section short immediately after referring to the "pretty, slender-necked, velvet-eyed girl" who received the greatest ovation on the night of the amateur theatricals (*P*, 179).

The link between the stuffed squirrel and Mira Belochkin's name may well have generated the whole story of Pnin's youthful love affair. The narrator never tells us exactly how he knows that Pnin was in love

[9]The relationship of this image with the Cinderella motif and other interesting cross-referential patterns in *Pnin* are discussed in Charles Nicol, "Pnin's History," in Roth, *Critical Essays*, pp. 93–105.

[10]Cf. Nabokov's discussion of Gogol's use of "irrelevant details" to mask the main structural idea of "The Overcoat" (*NG*, 148).

with Mira.[11] For all we know, the story of Pnin's first love may be correct, yet it may also be an invention based on the narrator's own "personal truth." As though in keeping with the principle proclaimed in "Spring in Fialta," the narrator allows his heart to imagine what it would feel like to have loved and to grieve for Mira—and then projects the imaginary experience onto the biography of Pnin.

Likewise, a great number of details that describe Pnin's life at Waindell College are traceable to the images and motifs of chapter 7 or to extratextual sources. Here are some examples.

1. The way chance remarks trigger Pnin's fascinating learned harangues on *Anna Karenin* and on Cinderella's shoes, under circumstances that favor only small talk, is encoded in the bus scene recollected in chapter 7: "As we hung from adjacent straps in the crowded and spasmodic vehicle, my good friend managed to combine a vigorous twisting of the head (in his continuous attempts to check and recheck the numbers of cross streets) with a magnificent account of all he had not had sufficient time to say at the celebration on Homer's and Gogol's use of the Rambling Comparison" (*P*, 186).[12] The same incident seems to have given the narrator the idea of Pnin's wariness concerning the logistics of "average reality" and to have generated his adventures on the way to Cremona.

2. The easy charm of Pnin's manner and conversation in congenial company is based on the narrator's observation of him in the Russian circles of prewar Paris.

3. The toy monoplane with *linen* wings and a *rubber* motor, which produced "fascinating thick whorls" when wound up, may be responsible for Pnin's "passionate intrigue" with Joan's washing machine (*P*, 40): he loves to watch the storms through the machine's porthole and on one occasion feeds it his *rubber*-soled *canvas* shoes.

4. The bus station employee who in chapter 1 takes his wife to a maternity hospital on a premature alarm, is named Bob Horn—in memory, as it were, of Robert Karlovich Horn, the likable estate

[11]During the episode at the Pines this piece of information seems to be confirmed by Madame Shpolyanski, yet her dialogue with Pnin is paraleptic (see n. 5 above), and there is no additional evidence that it ever took place.

[12]The content of this "magnificent account" can be found in the chapter "The Homeric Simile in *Dead Souls*," in Carl R. Proffer, *The Simile and Gogol's "Dead Souls"* (The Hague, 1967) pp. 67–94; Pnin's comments on *Anna Karenin* (*P*, 122, 129–30) may be found in a more detailed form in *LRL*, 190–98. (Nabokov insisted on "Karenin" as the correct form of the heroine's name in English.)

steward who applauds at the wrong moments during Pnin's amateur theatricals in chapter 7.

5. The bells that accompany the Clementses' breakfast, as well as the menu of "oranges and lemons" (*P*, 30), seem to be conjured up by associaton with the rhyme "The Bells of London": "Oranges and lemons / Say the bells of St. Clemens."[13]

Some of the patterns, however, appear to be imposed not by the narrator but by life itself: that is, by the omniscient novelist. For instance, the Russian books that Pnin uses for his research at Waindell have been donated by the millionaire Todd, and the house in which Pnin makes his home just before being fired is the former residence of the caretaker of Todd's estate. Thus, in a way, Pnin becomes the caretaker of Todd's cultural estate, and it is from this menial service that he is dismissed through the intervention of the narrator. Such a consideration may be soothing to the narrator's conscience, yet he may be suspected of inventing these "verifiable" facts precisely for the purpose of presenting Pnin's departure from Waindell as a promotion, or at least a liberation, rather than a setback; in fact, Pnin appears in *Pale Fire* as the head of the Russian department in another provincial college.

III

The more links we establish between the "imagined" scenes of chapters 1–6 and the eyewitness information, the more difficult it becomes to separate the narrator from the protagonist, and the more consistently does the narrator seem to project himself into Pnin's life story. This becomes especially clear when we examine the sequences of images and the shifts in tone within short narrative blocks.

When at the beginning of the novel the narrator presents Pnin as an anticlassical variety of the "*zerstreute Professor,*" he pretends to be try-

[13]For this observation I am indebted to Jessie Thomas Lokrantz, *The Underside of the Weave: Some Stylistic Devices Used by Vladimir Nabokov* (Uppsala, 1973), p. 79. However, I totally disagree with Lokrantz's repeated statement that *Pnin* is a relatively simple story and that its narrative is characterized by two voices. The latter view is shared by Herbert Grabes in his *Fictitious Biographies: Vladimir Nabokov's English Novels*, trans. Pamela Gliniars and Herbert Grabes (The Hague, 1977), p. 51, though not by Andrew Field, who, by using a similar expression, actually suggests that the narrator uses two tones of voice; see *Nabokov: His Life in Art*, pp. 135–36.

ing to "diagnose his sad case" (*P*, 13). However, a really serious attempt to diagnose Pnin's case and reveal the secret of his resilience comes in conjunction with the Mira Belochkin theme. Pnin is shown deliberately controlling his thoughts and suppressing memories that could rekindle old wounds:

> In order to exist rationally, Pnin had taught himself, during the last ten years, never to remember Mira Belochkin . . . because, if one were quite sincere with oneself, no conscience, and hence no consciousness, could be expected to subsist in a world where such things as Mira's death were possible. One had to forget—because one could not live with the thought that this graceful, fragile, tender young woman with those eyes, that smile, those gardens and snows in the background, had been brought in a cattle car to an extermination camp and killed by an injection of phenol into the heart, into the gentle heart one had heard beating under one's lips in the dusk of the past. [*P*, 134–35]

The effort not to dwell on painful matters has turned into a mental habit; it is almost automatically that Pnin's mind shifts from the thoughts of death, which creep in disguised as a line from Pushkin, to the physical realities of everyday existence: "*V boyu li, v stranstvii, v volnah?* In fight, in travel, or in waves? Or on the Waindell campus? Gently champing his dentures, which retained a sticky layer of cottage cheese, Pnin went up the slippery library steps" (*P*, 73–74).

Aided by this self-protective habit, Pnin blocks his awareness of Mrs. Thayer's hint that Isabel Clements may claim the room in which he lodges. Subliminally, however, he is conscious of the menace and almost allows his physical fatigue to bring it to the surface: "Pnin suddenly felt very tired. Not only had the *Zol. Fond* tome become even heavier after its unnecessary visit to the library, but something that Pnin had half heard in the course of the day, and had been reluctant to follow up, now bothered and oppressed him, as does, in retrospection, a blunder we have made, a piece of rudeness we have allowed ourselves, or a threat we have chosen to ignore" (*P*, 79–80). The strenuous repression of unwelcome thoughts is one of the causes of Pnin's breakdown during a Soviet movie.

Like Wordsworth's Wanderer, Pnin cannot "afford to suffer," because—as suggested in the foregoing quotation—his emotional and physical states are closely linked. Indeed his cardiac fits always conjure up the loved faces of the dead; conversely, memories of the past—such as those evoked by the game of croquet at the Pines—lead to seizures. Pnin's heart condition is the result of grieving over the fate of parents and friends. His reluctance to remember the past is traceable to the episode in which he denies the narrator's story of former meetings, yet it also seems to be the secret bond between him and the narrator—just as the wave of happiness is the secret bond between the narrator and the protagonist of "Recruiting." Dissimilar in many ways, both the narrator and the protagonist of *Pnin* are fugitives from pain. While Pnin attempts to control the flow of his thoughts, the narrator strives to regulate the flow of his imagination so that he will not lose his aesthetic detachment in the face of matters pregnant with "human appeal."

This is especially evident in the narrator's handling of the scene in which Joan Clements finds Pnin shattered by his ex-wife's visit. The preceding section discloses the pain that Liza had once again inflicted on Pnin. Now, however, the moving though economical account of his state of mind is discontinued; as Pnin is approaching an emotional breakdown, he suddenly turns into a buffoon, rummaging through Joan's cupboard in search, as he reportedly tells her, of "viscous and sawdust" (*P*, 59). The transliteration "viscous" for "whiskey" is fantastic enough—the typical Russian distortion would have been something like "veeski"—but the substitution of "sawdust" for "soda" is impossible: the Russian word for "soda" sounds much the same as the English one. This pseudo-Pninism strikingly differs from the other records of the protagonist's speech, which call for at least a brief survey.

At the beginning of the novel Pnin's sentences are faithful word-for-word translations from corresponding Russian phrases: "And where possible to leave baggage?" (*P*, 18)—*A gde mozhno ostavit' bagazh?* Later Pnin inserts carefully stored colloquialisms into his conversation, or speaks in a funny yet credible mixture of solecisms and quotations from a curriculum vitae (see *P*, 33–34). By the end of the novel, under the influence of new friendships, his English is considerably improved, though not his pronunciation. The narrator, who discusses the regularities of the Russian accent (see *P*, 66–67) with a precision matching only Pnin's own phonetic analysis of his name and patronymic (see *P*, 104), generally refrains from transliterating his speech. Among the few exceptions is the account of the road directions that Pnin, in the comedy of errors in chapter 6, gives to Professor Thomas, taking him for the ornithologist Wynn (see *P*, 151). Connected as it is with the disconcerting-likenesses motif, the episode seems to be the narrator's little revenge on Pnin for having caught a glimpse of things which, until the publication of *Look at the Harlequins!*, no one was supposed to see.

Pnin's conversations with his Russian friends are rendered in impeccable English, because then it is the narrator and not the protagonist who performs the translation; so are Pnin's thoughts, because they are not supposed to be entirely verbal: "we do not usually think in words" (*LATH*, 123). Therefore, the "viscous and sawdust" deviation from verisimilitude can be accounted for only as a facetious quotation from Jack Cockerell, who tends to impute to Pnin such impossible mistakes as "shot" instead of "fired" (*P*, 188). Pnin's failure to understand the humor of comic strips in the same episode is another blatant Cockerellian exaggeration.

At one of the most pathetic moments of the story, then, the narrator refuses to face the acuteness of the protagonist's suffering. He jams the potentially tragic note and, through Cockerell's parody on Pnin, moves to a parody on Cockerell. To further counterpoise Pnin's pain he imagines the sympathetic Clementses secretly rejoicing over a happy letter from their daughter Isabel. A similar artificial consolation is imputed to Pnin: thinking about Mira's arrival in Buchenwald, he imagines her "still smiling, still able to help other Jewish women" (*P*, 135). However, it is not clear whether the paragraph that deals with Mira's death is supposed to be a record of Pnin's thought process or the narrator's commentary filling in the span of time during which Pnin fights his seizure at the Pines. Perhaps it is a combination of both: Pnin and the narrator join forces in order to extricate themselves from pain by letting the string of associations wander to Hagen's already commonplace lamentation about Buchenwald's proximity to Weimar. The historical irony is easier to brook than the fate of a concrete person; it places a distance between the object of perception and the perceiving mind. Through the image of the mortified Hagen, Pnin and the narrator safely pass over to the ridicule of academic absurdities, recalling the president of Waindell's reference to Germany as "the nation of universities" and, in the same speech, his compliment to "another torture house, 'Russia—the country of Tolstoy, Stanislavski, Raskolnikov, and other great and good men'" (*P*, 136). The narrative has again moved away from tragedy into farce.

A semirational sense of guilt, especially evident in his thoughts about Mira, turns Pnin's memories into a menace. During the residue of his Cremona seizure, he has a vision of long-dead friends, "murdered, forgotten, unrevenged, incorrupt, immortal" (*P*, 27), among the audience in the lecture hall. The word "unrevenged" shows that Pnin's conscience is troubled by his having made peace with the world "in which such things as Mira's death were possible." The epithet "incorrupt" suggests that the victims of history's sinister bends preserve their integrity, whereas an emigrant survivor becomes almost a renegade: his life, persistence, resilience in a foreign country or culture are in some way corruptions of early values, compromises with the self. By the same token, the Anglo-Russian narrator, who seems to have escaped the fate of a "writer in exile, sans fame, sans future, sans audience, sans anything but his art" (*PF*, 301), is a still graver renegade.[14] The narrator is not immune to a Pnin-like sense of guilt. He imagines Pnin recalling "Vanya Bednyashkin, shot by the Reds in 1919 in Odessa because his father had been a Liberal" (*P*, 27). The executed young man's name is so patently derived from an expression of pity (*Bednyashka!*) that its origin is surely in the narrator's "easy art" (*P*, 136) rather than in the "historical truth." Like Pnin, the narrator wishes both to keep the dead ones "immortal" and to survive and forget.

On the other hand, the narrator dramatizes his sense of guilt in the story of his ousting Pnin from Waindell, invading his privacy, and so on. The projection of the sense of guilt and the desire to cope with it (while also coping with exile and approaching old age) is what the reader is left with when the complexities of the point of view cancel out both protagonist and narrator. Like most self-conscious fiction,

---

[14]In " 'The Rapture of Endless Approximation': The Role of the Narrator in *Pnin*," *Journal of Narrative Technique*, 16 (1986), 192–203, J. H. Garrett-Goodyear discusses some implications of the contrast between the "inelegant spontaneity" of Pnin and "the stylish sophistication" of the narrator; among other things he raises the problem of the narrative's sometimes "conveying both Pnin and the narrator at once" (pp. 192, 197). The comic touch in the narrator's description of Pnin is largely a distancing device, dictated by a fear akin to that of Osip Mandelstam's "The Egyptian Stamp," in which the narrator prays not to be made similar to his protagonist Parnok; see *The Prose of Osip Mandelstam*, trans. Clarence Brown (Princeton, N.J., 1967), p 171. Mandelstam's narrator's emotional life often seems to merge with that of Parnok, just as the experience of the narrator of *Pnin* sometimes seems to overlap with the pain of the protagonist. Under such circumstances the function of the distancing comic relief is therapeutic.

Pnin induces us to seek the "truth" not on the literal but on the moral and emotional plane: the real thing in it is the confession of the love of life despite vicissitudes and compromises, the wish to walk away from the tragic in order to enjoy what life and art can offer. The peculiar achievement of this novel lies not only in its brilliant character portrayal, in its subtlety and wit, and in the richness and density of its texture but also in the exploration of a specific modern predicament—the precarious balance between aesthetic reveling and intellectual self-castigation, between the joy of life and remorse.

Life asserts itself in *Pnin* even if its triumph is not ostentatious or proud. "This is the earth," the narrator seems to think, together with the protagonist, "and I am, curiously enough, alive, and there is something in me and in life—" (*P*, 58): a handy squirrel breaks the generalization short. It is only in a genius that the struggle with despair can lead to a profound metaphysical insight, and Pnin, as he admits in his letter to Liza, is not a genius. He is too humane, and humanity is burdened with clay. The narrator's turning away from Pnin's pain at Liza's departure is likewise, in a sense, an act of humanity, a response to Pnin's appeal for the privacy of sorrow: "Why not leave their private sorrows to people? Is sorrow not, one asks, the only thing in the world people really possess?" (*P*, 52). Whether too humane or too weak to respond to the challenge of the tragic, the narrator of *Pnin* seems to join the narrator of *Look at the Harlequins!* in admitting his lack of genius. The superior writer whom Vadim Vadimich imitates despite himself is perhaps not the real Nabokov but an imaginary might-have-been Nabokov, a much crueler man whose imagination would not balk at the approach of the tragic. It is by a voluntary loss of tragic power that Nabokov seems to have purchased his subtle knowledge of the human heart: his own, his character's, his reader's—any heart behind which (according to the diagnosis of Pnin's doctors) there is, symbolically, "a shadow" (*P*, 126). For such a loss (to borrow a phrase from Wordsworth), the slow sad music of humanity has proved abundant recompense.

Pnin is characteristic of Nabokov's major fiction in that its highly self-referential narrative points to something beyond itself, to human experience renderd universal by the cancellation of the discrete identities of the characters. At the same time the narrative creates an aesthetic (anaesthetic) distance between that experience and the reader. "I think there's a pain somewhere in the room," says the dying Mrs. Gradgrind to her daughter Louisa in Dicken's *Hard Times*, "but I couldn't positively say that I have got it."[15] Opiates have distanced Mrs. Gradgrind's pain; it has become weaker—removed, as it were, from her body to "somewhere in the room." Yet there is also Louisa's pain in the room, and the painful sympathy of the reader, which Dickens alleviates by the distancing effect of the grotesque touch. The notorious virtuoso technique of Nabokov's novels, his elaborate patterns, his hilarious comic relief, and the vertigo of his self-referentiality are likewise anaesthetic distancing devices. Their specific effects are not identical in any two novels, but their overall significance lies in the paradox that concerns the whole of Nabokov's canon: his aestheticism, which many critics tent to oppose to the humanistic content of his works, is in fact the humanistic form singularly appropriate to this content.

[15]Charles Dickens, *Hard Times*, ed. David Craig (Harmondsworth, 1978), p. 224.

3

Mary: "Without Any Passport"

> We know each for himself, that none of us would perpetrate such a
> folly, yet feel as if some other might.
>
> Nathaniel Hawthorne, "Wakefield"

Nabokov's first novel, *Mary* (*Mashen'ka,* 1926), initiates the
theme of the need for a balance between human commitment and
aesthetic pursuit, focusing on the conflict between sympathy and self-
protective detachment. This conflict is reproduced in the tension between the different layers of the novel's meaning: the moral value of
the protagonist's actions clashes with their aesthetic value and their
symbolic significance.

I

Mary is set in a Russian *pension* in Berlin in the mid-twenties.[1]
Nabokov breathes new life into the conventional *pension* setting (as
of Balzac's *Père Goriot*) by exploring the significance of the proximity
imposed on the characters. People from different social and cultural
circles suddenly find themselves brought together in shared premises.
The partitions between the rooms are thin, and a great deal of the
protagonist's irritation with his well-meaning neighbors stems from
his want of privacy. The son of a rich upper-class family, Lev Ganin is
accustomed not just to greater spaces but also to protected spaces in
which he can dream undisturbed.[2] Therefore, when he starts reliving

[1]The doors to the rooms of the *pension* are labeled with calendar pages bearing the
dates of April 1 to April 6. This is discussed by Alex de Jonge as the first of the
elaborate patterns in Nabokov's novels; see "Nabokov's Uses of Pattern," in Peter
Quennel, ed., *Vladimir Nabokov: A Tribute* (New York, 1980), p. 60.

[2]The *pension* thus presents a marked contrast to the house on Ganin's country estate,
which is a perfect illustration of Bachelard's "oneiric house" (*The Poetics of Space,* pp.

his past in memory, he spends most of his time outdoors, away from noisy rooms and neighbors knocking at the door.

The use of the outdoors as the arena of the action is a major feature of the carnivalistic mode in fiction.[3] The collapse of social barriers between exiles sharing an apartment is another expression of this mode. Finding themselves in unwonted proximity, the characters are exposed to the temptation of intimacy, of Dostoevskian confidences and confessions during which the partitions between individual identities are likewise knocked down. Such a carnivalization is threatening to Ganin, as it is to most of Nabokov's protagonists and narrators: if death is "divestment" and "communion" (*P*, 20), then unrestrained communion is deathlike. Yet Ganin's uncompromising attempts to preserve the discreteness of his emotional life lead him to the opposite error: his inner life becomes hermetic, and his solipsism threatens to become as destructive to others as communion is to him.

At the beginning of the novel, Lev Ganin, a former White Guard officer, learns that a fellow boarder by the name Alfyorov is expecting his wife to arrive from Russia in a few days. Shown a picture of this woman, Ganin thinks he recognizes her as his first love, Mary. A sudden influx of emotion enables him to terminate a burdensome affair with a woman called Lyudmila, after which he spends four days in blissful recollection of his lost love. He plans to meet Mary at the railway station and carry her off. Yet as the hour of her arrival draws near, the remaining portion of the novel becomes disconcertingly thin under the reader's fingers.[4] As Ganin is waiting for Mary's train, the sordid parting with Lyudmila flashes through his memory. Her words "I know he won't be able to forget me as quickly as he may think" (*M*, 76) prove to be perversely prophetic. The aftertaste of the recent liaison suggests that even Mary may turn out to be different from Ganin's Galatea. Realizing "with merciless clarity that his affair with Mary was ended forever" (*M*, 114) and remaining true to the fantasy,[5]

6–7), which shelters daydreaming, protects the dreamer, allows one to dream in peace.

[3]The carnivalistic mode and its expression in the works of Dostoevsky are described in Mikhail Bakhtin, *Problems of Dostoevsky's Poetics*, ed. and trans. Caryl Emerson (Minneapolis, Minn., 1984), pp. 122–70. The intensity of the carnivalistic element in Dostoevsky's work must have been one cause for Nabokov's wary dislike of this writer.

[4]Cf. the metaphor of the still-thick remainder of a novel at the beginning of *Invitation to a Beheading* (*IB*, 12)

[5]Cf. *The Gift*: "O swear to me that while the heartblood stirs, you will be true to what we shall invent" (*G*, 169). Fyodor Godunov-Cherdyntsev's fidelity to fantasy has a different meaning from Ganin's: the lovers must live authentically in a creatively

he beats a hasty retreat, which is almost unanimously applauded by Nabokov's critics.

A young novelist may be suspected of sabotaging a long-anticipated reunion merely in order to avoid the triteness of "happily-ever-aftering." This, however, is not the case with Nabokov, who will eventually show great inventiveness in tackling this overworked theme (see, for instance, the liberating effect of a frustrating reunion in "The Doorbell," 1927; the partial success that looks like failure in "The Reunion," 1932; and the triumph that masks itself as a failure in *Ada*, 1969). The strange ending of *Mary* is not due to the fear of a cliché; aesthetically and symbolically it is appropriate that Ganin should not meet Mary in the fictional present. Still, this appropriateness does not justify the callous attitude of the protagonist, an attitude that masks itself as a version of moral autonomy.

II

The reunion, indeed, can hardly take place in the novel without disrupting the elegance of the pattern of events. Ganin remembers falling in love with Mary during a summer's stay on his family's country estate in prerevolutionary Russia. In the happy days of his recuperation after typhus he conceived for the first time the image of a girl that he would like to meet: "Now, many years later, he felt that their imaginary meeting and the meeting which took place in reality had blended and merged imperceptibly into one another, since as a living person she was only an uninterrupted continuation of the image which had foreshadowed her" (*M*, 44). Unlike Ganin's original meeting with Mary, a reunion has not been rehearsed imaginatively and has nothing to blend with. It is therefore appropriate that the romance which started solipsistically in the imagination should end, no less solipsistically, in the memory, with the events of "real life" sandwiched between.

Like all his subsequent writing, Nabokov's first novel thus describes a circle. Unlike Kurt Dreyer of *King, Queen, Knave*, who regrets meeting his former mistress because afterward he can never remember Erica as he remembered her before—"Erica number two will always

---

perceived world of their own and keep this world from becoming soiled by plagiaristic conformism.

be in the way" (*KQK*, 176)—Ganin retains his image of Mary intact. He wishes to believe that this image will not die with him—and indeed it does not, though it takes the real artist, Nabokov, rather than the fictional artist *manqué*, Ganin, to ensure its survival. "Beauty is momentary in the mind," as Peter Quince thinks at Wallace Stevens's clavier, "but in the flesh it is immortal." The flesh is, of course, the written word.

The reunion might also have been inappropriate symbolically. Ganin's decision to avoid meeting Mary is parallel to giving up hope of returning to his motherland: he can go there only in his memories—without any passport (see *M*, 109). Never appearing in the drab fictional present, Mary can be understood to stand for Mother Russia.[6] The resurrection that the crucifix in young Ganin's sickroom suggests is, here, a resurrection of (and in) memory. When in chapter 1 the elevator in which Ganin and Alfyorov are stuck suddenly revives and takes them to their destination, Alfyorov comments, "I thought someone had pressed the button and brought us up, but there's no one here. . . . Up we came and yet there's no one here. That's symbolic too" (*M*, 4). The words are oddly prophetic: scores of emigrants who succumbed to the temptation to return to their native country found "no one there"—Russia had changed beyond recognition. Yet the symbolism of *Mary* is held in check: symptomatically, the quoted remark, as well as one about the stalled elevator as a symbol of émigré existence (see *M*, 3), comes from a philistine character,[7] an apt exponent of the theme of *poshlost'* (or "*posh-lust*": see *NG*, 63–74), the smug phoniness ridiculed throughout Nabokov's fiction. Moreover, unknown to Alfyorov, his words "up we came and yet there's no one here" also apply to Mary's arrival at the Berlin railway station after the curtain falls. The "merciless clarity" of Ganin's last-minute insight suggests not only the rigid self-discipline of an aesthetician but also a touch of cruelty that invites moral criticism of Ganin's conduct.

III

Because of the autobiographical element of *Mary* (its story of the protagonist's first love is similar to the material of chapter 12 of

[6]See Field, *Nabokov: His Life in Art*, p. 128.
[7]Cf. Hyde, *Vladimir Nabokov*, p. 39.

Speak, Memory), readers tend to be uncritical of Ganin's conduct. Yet it is Nabokov's general practice to bestow parts of his own experience upon his characters, much as they may otherwise differ from himself. Ganin is not a Nabokovian lyrical hero; to a large extent he is Nabokov's version of a charismatic villain, a dynamic force of infinite potentialities for the world of fiction. In *Mary* this force is used to explore the tension between the moral and the pseudoaesthetic, as well as the tension between sympathy and detachment.

The idea of detachment is explored through the motifs of proximity versus distance—distance in time, space, and personal relationships. On the last page Ganin realizes the metaphor of distance by boarding a train that will take him far away from Berlin. This act, like his attempts to maintain a sort of aesthetic detachment from actual experience, is associated with the rudimentary nature of his power of sympathy.

Ganin, indeed, passes through the novel leaving pain and confusion in his wake. The romantic lover of the fictional past is an inconsiderate and somewhat rude drifter in the fictional present. When his memories are first evoked, he takes care to "re-creat[e] a world that had perished" in order to "please the girl whom he did not dare to place in it until it was absolutely complete" (*M,* 33). Ironically, in the fictional present he also creates a setting for her arrival, yet not one that could please her. As the novel ends, the reader is left to imagine how Mary would painfully seek out the *pension*[8] only to find the poet Podtyagin dying, the landlady exhausted by his bedside, the "cosy" Klara brokenhearted after Ganin's departure, and her husband Alfyorov insensible—because Ganin had gotten him drunk and set his alarm clock to a late hour in order to forestall him at the railway station.

Ganin's romantic image of himself is quite remote from his image in the eyes of his fellow boarders (Nabokov will develop such a contrast more fully in *The Eye,* 1930). Klara, who has seen him opening Alfyorov's drawer and been offered no explanation, will remain convinced that she has been in love with a thief; the others will regard his tampering with Alfyorov's alarm clock as a piece of wanton hooliganism. Like Ganin's self-image, the latter view is not completely devoid of truth: in the past Ganin had played with his will power by "making himself, for instance, get out of bed in the middle of the night in order to go down and throw a cigarette butt into a postbox"

---

[8]In chapter 1 Alfyorov mentions that Mary "wrote the address in a very funny way" (*M,* 2), suggesting that she does not know German.

(*M*, 10), without even regarding his experiment as a practical joke on the owners of the box. This is a self-emulating game rather than a Schopenhauerian exercise in subduing one's will by forcing oneself to do things contrary to the desires of the flesh. By his entropy-promoting unconcern for the discomfort of his neighbor, whom he does not bother to love as himself, Ganin increases the gulf between himself and others.[9] In effect, he becomes as consummate a solipsist as Van Veen in *Ada*, and it is not accidental that Van Veen elaborates on Ganin's youthful trick of walking on his hands, turning the world upside down.

Ganin never seems to think about Mary's unhappiness. At the cinema he is annoyed with Lyudmila's whispering to Klara something about the material for a dress but never notices how sick Klara is of wearing the same dress every day. Having little else to do, he helps Podtyagin get his exit visa for France but does not prevent the old man from losing his precious passport; the reader, however, is allowed to notice the precise moment when Podtyagin lays his passport on the seat of a bus, never to pick it up (see *M*, 80). Podtyagin suffers his fatal heart attack as a result of the setback, yet Ganin has no feelings of guilt on leaving him. For the sake of the poetic image of Mary he not only sacrifices Mary herself but also spurns commitment to the essentially kind people around him. Such solipsistic single-mindedness prefigures that of Martin Edelweiss in *Glory*: in his pursuit of victory over fear, Martin does not regard his mother's anguish as too high a price for his self-emulating exploit.

Ganin's personal standard is not ethical, like Martin's, but aesthetic. He is repelled by anything that smacks of banality, of *poshlost'*; he is annoyed by Alfyorov and Lyudmila, and even by Mary when she uses the heavy-duty formula of surrender ("I am yours, . . . do what you

---

[9]According to Schopenhauer, a truly virtuous man is one who "*makes less distinction than is usually made between himself and others*. . . . He perceives that the distinction between himself and others, which to a wicked man is so great a gulf, belongs only to a fleeting, deceptive phenomenon. He recognizes immediately, and without reasons or arguments, that the in-itself of his own phenomenon is also that of others, namely that will-to-live which constitutes the inner nature of everything and lives in all" (*The World as Will and Representation*, 1:372). Ganin, the artist *manqué*, is to some extent a wicked person, yet in Nabokov (as in Joyce) the image of the true artist almost invariably contains a touch of cruelty. This is not a Nietzschean reinterpretation of Schopenhauer; rather, it is the consequence of art's mandatory emphasis on difference, on distinctive features. Art cannot reveal the universal inner nature of things without first capturing the "fleeting, deceptive phenomenon," the uniqueness of individual identities that increases distance at the expense of carnivalistic sympathy.

like with me": *M*, 73) during their tryst in the park. At the same time Ganin is almost as shallow as another fictional salesman, Kurt Dreyer of *King, Queen, Knave*; the touch of artistic sensibility is wasted on him if he cannot appreciate the motives of Mary's strained submission or the proud humility with which she (unlike Lyudmila) accepts their rupture. Like Dreyer, Ganin dreams of outlandish adventures because he is incapable of achieving a defamiliarizing perception of ordinary life. "Average reality" does, indeed, begin "to rot and stink as soon as the act of individual creation ceases to animate a subjectively perceived texture" (*SO*, 118). The divorce of average reality from the act of creation compliments Ganin's solipsism. He leads a rich and intense inner life, but instead of letting this life irradiate upon the world given to perception, he leaves average reality to rot (like the cigarette butt in the mailbox) and replaces it with strictly internalized processes. He elevates memory to the status of art—not undeservedly—yet makes the mistake (to be repeated, in another way, by the protagonist of *The Defense*) of using art as a surrogate for life.

The blurred borderlines between the description of the Berlin scene and Ganin's memories of recuperating after typhus suggest that the memories are not embedded in the present experience but rather take its place. The image of clean, ample clothes, which replaces the reader's memory of Ganin's dusty and sweaty ones of the previous morning, signals the point at which a full transition from the fictional present to the fictional past has taken place:

> Wandering around Berlin on that Tuesday in spring, he recuperated all over again, felt what it was like to get out of bed for the first time, felt the weakness in his legs. He looked at himself in every mirror. His clothes seemed unusually clean, singularly ample, and slightly unfamiliar. He walked slowly down the wide avenue leading from the garden terrace into the depths of the park. Here and there the earth, empurpled by the shadows of leaves, broke into molehills that looked like heaps of black worms. He had put on white trousers and lilac socks, dreaming of meeting someone, not yet knowing who it would be. [*M*, 33–34]

Ganin's error is indirectly commented on by Podtyagin, who regrets having put into poems what he should have put into life (*M*, 42). Podtyagin, however, is not a solipsist; and the spark of talent with which he is endowed redeems even his dependence on the quotidian, which he accepts with a somewhat Dostoevskian, self-flagellating humility. He can still probe the meaning of the émigré existence, and it is to him that Ganin and Klara turn in an attempt to make sense of their lives. But Podtyagin is too tired to receive confessions: symbolically, Russian emigration can no longer find support in the regional literature of the past. He is a dying man; the dignity of his condition is not sufficiently recognized by the people around him, but it reasserts itself in his ironic farewell to Ganin: " 'You see—without any passport' " (*M*, 109). In repeated reading, Podtyagin, with his ironic self-pity, is a more endearing character than the presumptuously earnest Ganin.

IV

The ambivalence of Ganin's decision to avoid meeting Mary finds its parallel in the cautious touch of ambiguity concerning Mrs. Alfyorov herself. It is not quite clear whether this woman really is Ganin's Mary. The photograph that Ganin sees is not described, nor is the impression that it produces on him. While Ganin is looking at the picture, we hear only Alfyorov's comments[10]: "And that's Mary, my wife. Poor snapshot, but quite a good likeness all the same. And here's another, taken in our garden. Mary's the one sitting, in the white dress. I haven't seen her for four years. But I don't suppose she's changed much. I really don't know how I'll survive till Saturday. Wait! Where are you going, Lev Glebovich? Do stay!" (*M*, 25).

It is significant that though the English version of *Mary* follows the Russian original with a fidelity matched only by that of *Invitation to a Beheading*, the dress of Alfyorov's wife is described as "white," whereas it is "light" (*svetloe*) in the Russian text (*Ma*, 42). The word "light" can suggest "flimsy," which Nabokov might have wished to avoid, yet whatever considerations determined his choice, the epithet "white" brings to mind the white dress that Mary had worn for her intended bridal night with Ganin (see *M*, 72). Ganin may have merely projected familiar features onto the "poor snapshot," subconsciously prompted by the white dress and the mention of a yellow-bearded

[10]Nabokov may have encountered this technique in Dickens, with whose work he was made familiar in childhood. In *Bleak House*, for instance, it is only from Sir Leicester's belated reaction that we learn about Lady Dedlock's having fainted at the sight of a piece of writing.

admirer in Mary's letter to him (*M*, 92)—Alfyorov sports a little yellow beard. In the first chapter of the novel Ganin narrowly escapes being shown Mrs. Alfyorov's letter and thus loses his chance to recognize the handwriting.

Moreover, the concatenation of memories starts not with Mary herself but with Ganin's convalescence after typhus; just before showing Ganin his wife's picture, Alfyorov produces the picture of his sister who, he says, died of typhus. Typhus may therefore be the key to Pandora's box of memories, and the four days that Ganin spends reliving his romance may have originated in a mnemonic trick. In retrospect, *Mary* thus appears to contain elements of the "sources" (*Roots III*) technique that Nabokov perfected in his later fiction.

The touch of ambiguity suggests that no matter who Alfyorov's wife may turn out to be, she is not the Mary whom Ganin had loved. This could provide aesthetic justification for Ganin'a retreat at the end of the novel; therefore, Nabokov undermines the ambiguity by giving Ganin a few minutes to reexamine the photographs before Klara surprises him in Alfyorov's room (see *M*, 35). Moreover, in *The Defense*, Mrs. Luzhin admires Alfyorov's wife (see *D*, 203): there may, of course, be more than one nice woman by the name of Mashen'ka in "real life," but fiction does not usually imitate "real life" to that extent.

By the time Nabokov wrote *Mary* he had already translated *Alice in Wonderland* into Russian, and it would not be surprising to find him basing the most appealing part of the protagonist's experience on a mistake or a dream, as he would later do in "The Affair of Honor" (1927), *The Waltz Invention* (1938), and other works. Yet one must acknowledge the wisdom of his refraining from the use of this framework in *Mary*. Had the doubt about the identity of Alfyorov's wife been given greater force, the aesthetic aptness of Ganin's final choice would have eclipsed the ugliness of his decision to abandon the woman he had loved to the life of sordid compromise from which he himself escapes. The tentativeness of the ambiguity, especially when compared with the flourishing of this technique in *Invitation to a Beheading*, is indicative of the novelist's attitude toward Ganin: faced with the ambivalence of Ganin's conduct, Nabokov tips the scale in favor of criticism rather than justification.

V

Another Nabokovian technique, somewhat more clearly evident in *Mary*, is the ultimate cancelation of the protagonist by reminding the reader of his fictionality. At the end of the novel Ganin goes to the southwest of Germany, whence he intends to continue to France and the sea—"without a single visa" (*M*, 114). That cryptic remark refers either to the fact that, unlike Podtyagin, Ganin has a forged Polish passport (a counterfeit identity?), which gives him greater freedom, or else to the fact that he does not care about the legality of his transits. If the latter possibility is read figuratively, however, the remark may also be understood to mean that Ganin does not need a visa for where he is going—back to the "involute abode" (*PF*, 63) whence he has emerged—any more than Podtyagin needs a passport or Mr. Silbermann of *The Real Life of Sebastian Knight* needs money. Ganin is dismissed after having served his purpose as a beneficiary of one of the most touching parts of his creator's past. On seeing the movie in which he himself appears as an extra,[11] Ganin thinks that "the whole of life seem[s] like a piece of film-making where heedless extras [know] nothing of the picture in which they [are] taking part" (*M*, 22). The remark is more than a piece of homespun philosophy: at this point in the narrative Ganin does not yet know what the novelist (the "Assistant Producer"? See *ND*, 71) has in store for him, though only a short while later he will knock on Alfyorov's door and be shown some photographs. Nabokov is generous to Ganin; not only does he give him the love of Mary and four happy days of memories, but he also arranges the possibility that the lovers' paths will cross again. The rest, however, is left, as it were, for Ganin to decide. Nabokov does not seek out plausible accidents to prevent an aesthetically impossible reunion. Instead, he presents Ganin as the kind of person who would *choose* to renounce Mary—one whose choice is as much in character as Martha's decision to abort her husband's murder at the end of *King, Queen, Knave*.

Nabokov's last novel, *Look at the Harlequins!*, contains a significant allusion to Browning's "My Last Duchess," in which the Duke of Ferrara admires the beautiful portrait of his late wife much more than he had appreciated the original; he has, it is implied, deprived the lady of her young life and, so to say, turned her into the picture that he had commissioned. In *Mary*, Ganin prefers his beautiful internalized image of the woman he has loved to the woman herself. His decision not to

---

[11] By a "chance that mimics choice" (*TD*, 230), the English word "extra" for the Russian *statist* evokes an association with the notion of "superfluous person" (*lishnii chelovek*) that Russian criticism sometimes applies to those exiled romantic heroes: Pushkin's Onegin, Lermontov's Pechorin, Turgenev's Rudin.

see Mary at the end of the novel is motivated by his wish to separate his image of her from the real person that she may have become. This insistence on a strict partition is opposed to true creativity, which seeks to reduce the distance between the real and the ideal.

As Ganin is waiting for Mary's train to arrive, the corresponding span of the representational time is filled with the description of the splendid morning; this description is discontinued as soon as he decides against meeting Mary. Before his final resolution is made, Ganin's keen observation of the details of the scene is said to mean "a secret turning point for him, an awakening" (M, 113); yet in the last sentence, after he has boarded a Southbound train, he is shown falling into a doze, "his face buried in the folds of his mackintosh" (M, 114). Ganin's awakening is canceled, together with the protagonist himself: the dawn and the "curiously calming effect" (M, 114) of the sight of workmen building a house stand for *his author's* feelings upon completing the novel. In his introduction to *Mary*, Nabokov explains his use of autobiographical material as motivated by a writer's "relief of getting rid of oneself, before going on to better things" (M, xi). His criticism of Ganin may to some extent have exorcised the irrational feeling of guilt that transpires through the ending of the "Tamara" segment (chapter 12) of *Speak, Memory*, with its thought of "Tamara's" letters reaching the Crimea after the addressee has sailed away.

Be that as it may, though aesthetic appropriateness does not justify Ganin's decision, it does justify the narrative choices of the author. If it is Nabokov's imagination that balks at the penultimate moment and thus prevents the reunion, it does so in order to keep the carnivalistic element inherent in the theme of sympathy well under control. He is prepared to carry sympathy only to a certain point, and that point is the threshold beyond which sympathy denies detachment and contact threatens to become merger. The need for a balance between sympathy and detachment is the structural idea that governs the relationship between the themes and techniques of *Mary*.

4

King, Queen, Knave, or
Lust under the Linden

Lovers and madmen have such seething brains,
Such shaping fantasies, that apprehend
More than cool reason ever comprehends.
The lunatic, the lover, and the poet,
Are of imagination all compact.
William Shakespeare, *A Midsummer Night's Dream* 5.1

Nabokov's second novel, *King, Queen, Knave* (*Korol', dama, valet,* 1928), a self-reflexive satirical version of the novel of adultery, asserted his intellectual and artistic independence, his refusal to restrict himself to the genre of the "human document" (*KQK,* viii), or to cater to the émigré readers' need for explicit moral and ideological support.

The characters of *King, Queen, Knave* are Germans, people whom Nabokov during his stay in Berlin did not bother to observe as closely as he would later observe his new compatriots across the Atlantic. "I spoke no German," he says in the foreword, "had no German friends, had not read a single German novel either in the original, or in translation. But in art, as in nature, a glaring disadvantage may turn out to be a subtle protective device" (*KQK,* viii). Protective from what? Perhaps from "human humidity" (*KQK,* viii), the potentially overwhelming compassion which, but for a timely exercise in detachment, would have become difficult to control.[1] Perhaps also from the duty to deal with issues of the recent political agenda, which—in particular the Russian revolution—were almost "an encroachment upon creative

---

[1] See also Pifer's excellent discussion (*Nabokov and the Novel,* pp. 14–18) of Nabokov's detachment from his characters in *King, Queen, Knave* as a break with the formal tradition.

47

freedom" (*D*, 79); according to *The Defense*, "The general opinion was that [the revolution] had influenced the course of every Russian's life; an author could not have his hero go through it without getting scorched, and to dodge it was impossible" (*D*, 80). A non-Russian environment, however, allowed a respite from this predicament. "The fairytale freedom inherent in an unknown milieu," notes Nabokov in the foreword, "answered my dream of pure invention" (*KQK*, viii). It was freedom to deal with a subject of universal, transnational significance.

The major theme of *King, Queen, Knave* is the rejection of spiritual life. Whereas the protagonist of *Mary* rejects human commitment for the sake of the perfection of a disembodied spiritualized image, the main characters of *King, Queen, Knave* spurn fate's offer of an experience that could have raised them above the satisfaction of carnal desires. The "bright brute," as Nabokov called the book (*KQK*, vii), is an inquiry into the mechanics of the devaluation of love and the substitution for it of lust.

The flippant heroine of Nabokov's *Ada* has occasion to criticize a book called *Love under the Lindens* (*A*, 403): the title is an Antiterran hybrid of Eugene O'Neill's *Desire under the Elms* and the name of Berlin's (now East Berlin's) main street, Unter den Linden. Lust, rather than love, under the lindens, is examined in *King, Queen, Knave*, a narrative whose coloration is influenced by "the map and weather of Berlin" (*KQK*, viii). The characters' bondage to lust gradually reveals its horrifying aspects, yet the grim logic of their fate is counteracted by the comic mode in which their experience is rendered.

According to Henri Bergson, the admixture of the mechanical with the living is an infallible source of comedy.[2] Nabokov maintains the comic spirit of *King, Queen, Knave* by fully developing one of the aspects of nonauthentic life—its imitative, artificial, mechanical features. Moreover, the novel flaunts the machinery through which it brings about its comic ending, subverting the mechanics of causality by the countermoves of coincidence through which the novelist self-consciously monitors the plot.

I

The consciously self-imposed artificiality of the characters' lives is brought into relief with the help of a "fellow artist," the name-

---

[2]See Henri Bergson, "Laughter," in *Comedy* (Garden City, N.Y., 1956), pp. 61–190.

less, mysterious, and somewhat pathetic Inventor (Herr Frankenstein?) who creates walking mannequins for the department store owned by the "King." The automannequins are impelled not by a robotlike imitation of a brain but by a network of currents that pass through *voskin*, the waxlike material out of which they are made (*vosk* is the Russian for "wax"). These currents simulate the "self-awareness" of human muscles, a phenomenon which, according to one of the Inventor's assistants, may account for one's "well-known capacity of waking up at a self-imposed hour" (*KQK*, 194). The "Knave" of the novel, Franz Bubendorf, exemplifies this capacity by waking up at exactly the predetermined time on the day when his self-conscious body is to be used as a murder weapon (see *KQK*, 238).

The cast of automannequins—the mature gentleman, the lady, and the young sleepwalker—reproduces the human trio of King-Queen-Knave, so that the moving dummies come to symbolize the state to which the main characters of the novel are likely to degenerate. The "Knave" comes closest to doing so.

Franz arrives in Berlin from the province and is given employment by his uncle Kurt Dreyer (the "King"), out of whom he is self-consciously, and first not without a tingle of shame, determined to "squeeze everything he possibly [can]" (*KQK*, 27). He falls in love with Dreyer's wife Martha (the "Queen") and, soon after the affair is consummated, surrenders to her his body and his will. His lovemaking becomes mechanical ("to work, old soldier": *KQK*, 166), and the perceptions and thoughts of his everyday life become completely automatic:

He would rise; shuffle to the smelly toilet . . . , shuffle back, wash his hands, brush his teeth, shave, wipe the soap from his ears, dress, walk to the subway station, get on a non-smoking car, read the same old advertisement ditty overhead, and to the rhythm of its crude trochee reach his destination, climb the stone staircase, squint at the mottled pansies in the bright sun on a large flowerbed in front of the exit, cross the street, and do everything in the store that he was supposed to do. Returning home in the same way, he would do once again all that was expected of him. After her departure, he would read the newspaper for a quarter of an hour or so because it was customary to read newspapers. Then he would walk over to his uncle's villa. At supper he would sometimes repeat what he had read in the paper, reproducing every other sentence verbatim but strangely jumbling the facts in between. . . .

His thoughts were characterized by the same monotony as his actions, and their order corresponded to the order of his day. Why has he stopped

the coffee? Can't flush if the chain comes off every time. Dull blade.
Piffke shaves with his collar on in the public washroom. These white
shorts are not practical. Today is the ninth—no, the tenth—no, the elev-
enth of June. She's again on the balcony. Bare arms, parched geraniums.
Train more crowded every morning. Clean your teeth with Dentophile,
every minute you will smile. They are fools who offer their seats to big
strong women. Clean your teeth with Dentophile, clean your minute
with your smile. Out we file. [*KQK*, 200–201]

The mechanization of his mental life is welcome to Franz because in
waking hours (his nights are "full of terror": *KQK*, 200) it suppresses
the desires and adolescent disgust between which his consciousness
oscillates when not dulled by routine. He shrinks from creative, defamiliarizing perception for fear that it may expand his "chamber of
horrors" (*KQK*, 3), the repository of disgusting memories formed in
his brain at more impressionable times. Lacking the courage to con-
front "average reality," he becomes part of that reality; indeed, the
smell that Dreyer notices around Franz (*KQK*, 185) is more than a
symptom of the latter's rudimentary hygiene.[3]

"The slow motion of a sleepwalker" (*KQK*, 74), which at the beginning of the novel was caused by Franz's erotic languor, eventually
becomes one of the symptoms of his lack of control over his life.[4] His
stultification is brought into high relief in the episode in which amid
the hilarious interplay of the author's imagination with that of the
characters, Franz is confused with a mannequin, while Dreyer appears
in the role of a fitter (see *KQK*, 186).

In the best tradition of literary adultery,[5] Franz soon gets tired of
his affair with Martha, yet he not only obediently continues the affair
but is also prepared to carry out her plan to murder Dreyer. His
mental debility progresses. In the last chapter, when the Inventor's
automannequins are demonstrated to a potential buyer, the young

[3]"Average reality begins to rot and stink as soon as the act of individual creation
ceases to animate a subjectively perceived texture" (*SO*, 118). See also the discussion
of this statement in Chapters 1 and 3 above.

[4]Cf. Nabokov's development of the theme of sleepwalking in *Transparent Things*.

[5]*King, Queen, Knave* is in many ways a parody on the genre of literary adultery as
well as a reinterpretation of some of its conventions. For an interesting analysis of such
conventions, see Carol Bensick, "His Folly, Her Weakness: Demystified Adultery in
The Scarlet Letter," in Michael Colacurcio, ed., *New Essays on "The Scarlet Letter"*
(Cambridge, 1985), pp. 137–59; Martha, however, gains weight by the end of the novel
(like Anna Karenin) not because adultery is "illegal, immoral, *and* fattening" (p. 159),
but because she has a heart condition and is a greedy eater.

sleepwalker is not among them—perhaps because, realizing a metaphor, he has completely merged with the dehumanized Franz.

Of the three main characters, Franz comes closest to matching the state of the automannequins; his uncle and potential victim Kurt Dreyer manifests the least resemblance to his own waxwork portrait. His frequently unconventional conduct and avid love of life may even mislead the reader into considering him an artist *manqué*, one of the Nabokovian avatars of the artist,[6] but Dreyer is a true artist as far as business is concerned. Reading such modern novelists as Robertson Davies and Walker Percy, we have become accustomed to the idea that moneymaking is a talent in its own right; in the case of Dreyer, who gets rich by successfully translating his fantasies into commercial ventures during a period of inflation, this talent is definitely artistic. (Ironically, his wife Martha is the only person to appreciate this, although for the wrong reason.) Dreyer considers himself a "happy and healthy failure": "What prevented him from seeing the world? He had the means—but there was some fatal veil between him and every dream that beckoned to him" (*KQK*, 223–24).

Dreyer's "fatal veil" is also the Coleridgean "film of familiarity" (both expressions appear only in the revised version of the novel), which cancels the "thrill" of perception: "Natures like his spend enough energy in tackling with all the weapons and vessels of the mind the enforced impressions of existence to be grateful for the neutral film of familiarity that soon forms between the newness and the consumer. It was too boring to think that the object might change of its own accord and assume unforeseen characteristics. That would mean having to enjoy it again, and he was no longer young" (*KQK*, 106).[7]

Whereas Franz embraces the automatic way of life out of moral cowardice, it is out of indolence and premature intellectual fatigue that Dreyer allows his mental life to acquire the automatic quality that his adventurous physical life successfully escapes. Dreyer fancies himself a

---

[6]Cf. Vladislav Khodasevich: "The life of the artist and the life of a device in the consciousness of the artist—this is Sirin's theme, revealing itself to some degree or other in almost every one of his writings, beginning with *The Defense*. However, the artist (and more concretely speaking, the writer) is never shown by him directly, but always behind a mask: a chess-player, a businessman, etc." ("On Sirin," in Appel and Newman, *Nabokov*, p. 100).

[7]In this respect, Dreyer is the diametrical opposite of Nabokov's Martin Edelweiss, who finds a "thrill" and "glamour" in "the most ordinary pleasures as well as in the seemingly meaningless adventures of a lonely life" (*Gl*, x.).

born artist who is "a businessman by accident" (*KQK*, 223); he is, in fact, a talented businessman and an avid yet lazy audience for artistic performances (including the Almighty's), a superficial "consumer" of the kind that would enjoy and pigeonhole the novel in which he himself appears but would neither reread or remember it nor deepen or modify his understanding. As his former mistress Erica complains, he treats living people like statuettes: "You seat a person on a little shelf and think she'll keep sitting like that forever" (*KQK*, 175). Thus Dreyer's aesthetic failure turns into a moral one. His insufficient respect for the autonomous development of others also blinds him to the plot hatched against him by Martha and Franz.

The motif of consciously self-imposed artificiality is reflected in Dreyer's love life. Like most husbands in novels of adultery, he is married to a woman who, he well knows, cannot really love him; it is by gifts and compromises that he coaxes her into counterfeit eroticism. His extramarital sex is characterized by a quest for novelty—such as skiing (*"shee-ing,"*: *KQK*, 160) trips with both identical twin girls instead of just one—in order to achieve artificial stimulation in the absence of genuine feelings. His love for his wife has an element of genuineness about it, but the Martha he loves is the image he has conceived in his brain, an image left far behind by the woman who cannot remain "on the little shelf" where she was seated in the placid early days of their marriage. And yet, because of this glimmer of genuine feeling, Dreyer is felt to deserve the rescue that the self-conscious artifice of the novelist grants him.

As to Martha, artificiality is her chosen way of life. It is she who gives a new expression to the Nabokovian theme of artistic creativity, but she is an anti-artist rather than an artist *manqué*. She represents the kind of destructive militant banality that one day may just slip into crime.

Martha starts by plagiarism. She furnishes the villa that Dreyer has bought for her out of the contemporary German version of *Better Homes and Gardens*, demands of him conventional behavior and respectable savings accounts, chooses a lover who resembles a famous actor (a contemporary sex symbol), and conducts the affair "strictly adhering to every rule of adultery" (*KQK*, 115). Plagiarism yields to a grim parody on artistic creation. Regarding Franz as "warm, healthy young wax that one can manipulate and mold till its shape suits your pleasure" (*KQK*, 31), Martha proceeds not to create a person out of

clay—as two real artists, God and Pygmalion, are said to have done—
but to reduce a living human being to the state of mechanical dummy.

Besides serving as the sinister mirror image of the Inventor, who
creates dummies from a different sort of wax, Martha enters, as it
were, into a presumptuous competition with the novelist himself. She
undertakes to usurp his prerogative of determining his characters' fate:
"She needed a sedentary husband. A subdued and grave husband. She
needed a dead husband" (*KQK*, 197)—the word "dead" suddenly
stops being a figurative synonym for "sedentary" and "subdued" and
recovers its literal meaning. Having passed from exercises in domestic
artifice to the pseudocreative act of "molding" Franz, Martha now
engages in the glaringly anticreative pursuit of her husband's death. At
first she half believes that she can get rid of Dreyer by just intensely
wishing him gone, but unlike the black magic of the novelist during
the automannequin demonstration (the female mannequin collapses
behind the stage at the exact time when Martha enters the final stage
of her illness), her voodoo exercises fail ("My spells don't work":
KQK, 128). She then starts planning a murder, calculating details,
choosing weapons, seeking for clues in detective novelettes, "and
thereby plagiarizing villainy (an act which after all had been avoided
only by Cain)" (*KQK*, 178). Leaving an exhibition of criminology,
Dreyer thinks "what a talentless person one must be, what a poor
thinker or hysterical fool, to murder one's neighbor" (*KQK*, 207). His
"veil of familiarity" prevents him from applying this insight to his
nephew and wife.

By concocting different murder plans and rejecting them as unsafe,
Martha plagiarizes, as it were, the trial-and-error workings of Fate in
The Gift or of the invisible matchmaker in *The Defense*.[8] Like these
two agents of the novelist, she later evolves a workable plan by adjust-
ing all the details to Dreyer's character: Dreyer cannot swim, so he can
be drowned; he likes bets and games, so he can be lured into a dangerous situation. Even these ideas are not quite her own: it is Dreyer
who offers her a vacation at the seaside and laments his helplessness in
water. At this point, however, the self-conscious countermoves of the
novelist rescue Dreyer from his "logical fate" (*BS*, 233).

[8] In these two novels (as in Sebastian Knight's novel *Success*) Fate seems to miscal-
culate in its first attempts to bring two potential lovers together: e. g., early in the novel
Fyodor fails to meet Zina because he does not like to make German translations;
Luzhin is not led to his future wife either by his classmate or by his geography teacher
because he avoids their company.

II

The installation of this countermechanism is delegated to none other than the Inventor of the automannequins, whose function is thus not limited to providing an indirect commentary on the main characters of the novel.

While Martha believes that destiny is on her side (see *KQK*, 156), "wise fate" (*KQK*, 160) is quietly preparing to sabotage her plans. One of the guests at a party in the Dreyers' house is the director of the Fatum Insurance Company, later referred to as Mr. Fatum (see *KQK*, 145). Insofar as characters are "methods of composition" (*RLSK*, 95), Fate is thus a member of the cast. It has aliases: "the imp of coincidence" (*KQK*, 38); the "god of chance (Cazelty of Sluch, or whatever his real name was), once you imagined that god in the role of a novelist or a playwright, as Goldemar had in his most famous work" (*KQK*, 224).[9] The word "Sluch" is sometimes incorrectly understood as the Russian for "rumor."[10] According to the "Notes on Transliteration" in Nabokov's volumes on *Eugene Onegin*, however, the Russian word for "rumor" would be transliterated as *sluh* or *slukh*. The "sluch" of *King, Queen, Knave* is a truncated (bastard) form of the Russian *sluchai*, meaning "chance event, random occurrence."[11] Just as "Cazelty" is the plain-folk distortion of "casualty" ("plain-folk" being Nabokov's translation of *prostonarodnykh* in the Prefatory Piece of *Eugene Onegin*), "Sluch" is the slick double of the good-natured slouchy Fate of *The Gift*.

Unlike Franz, this mysterious character refuses to be manipulated by anyone except the novelist himself. Aided and abetted by the novelist, Sluch sends the "fifth business,"[12] the actual writer's fictional fellow Inventor, in pursuit of the troublemaking Franz and even accommodates him in the same hotel room where Franz had spent his first night

---

[9]Goldemar is, of course, Vladimir, and his most famous work in 1928 is, of course, *King, Queen, Knave*, where "Sluch" is the puppeteer's *alter ego*.

[10]See Carl R. Proffer, "A New Deck for Nabokov's Knaves," in Appel and Newman, *Nabokov*, p. 300; and Lawrence L. Lee, *Vladimir Nabokov* (Boston, 1976), p. 39.

[11]Cf. Andrew Field's note on Pnin as the truncated form of Repnin bestowed upon illegitimate offspring (*Nabokov: His Life in Art*, p. 139).

[12]The "fifth business," made famous by Robertson Davies (in his novel bearing that title), is a character who stands aside from the central conflicts of the plot yet without whom the denouement would not be possible. Several such characters, including the Inventor of *King, Queen, Knave*, are discussed in my essay "A Nabokovian Character in Conrad's *Nostromo*," *Revue de littérature comparée*, no. 1 (1985), 15–29.

in Berlin: "It is significant that Fate should have lodged him there of all places. It was a road that Franz had travelled—and all at once Fate remembered and sent in pursuit this practically nameless man who of course knew nothing of his important assignment, and never found out anything about it, as for that matter no one else ever did, not even old Enricht" (*KQK*, 107–8).

The Inventor's assignment is, first and foremost, to provide Dreyer with one of his favorite escapes to other people's imagination, escapes that he has grown wise enough to conceal from his wife until they become remunerative. Aware of Martha's impatience with risky financial ventures, Dreyer has postponed mentioning the automannequin project to her until he is about to sell the patent to Mr. Ritter (a variation on the *"mon oncle d'Amérique"* theme; *L*, 29). The information is imparted to Martha a moment before she is supposed to give Franz the sign to push Dreyer into the waters of Pomerania Bay, and since the prospect of adding a hundred thousand dollars to her bank account is irresistible she deems it worthwhile to give her husband a reprieve and postpone her widowhood. This, as the narrator notes in another connection, is a "fatal postponement" (*KQK*, 220). Just as Dreyer never gets to tell Franz the end of a funny story that must be accompanied by "certain vehement gestures and extravagant attitudes" (*KQK*, 219–20), so Martha never gets to start the series of vehement movements that would lead to her husband's drowning. The chill and the overexcitement trigger the pneumonia of which she dies.

Her change of mind is consistent with Martha's stinginess and greed. She has married Dreyer for money; she meets Franz in a second-class railway car because, despite her husband's wealth, she grudges the expense of a first-class ticket; she haggles with old Enricht, Franz's landlord, over five marks a month, and does not send Franz to buy manuals on poisons because the "dutiful darling" (*KQK*, 164) may wind up with "ten volumes costing twenty-five marks each" (*KQK*, 163). Since she would not spend two hundred and fifty marks to get information on how to brew a poison for Dreyer, and since her potential willingness to "grant [Dreyer] a reprieve for some solid deal" is anticipated earlier in the novel (*KQK*, 196), Dreyer's escape is related as much to the patterns of her mind as to the danger itself. Nor is the reader unprepared for Martha's expedient sickbed exit at the end of the novel—and not only because the heroines of the novels of adultery usually die in the end: *King, Queen, Knave*, especially its revised version, contains a sufficient number of references to her ill health and susceptibility to colds. Thus Fate, or Sluch, turns the tables on Martha for having presumed to plan an "in character" death for the shallow yet essentially well-meaning Dreyer.

Yet Dreyer owes his rescue primarily to the timely mention of the automannequin deal and to the preparations for this deal: that is, to arrangements made a long time before the crisis. The self-conscious artifice of *King, Queen, Knave* thus takes the shape of insurance (the "Fatum Insurance Company"). The logical development of the situation is carrying Dreyer inexorably to destruction—as in the plays of Molière and in Fielding's *Tom Jones*, comedy threatens to yield to tragedy—but then it turns out that art is not governed by the same grim causality as the lives of the trio; that Dreyer is insured by the foresight of Fate, which has the Inventor (and Mr. Ritter, product of a generous literary convention) up its capacious sleeve.

The narrative does not conceal the artificiality of this insurance: the Inventor is explicitly presented as an emissary of Fate (see *KQK*, 107–8); after the aborted murder a restaurant singer keeps repeating a song about Montevideo, which also happens to be the name of the hotel in which the Inventor has succeeded Franz (see *KQK*, 253); then the automannequins begin to crumble and disintegrate (see *KQK*, 262–63)—not because the Inventor is a charlatan but because they have served their purpose and are no longer necessary. This is one of the improvements over the Russian version of the novel.[13] While editing the translation of his early work, Nabokov seems to have been compelled to transfer to it the method that he evolved much later in *Invitation to a Beheading*, in which the fictional setting frankly crumbles once the need for it is over. The accident that befalls the Inventor and his mannequins at the end of the novel (see *KQK*, 262–63) cannot be taken at face value; Mr. Ritter, who is watching the demonstration, does not seem to notice anything wrong and several pages later cables his wish to clinch the deal (see *KQK*, 270). In his grief over Martha's death Dreyer brushes aside the news of his financial success, and the novelist himself dismisses the "fifth business" just as he would have

[13]Most of thes changes are surveyed in Jane Grayson, *Nabokov Translated: A Comparison of Nabokov's Russian and English Prose* (Oxford, 1977); and Proffer, "A New Deck for Nabokov's Knaves," pp. 293–309. One amusing detail: the strawberries that Dreyer wants but cannot buy in the first chapter (*KQK*, p. 6) were plums in the Russian version. Why the change? Perhaps because in 1967 Nabokov, unlike the Sirin of 1928, was familiar with the sinners reaching out for strawberries in Hieronymus Bosch's *Garden of Earthly Delights*.

discarded a used Kleenex tissue—the absence of which is anachronis-
tically lamented in the English version of *King, Queen, Knave* (see
KQK, 108).

III

Franz, Martha and Dreyer are not, in general, the lifeless cardboard figures that the title of the novel may suggest.[14] The title *King,
Queen, Knave* outlines the conventional triangle about which—after
*Anna Karenin, Madame Bovary, La Princesse de Clèves, Le bal du compte
d'Orgel*,[15] *The Scarlet Letter*, and so on—there is little left to say in
terms of the "human interest" that V. Sirin demonstratively re-
strained. The images of playing cards refer, moreover, not only to the
three cards in Hans Christian Andersen's fairytale but also to Lewis
Carroll's *Alice in Wonderland* and the obnoxious Queen of Hearts, who
orders heads off until Alice cancels her illusion of grandeur together
with the whole Wonderland dream. In other words, the title should not
be taken as an admission of the main trio's flatness. In fact, they are
fully realized characters (national coloration excepted): we know more
than we sometimes wish to know about their appearance, age, ante-
cedents, occupations, wardrobe, personal habits, preferences, manner
of speaking, capacities and limitations, state of health and its changes,

[14]Nabokov's titles are often deceptive: though *Despair* holds the promise of a Dostoevskian murky gloom, the novel turns out to be pointedly anti-Dostoevskian; "Lik"
(1939), which is the Russian for "image" in a religious or poetic context, turns out to
be the acrostical soubriquet of a character shaped almost as a sarcastic answer to
Dostoevsky's Myshkin; "Recruiting" (1935) contains no human interest story about
would-be soldiers; and "A Matter of Chance" (1924) deals not with chance as such but
with different kinds of wickedness masquerading as chance.

[15]*Le bal du compte d'Orgel*, a subtle variant of the novel of adultery, was published in
1924, shortly after the death of its author, Raymond Radiguet, at the age of twenty. In
Nabokov's 1935 story "Torpid Smoke" it is mentioned as one of the protagonist's
favorite books (see *RB*, 31). There is no similarity between Radiguet's protagonist,
François de Séryeuse, and Franz Bubendorf, yet their first names may have been
connected in a naughty cell of Nabokov's brain—though it seems that he foresaw such
observations: "The greatest happiness I experience in composing is when I feel I cannot
understand, or rather catch myself not understanding (without the presupposition of an
already existing creation) how or why that image or structural move or exact formulation of phrase has just come to me. It is sometimes rather amusing to find my readers
trying to elucidate in a matter-of-fact way these wild workings of my not very efficient
mind" (*SO*, 69).

sexual performance, and means of contraception. They are, in sum, as rounded, or three-dimensional as the Inventor's automannequins. What they lack is "only" the fourth dimension, the something else that arrests Nabokov at the end of "Mademoiselle O" (see *SM*, 117). In plainer words, they lack what is commonly called the soul—not because Nabokov failed to endow them with one but because the central theme of the novel is the suppression of the spiritual part of the self, a suppression that is, moreover, self-imposed.

This theme is related to the main moral issue that Nabokov diagnoses in Tolstoy's *Anna Karenin*:

> Lyovin's marriage is based on a metaphysical, not only physical, concept of love, on willingness for self-sacrifice, on mutual respect. The Anna-Vronski alliance was founded only in carnal love and therein lay its doom.
>
> It might seem, at first blush, that Anna was punished by society for falling in love with a man who was not her husband. Now such a "moral" would be of course completely "immoral," and completely inartistic, incidentally, since other ladies of fashion, in that same society, were having as many love-affairs as they liked but having them in secrecy. . . . The decrees of society are temporary ones; what Tolstoy is interested in are the eternal demands of morality. And now comes the real moral point that he makes: Love cannot be exclusively carnal because then it is egotistic, and being egotistic it destroys instead of creating. It is thus sinful. And in order to make his point as artistically clear as possible, Tolstoy in a flow of extraordinary imagery depicts and places side by side, in vivid contrast, two loves: the carnal love of the Vronski-Anna couple (struggling amid their richly sensual but fateful and spiritually sterile emotions) and on the other hand the authentic, Christian love, as Tolstoy termed it, of the Lyovin-Kitty couple with the riches of sensual nature still there but balanced and harmonious in the pure atmosphere of responsibility, tenderness, truth, and family joys. [*LRL*, 146–47]

Nabokov develops Tolstoy's theme by presenting a group of people who are averse to the life of the spirit; love gives them a chance to embark on this life, but they reject the gift and thus profane that fragment of the divine which is hidden in every human being.

This is also a variation on the theme of Mystery that runs through most of Nabokov's writings. In the worlds of his novels, as in the world of *A Midsummer Night's Dream*, the poet, the lover, and the lunatic are allowed to perceive more than the daily reality known to the uninitiated. Most of Nabokov's fictional heroes are lovers, artists, madmen, or any combination of the three; and they do, indeed, seem to be made aware of "something else," of something that transcends the familiar. In *King, Queen, Knave*, falling in love is presented as just such an extraordinary experience, yet the stereotypic consciousness of the characters immediately attempts to pigeonhole and debase it. Franz Bubendorf, for instance, does not realize how beautiful (despite the bafflement and the pain) his world becomes after he has broken his glasses. The outlines of objects disappear, and the world picture, formerly a mosaic of concepts,[16] acquires an artistic integrity: "Once in the street he was engulfed in streaming radiance. Outlines did not exist, colors had no substance. Like a woman's wispy dress that has slipped off its hanger, the city shimmered and fell in fantastic folds, not held up by anything, a discarnate iridescence limply suspended in the azure autumnal air. Beyond the nacrine desert of the square, across which a car sped now and then with a new metropolitan trumpeting, great pink edifices loomed, and suddenly a sunbeam, a gleam of·glass, would stab him painfully in the pupil" (*KQK*, 23).

It is on this day, "in the unsubstantial radiance of his myopia" (which now has more meanings than one) that Franz really falls in love with Martha, whom he had seen, and lusted for, on the train the previous day. At that first meeting, fascinated by her glamour, he "eagerly started to seek human, everyday tokens that would break the spell" (*KQK*, 11); his petit bourgeois upbringing makes him impatient with every sort of enchantment. Therefore, as soon as his spectacles are repaired, "Franz experienc[es] at once a feeling of comfort and peace in his heart as well as behind his ears. The haze dissolv[es]. The unruly colors of the univers [are] confined once more to their official compartments and cells" (*KQK*, 45).

The motif of the compartments and cells involves a determined exclusion of the carnivalistic element in which partitions are knocked down and communion becomes possible. As noted in Chapter 3, Nabokov is wary of a too enthusiastic removal of partitions. He would

[16]It may be interesting to read the passage describing Franz's first (myopic) view of Berlin in the light of the following remarks of Schopenhauer: "However fine the mosaic may be, the edges of the stones always remain, so that no continuous transition from one tint to another is possible. In the same way, concepts, with their rigidity and sharp delineation, however finely they may be split by closer defintion, are always incapable of reaching the fine modifications of perception. . . . This same property in concepts which makes them similar to the stones of a mosaic, and by virtue of which perception always remains their asymptote, is also the reason why nothing good is achieved through them in art" (*The World as Will and Representation*, 1:57).

respond to Whitman's urge to "unscrew the locks from the doors" but would not go on and "unscrew the doors themselves from their jambs."[17] In fact, one of the most important images in the Nabokov *oeuvre* is that of a nonhermetic partition, of a door that has come ajar. This image is brought into high relief in the poem "*Vlyublyonnost'*"("The Being in Love") included in his *Look at the Harlequins!* (1974). The last stanza of the poem provides a crucial clue to the treatment of falling in love in Nabokov's fiction—the claim that "being in love" opens the door on the beyond:

> *Napomináyu chto vlyublyónnost',*
> *Ne yáv', chto métiny ne té.*
> *Chto mózhet-byt' potustorónnost'*
> *Priotvorílas' v temnoté.*
>
> [*LATH*, 25]

In an attempt to explain the meaning of this stanza, the protagonist of *Look at the Harlequins!* translates the word *potustoronnost'* as "the hereafter":[18] "*Napomiñayu*, I remind you, that *vlyublyonnost'* is not wide-awake reality, that the markings are not the same (a moon-striped ceiling, *polosatyy ot luny potolok*, is, for instance, not the same kind of reality as a ceiling by day), and that, maybe, the hereafter stands slightly ajar in the dark" (*LATH*, 26).

Vera Nabokov cites this poem as one of the texts that most clearly reveal Nabokov's preoccupation with the theme of Mystery (see *S*, 3). In *Look at the Harlequins!* it appears in the episode that parallels the so-called "detective" phase of Nabokov's work, the phase that includes *King, Queen, Knave*.[19] It may thus be read as an indirect commentary on the image of doors that recurs persistently throughout the novel. Some doors in *King, Queen, Knave* are ajar in the light or in the darkness, but most are closed, slammed, locked or unlocked with keys or latches. Martha musters all her strength to keep the door of Franz's room closed against her husband's intrusion, shuts the door abruptly behind Dreyer's dog, imagines herself snatching Dreyer's book of poems and locking it away in a suitcase. The shutting of doors (and

---

[17]Walt Whitman, "Song of Myself," section 24.

[18]This may be a subversive allusion to "What is Love? 'Tis not hereafter" from Shakespeare's carnivalistic *Twelfth Night* (2.3).

[19]See Charles S. Ross, "Nabokov's Mistress-Muse Metaphor: Some Recent Books," *Modern Fiction Studies*, 25 (1979), 515.

lids) is endowed with unmistakably symbolic significance when, after Franz's first visit to the Dreyers, Martha locks the door behind her husband with unwonted violence:

> As soon as the door had noiselessly closed behind him, Martha sprang up and furiously, with a wrenching twist, locked it. This was utterly out of character: a singular impulse she would have been at a loss to explain, and all the more senseless since she would need the maid in a minute, and would have to unlock the door anyway. Much later, when many months had passed, and she was trying to reconstruct that day, it was this door and this key that she recalled most vividly, as if an ordinary door key happened to be the correct key to that not quite ordinary day. However, in wringing the neck of the lock she failed to dispel her anger. [*KQK*, 41]

Martha attempts to translate this "not quite ordinary" experience into the "in character" notion of respectable middle-class adultery. Her love for Franz is genuine at first and therefore not reducible to the familiar order of things. Martha resents this loss of control and, misinterpreting its nature, directs her anger against her husband, the only person who has been eluding her reins. Slamming the door, she rejects the exquisite gift offered by "the being in love."

Franz, a prisoner of physical sensation,[20] profanes his love for Martha by his insistence on translating it into plain carnal lust. Because he is genuinely in love with her at first, he abstains from adventures with prostitutes, and his languor infuses the city with sordid yet mysterious splendor. Yet when sleep hands him "the key of its city" (*KQK* 74), the passage that Franz chooses to open leads him only to the "solitary practice" (*KQK*, 22) that he has been promising himself to give up. He is not aware that his restlessness is not entirely libidinous and that, unlike Alice in a Wonderland hall, he has chosen the wrong door.

A loud motorcycle that Martha and Franz dream of at the same time (see *KQK*, 75) suggests that, when in love, they are capable of unusual experience without wishing it or recognizing its nature. It is noteworthy, however, that Nabokov inserts the motorcycle into Martha's dream only in the revised edition (in the original only Franz dreams of it), wishing, as it were, to intensify the sense of the mysterious gift

---

[20]See Pifer, *Nabokov and the Novel*, pp. 18–22.

offered to the lovers.[21] They do not accept the gift. A door on the beyond has come ajar, yet they promptly shut it by consciously seeking only satisfaction of physical desire. Martha regrets that November is "being squandered on trifles as money is squandered on trifles when you get stranded in some dull town," and Franz regrets that he is "draining his passion in useless fantasies" (*KQK*, 84). Soon after the affair is consummated, Martha's lovemaking turns into a kind of masturbation: she seeks to appropriate Franz's body and treat it as her own appurtenance—"my dining room, my earrings, my silver, my Franz" (*KQK*, 124). Her visits to Franz take place when she is supposed to be attending classes in "rhythmic inclinations and gesticulations"(*KQK*, 131); instead of improving her control over her own body (which lets her down by the end of the novel), she learns to manipulate the body and the will of the subdued lover.

Only the shallow, egotistical, yet rather well-meaning Dreyer— who, despite his eccentric infidelities, still loves his wife—does not seek to shut himself off hermetically from mystery. Consciously, he looks for it in the wrong places: when in her delirium Martha talks of their dog's death, Dreyer takes that for evidence of "second sight" (*KQK*, 271) because he does not know that Martha has given orders for Tom to be poisoned. Like Franz, Dreyer tends to choose the wrong doors. Symbolically, it is not through the front door but through a squalid back entrance that he first leads Franz into his emporium (see *KQK*, 68).

Yet not all doors fail Dreyer. The night before the boating expedition during which Martha plans to drown him, he is tortured by the "upright glare of a door ajar" (*KQK*, 236). The glare comes from Martha's room and merges with the scorching pain in his sunburned back. Dreyer is too sane to realize that it is a danger signal, warning him that he is on the brink of the "hereafter," yet something deep within him responds to the writing on the wall: the next day he pronounces the magic formula, "Tomorrow . . . I'm making a hundred thousand dollars at one stroke" (*KQK*, 247), just in time to save his life. One may recall that Dreyer has met Franz's landlord, the self-styled Menetek el Pharsin, whose variant of the magic "Close, Sesame" ("Your girl is in there": *KQK*, 221) prevented him from forcing the door open and discovering Martha in Franz's room.

[21]Nabokov's lecture on *Anna Karenin* comments on Anna's and Vronski's double nightmare (*LRL*, 175–77).

IV

At the very end of the novel it is from behind a partition (a "thin wall": *KQK*, 272) that we listen to the frenzied laughter of Franz. Among the most significant revisions made in 1966, when Nabokov was preparing the English edition, is a greater emphasis on the gradual and thorough dehumanization of Franz Bubendorf. Consider, for instance, the treatment of the "visits of inspection" (*KQK*, viii) that "Nabokov" and his wife (equipped with their butterfly net, which is absent from the Russian original; see *KQK*, 232) pay to the world of *King, Queen, Knave* in the last two chapters. In the original the foreign couple that Franz notices at Pomerania Bay is given less narrative space, yet Franz suddenly understands what their image means (*Kdv*, 239–40). This scene hints at the role played by the Lyovin-Kitty marriage in *Anna Karenin*: the two young foreigners genuinely love each other; their feeling is much more than the carnal lust that Franz had known. In the revised version of the novel Franz is never granted this insight; he is too degenerate even to recognize what he can no longer be.

The fact that the foreign couple seem to be discussing Franz in the last chapter is given greater prominence in the revised edition. As a result, their appearance functions less as emphasis on the theme of love and more as a structural device, an embryonic form of the *Roots III* technique that is brought to perfection in *Pnin*. The brief encounter that takes place between the novelist and the characters at Pomerania Bay is, to some extent, a counterpart of chapter 7 of *Pnin*, where the narrator recounts his contacts with Pnin and the firsthand information that seems to have been transformed into various motifs of Pnin's life. Indeed, the foreword to *King, Queen, Knave* informs us that the novel was conceived "on the coastal sands of Pomerania Bay" (*KQK*, vii).

Franz's development anticipates the development that thousands of German youths would undergo in the next two decades: from satisfaction of basic physical needs through brainwashing, stultification, and habitual unquestioning obedience to the routine commission of atrocious crimes. The novel presents the mechanical round of lower-middle-class life as one of the factors conducive to the eventually enormous sway of Hitler's propaganda. While revising *King, Queen, Knave* in 1966, Nabokov was moved to insert into it the remark that in the future Franz would be "guilty of worse sins than avunculicide" (*KQK*, 138). Yet it is interesting that even in the Russian original, Franz is ominously singled out from the rest of the trio. At the end, when Martha dies and Dreyer goes to pieces with grief (figuratively reenacting the literal fate of the automannequins in the last demonstration), Franz remains disconcertingly alive. Nabokov does not use the self-conscious artifice of the novel to cancel this character as he cancels the protagonists of *Pnin*, *Mary*, *Bend Sinister*, and *Pale Fire*; the story of Franz is not over when the curtain falls. As in *Mary* and *The Gift*, we are invited to follow the character in our own imagination for a short while after the narrative ends.

We can, moreover, construct not one but two sequels to Franz's story. The first involves the sleepy girl in the next room who overhears Franz's wild rejoicing in the last paragraph of the novel. Since Franz has been waiting for a chance to get free of Martha and pursue other women, the reader expects him to start an affair with a chance neighbor. In the revised version Nabokov brings out the potentialities of this situation: the girl in the next room becomes "a miserable tramp whom a commercial traveller had jilted" (*KQK*, 272). The promiscuous "commercial traveller" looks forward to Nabokov's story "A Dashing Fellow," published in 1930 (that is, shortly after the Russian version of *King, Queen, Knave*); the protagonist of that story has syphilis, which Franz would carry away from the encounter with the "miserable tramp." The noseless face that terrifies Franz on the train is probably his own future in which, according to the revised version of the novel, he will be very ill (see *KQK*, 138).

It seems that the waxlike Franz is about to step out of the fictional gallery of waxworks into the historical chamber of horrors: the other implicit sequel is suggested by the remark that in his more mature life Franz would be "guilty of worse sins than avunculicide" (*KQK*, 138); he is presented as a Nazi in the making. In 1927 V. Sirin was only intuitively aware of what Vladimir Nabokov would highlight in 1967. The implied connection between Franz's progress through the novel and his Nazi future is retrospectively intensified not only by the revisions that Nabokov eventually made in the novel itself but also by his description in his postwar autobiography of Dietrich, a young German he had known during his years in Berlin, a "well-bred, quiet, bespectacled" university student "whose hobby was capital punishment" (*SM*, 278). He collected grisly pictures, traveled with his camera from one active execution site to another, and was disappointed when a friend of his got drunk instead of committing the suicide he had been looking forward to witnessing. The segment concludes: "I can well imagine the look of calm satisfaction in his fish-blue eyes as he shows, nowadays (perhaps at the very minute I am writing this), a never-expected profusion of treasures to his thigh-clapping, guffawing co-veterans—the absolutely *wunderbar* pictures he took during Hitler's reign" (*SM*, 279).

The motif of the victim's expected cooperation with the executioner relates this description to *Invitation to a Beheading*, yet it may also be read as containing the motif of poker cards alluded to in the 1967 foreword to *King, Queen, Knave* (*KQK*, xi): it is out of the "meager stack" (*SM*, 278) of his non-Russian and non-Jewish acquaintances of the period spanning the two world wars that Nabokov sorts out the image of Dietrich. It may at first seem that Dietrich and Franz share only their quietness and spectacles, yet if one thinks about the psychological origins of sadism, the gap between them is bridged. Here is Schopenhauer's explanation of cruelty as an end in itself:

a person filled with an extremely intense pressure of will wants with burning eagerness to accumulate everything, in order to slake the thirst of egoism. As is inevitable, he is bound to see that all satisfaction is only apparent, and that the attained object never fulfils the promise held out by the desired object, namely the final appeasement of the excessive pressure of will. He sees that, with fulfilment, the wish changes only its form, and now torments under another form; indeed, when at last all wishes are exhausted, the pressure of will itself remains, even without any recognized motive, and makes itself known with terrible pain as a feeling of the most frightful desolation and emptiness. . . . he then seeks indirectly the alleviation of which he is incapable directly, in other words, he tries to mitigate his own suffering by the sight of another's, and at the same time recognizes this as an expression of his power. The suffering of another becomes for him an end in itself; it is a spectacle over which he gloats; and so arises the phenomenon of cruelty proper, of bloodthirstiness, so often revealed by history in the Neros and Domitians, in the African Deys, in Robespierre and others.[22]

At the end of the novel Franz Bubendorf is on his way not only to the satisfaction of desires but also to the loss of the capacity for further direct satisfaction—the psychological grounds for sadistic enjoyment are being laid. Together with a defenselessness against the authority of the rulers, produced by habitual obedience to orders and absence of an

[22]Schopenhauer, *The World as Will and Representation*, 1:364.

independent moral or ideological stand, Franz's disposition presents him as the stuff that war criminals are made of. It is characteristic of all totalitarian regimes (Nabokov notes that there is nothing intrinsically German about his characters; see *KQK*, viii) that they thus promise their subjects material well-being and seek to suppress those aspects of their spiritual lives that could counteract the frightening outcome of the scramble for the gratification of desires.

Thus, paradoxically, Nabokov's "bright brute" did come after all to bear an imprint of the political agenda. From the frying pan into the fire: if in 1927 V. Sirin chose a German milieu so as not to be obliged to deal with the Russian Revolution, in 1967 that choice forced Nabokov to deal with the problem of World War II. Before 1967 this subject had been partly "got rid of" in *Bend Sinister* and *Pnin*. Yet it would, it seems, always lurk close by, a "shadow behind the heart" (*P*, 126; *KQK*, 251).

5

The Defense:
Secret Asymmetries

What immortal hand or eye
Could frame thy fearful symmetry?
William Blake, "The Tyger"

God moves the player and he, the piece.
What god behind God originates the scheme
Of dust and time and dream and agony?
Jorge Luis Borges, "The Game of Chess"

The human "warmth" (*D*, 10) that was largely kept out of *King, Queen, Knave* erupted in Nabokov's so-called "chess novel," *The Defense* (*Zashchita Luzhina*, 1929), a novel that deals more directly than any other of Nabokov's works with the problem of balance between intellectual pursuit and human commitment.

It would be an oversimplification to say that the major conflict of *The Defense* is between art and life. Chess is a game that explores the infinite potentialities of its own medium, whereas a truly great work of art explores its medium in order to reveal insufficiencies in the existing patterns of thought about the world.[1] *The Defense* is an example of such a work of art. Its chess patterns stand for all the patterns and systems that prove tragically inadequate when preferred to or violently superimposed on the natural flow of life. Yet the game of

[1] Nabokov would, it seems, agree with Wolfgang Iser's view that a literary text refers not to a contingent world but to "the ordered pattern of systems," or models of reality, through which the mind attempts to organize this world. The literary text "represents a reaction to the thought systems which it has chosen and incorporated in its own repertoire"(*The Act of Reading: A Theory of Aesthetic Response* [Baltimore, 1978], p. 72).

67

chess is not used allegorically. The chess imagery and the human situations related to the game lend the novel its peculiar coloration without forcing it into a constrictive structural pattern.

In other words, the analogies between chess concepts and the features of *The Defense* are loosely general. The most salient of these analogies is the paradoxical symmetry (a chess phenomenon) of the plot and the structure of the novel: the protagonist's life *only seems* to submit to the rules of a chess game, and the novel itself *only seems* to be structured as a chess problem. Both the reality of Luzhin's predicament and the shape of the novel present too great a complexity to be described in terms of chess.

I

In his 1963 foreword Nabokov mentions that *The Defense* is endowed with some features of chess problems (see *D*, 10). A chess problem contains the semblance of a competition between the hypothetical White and Black; in reality, however, it is a competition between the composer and the solver—"just as in a first-rate work of fiction, " Nabokov points out in *Speak, Memory*, "the real clash is not between the characters but between the author and the world" (*SM*, 290). The "world" here should stand not only for the audience that must solve the problem but also for chaotic contemporary reality and the various systems of thought that attempt to reduce it to organized patterns. The novel not merely rivals these systems of thought but also highlights the insufficiency of any man-made model that seeks either to mimic or to replace the contingent actuality that defies predetermination.

The Defense indirectly reflects the intellectual confusion into which Europe and, in particular, its Russian population were cast by World War I and the revolution. In Europe the war seemed to put an end to the lingering nineteenth century; in Russia it joined forces with the revolution to put an end to a cultural world. The Russia of liberal intellectuals ceased to exist; for them, exile proved to be the least of the possible evils. *The Defense* mentions, *en passant,* the approaches of various social and cultural groups to the "science of exile" (*D*, 222): the standard bragging lies of Soviet newspapers and tourists, the occasional "viperous hostility" (*D*, 226) of the émigré press, gaudy fake-Russian decor in the apartment of Mrs. Luzhin's wealthy parents, fashionable theosophy (see *D*, 129), and so on. Paradoxically, the protagonist of the novel, the chess player Luzhin, is minimally affected by the irreversible changes in his fatherland: had the revolution never taken place, he would most probably still have spent the greater part of his life shuttling between the chess cafés of middle and western Europe. And yet Luzhin is the kind of person whose fate literalizes the fate of his generation. His image is similar to that of the mad Jewish boy in Nabokov's "Signs and Symbols" (1948): even though the boy's family has escaped from Germany to America, his acute paranoia, his sense of the systematic hostility of the world, is a morbidly condensed literalization of the Jewish experience in Europe at the time of the Holocaust.

Thanks to his touch of genius and, perhaps, prophetic madness, Luzhin likewise responds, unconsciously but accurately, to the period in which he lives. In his pampered prerevolutionary preschool days his fear of the "unknown and therefore hideous" (*D*, 22) outside world is far more intense than that of an ordinarily sensitive child; he senses the frightening confusion of the contemporary world long before the cataclysm breaks upon the consciousness of the ordinary people around him. In his thirties Luzhin maintains an ostrichlike defense against reality; symptomatically, he walks "half closing his eyes so that [a former schoolmate] would not notice him" (*D*, 200). He is not averse to accepting an invitation from Stalinist Russia and has no idea of what is happening there (a minimal knowledge of history allows the contemporary reader to imagine his fate had he, indeed, returned). His incompetence concerning everything except chess is, in fact, only a more pronounced form of the semivoluntary ignorance in which millions of people on both sides of the iron curtain have lived for at least four decades of the present century.

Luzhin's emotional and intellectual limitations stem from that "escape into aesthetics" of which his author was unjustly accused in early critical responses. The use of art as a compensation for the inadequacies of reality and the current systems of thought is an experience that this chess player shares with his novelist father, Ivan Luzhin. It is, moreover, precisely the theme that Ivan Luzhin vainly seeks for his would-be swansong. He never finds the theme, perhaps because it lies so close to him—in the circumstances under which he conceives the idea of his book, in his manner of sifting his material. In the empty conference room of a Berlin coffeehouse Luzhin senior mistakes a strident mixture of pleasure and pain for the return of literary inspiration (see *D*, 75–77). The delicate balance between sadness and pleasurable sensations and memories is disrupted by a painful thought about his estranged son, the "taciturn person who sometimes called upon him in Berlin, replied to questions monosyllabically, sat there with his eyes half closed, and then went away leaving an envelope with money in it on the windowsill" (*D*, 78). As if to exorcise the disharmonious intrusion, Ivan Luzhin decides to write a novel about a young chess player who would remain the angelic genius of his father's dreams. From this novel he would expunge all the jarring notes, dismiss such uncouth stumbling blocks as war and revolution, and drive out the "purely personal, unbidden recollections, of no use to him—starvation, arrest, and so forth" (*D*, 80–81). He fails to see, however, that, still indulging in the daydreams of his past, he is endowing his son "with the features of a musical rather than a chess-playing prodigy" (*D*, 78). The absence of harmony between the atmosphere and the contents of the projected book is one of the reasons it never gets written.

Luzhin senior never discovers the main theme of his hero's experience because, like his son, he refuses to grapple with confusing realities. According to the truncated dialogue between two intellectuals in a later part of the novel, he is not an untalented writer, yet his talent is vitiated by the didactic tendency of his "oleographic tales for youngsters" (*D*, 231), in which schoolboys feed their sandwiches to scruffy dogs and come to appreciate kind young stepmothers who nurse them through functional fevers. The elder Luzhin's sentimental species of humanism (*chelovekolyubiye*) is a widespread thought system with no provision for the violent fermentations of the prerevolutionary years or for the harsh realities of war and revolution. His wish-fulfilling tales seek to make up for the deficiency of this thought system by putting together a world to which it would apply.[2]

For old Luzhin, the writing of fiction is a defense against pain, a palliative for ills and wrongs. For his son, chess becomes a similar defense: if a telegraph pole is an eyesore, Luzhin junior imagines how it could be removed by "a Knight's move of this lime tree standing on a sunlit slope" (*D*, 99); while his future mother-in-law is scolding him, his attention is engrossed by an imaginary chess configuration on the squares of her drawing room floor (*D*, 127–28).[3] The form that his

[2]The function of didactic literature as represented by old Luzhin's books is "not to produce an aesthetic object that will rival the thought system of the social world, but to offer a *compensation* for specific deficiencies in specific thought systems" (Iser, *The Act of Reading*, p. 101).

[3]Despite his inbred culture, Luzhin becomes as limited (and as expressively inarticulate as Gogol's Akaky Akakievich, the master calligrapher of "The Overcoat," who sees the neat lines of his handwriting superimposed on the less satisfactory objects in

madness takes at the end of the novel is a fantastic transformation of the theme of attempts to replace genuine life by an artificially harmonious system.

The Defense is thus an appropriate yet very oblique response to the inner agenda of its period. This obliqueness is caused by the novel's centering upon the experience of the nonrepresentative individual. Paradoxically, preoccupation with the unique rather than the typical broadens the significance of the issues involved beyond the specific cultural-historical situation.

II

Returning to the émigré background of *Mary, The Defense* develops the idea expressed by the disillusioned poet Podtyagin: "I put everything into my poetry that I should have put into my life" (*M*, 42). The chessplayer Luzhin goes further than Podtyagin: obsessed with his sterile art he turns it into a defense against unmanageable reality. The symbolism and structure of the novel, however, show that such a defense is both unnecessary and ineffective.

The title refers to the theme of defense against life as well as to a specific element of the plot: grand master Luzhin has painstakingly prepared a response to the famous opening of his opponent Turati, but Turati surprises him by not launching the expected attack; thus the defense proves unnecessary. This event has wider implications. Whereas Luzhin has concentrated entirely on his chess homework, Turati has also taken into account the psychology of their confrontation; he has thought not only about the game but also about the player, foreseeing that Luzhin would not come to the match unprepared. In the end, other things being equal, it is the attention to human reality that wins the day; chess is not as "supremely abstract" as it "is supposed to be" (*D*, 10). The elaborate defense that Luzhin has constructed in his mind is a wild-goose chase: Turati's opening proves to be not merely a successful strategy used in previous games but also a diversionary device.

The motif of diversion is of crucial importance in the novel. In his 1963 foreword Nabokov cryptically remarks: "Rereading this novel today, replaying the moves of its plot, I feel rather like Anderssen

---

the street. There are many analogies between "The Overcoat" and *The Defense;* Nabokov's novel could be regarded, to some extent, as an answer to Gogol.

fondly recalling his sacrifice of both Rooks to the unfortunate and noble Kieseritsky—who is doomed to accept it over and over again through an infinity of textbooks, with a question mark for monument" (D, 8).

The double-rook sacrifice is, in fact, a diversion, a chess equivalent of a conjuror's patter. D. B. Johnson explains: "Rooks are not what double-rook sacrifices are about. Rooks can be sacrificed in various ways, but when chess players speak of double-rook sacrifices they have in mind the particular case when the opposing Queen is permitted to capture both Rooks stationed in their own back rank. The immediate purpose of the Rook sacrifice is the diversion of the opposing Queen far from the real scene of the action. The Rooks are simply irresistible decoys *to trap and neutralize the opposing Queen, thus depriving the King of its strongest defender.*"[4]

Thus the double-rook sacrifice is a metaphor for whatever decoy diverts attention from the central issues of the moment. There are several such diversions in the novel's plot: for instance, humdrum events divert Mrs. Luzhin's attention from her husband at the time when he is fighting insanity;[5] a love affair and a wish to have a *Wunderkind* divert Luzhin senior from seeing that chess has come to occupy an unnatural place in his son's life. But the major diversion proves to be the game itself. Instead of enriching Luzhin's life, chess impoverishes it by channeling his mental energies away from almost all other aspects of reality.

Luzhin, like Cincinnatus in *Invitation to a Beheading,* is different from most people even in his earliest days. His streak of genius enables him to feel something that is hidden from others and produces an almost unbearable "itch of being" (GI, xiii). A sensitive and undisciplined child "who at the slightest provocation would throw himself flat on the floor, screaming and drumming his feet" (D, 74), he would always walk through the same St. Petersburg streets, taking care to be at the farthest possible spot from the cannon of the Peter and Paul fortress when it was fired. In his fear of suffering he is preoccupied with staving off various kinds of torment. The dictation that his father gives him in the 1964 English version of the novel contains the quasi-Schopenhauerian phrase: "Being born in this world is hardly to be

---

[4]Johnson, *Worlds in Regression,* p. 90. Johnson presents, among other things, a very interesting account of the connotations of Turati's name and of the relevance of the actual Anderssen-Kieseritsky story for the motifs and the rhetoric of Nabokov's novel.
[5]See ibid.

borne" (*D*, 17). Subverting the exercise and, as it were, rejecting its concepts, Luzhin leaves blank spaces for the words "born" and "borne."

In the Russian original the dictation contains a different sentence: "It's a lie that there are no boxes in the theatre" (*ZL*, 25)—in Russian the words "lie"and "boxes" are homophones but not homographs. Whereas the English pun initiates the metaphysical theme of the novel, the Russian pun hints at the element of falsehood and theatricality in Luzhin's early home life. His father, a landowner and author of didactic books for children, a kindly and well-meaning person, is insincere with himself. He has keen insights but profanes them by stereotyped expressions; instead of living authentically, he identifies with standard roles. The child instinctively feels the falseness and withdraws into himself.

Luzhin's preschool days are sketched economically, but it is made clear that he uses the pattern of his daily routine to shield himself from the world (see *D*, 21–22). School disrupts his orderly pattern and exposes him to the collective malevolence of the Average Man, a phenomenon extensively treated in *Invitation to a Beheading* and *Bend Sinister*. Whether because he is introduced as the son of a well-known writer or because his classmates feel in him the "secret stir of talent" also recognized by his father (*D*, 25), young Luzhin is surrounded with "such hatred and derisive curiosity" that a "burning mist" confuses his senses, blurring his vision and making the teacher's voice "hollow and incomprehensible" (*D*, 29). This confusion is a concentrated expression of Luzhin's experience of incomprehensible reality. He seems to be seeking a solution that would be no less than an eschatological formula. In his early days he likes arithmetic because it simulates the discovery of solution: there is "mysterious sweetness in the fact that a long number, arrived at with difficulty, would at the decisive moment, after many adventures, be divided by nineteen without any remainder" (*D*, 17). For a similar reason he likes detective fiction, magic tricks, and cardboard puzzles—until he finds a model of harmony that can provide him with an escape: chess, the game of "infinite possibilities" (*D*, 43), a faked yet boundless world within a world. "Escape" here overlaps with "asylum"; Nabokov explores the double meaning of the latter in the preface to the English version of *Glory*, where he writes that an "escape" is "only a cleaner cell on a quieter floor" (*Gl*, xiii). Chess could have provided Luzhin not with an escape but with "relief from the itch of being" (*Gl*, xiii); mishandled, the gift turns into Pandora's box. It is not insignificant that the most recurrent class of "things" in this novel's world (compare the doors of *King, Queen, Knave)* is an assortment of boxes, chests, suitcases, and other containers of pseudomysteries.

Symptomatically, Luzhin is not interested in composing chess problems. As a competitive game chess gives him the sense of having a "militant, charging, bright force" (*D*, 68). He is equal to challenges during the game but does not develop courage away from the chessboard. Chess diverts him from his family, from the void in his emotional life, from the war and the revolution. In the game he finds his "sole harmony, for what else exists in the world beside chess? Fog, the unknown, non-being" (*D*, 139). The moves of his match with Turati are described in terms of melodies—Luzhin's version of the music of the spheres.

The space that life among people occupies in young Luzhin's consciousness steadily dwindles. He shirks duties, cuts classes, turns his back on the best of his classmates, ignores the unhappiness and appeals of his parents and his aunt. Leafing through old magazines in search of chess sections, he pays no attention to the pictures of starving Indian children (see *D*, 54). Because of his father's oversight and the impresario Valentinov's deliberate neglect, he learns nothing about personal and business relationships. Caught in a vicious circle, he escapes into chess because he cannot deal with his environment, but the escape increases his social inadequacies. Here, however, lies one of the secrets of his charm for his fiancée: despite the jumble of acquired formulations that make up his speech, she recognizes the childlike authenticity of his conduct and feelings.

A similar narrowing takes place in Luzhin's contacts with material reality. He grows fond of the taxing blind play, not because it is lucrative but because it frees him from "the palpable pieces whose quaint shape and wooden materiality [have] always disturbed him and [have] always seemed to him but the crude, mortal shape of exquisite, invisible chess forces" (*D*, 91). The cities where he plays become "as much a habitual and unnecessary integument as the wooden pieces and the black and white board, and he accept[s] this external life as something inevitable but completely uninteresting" (*D*, 95). He has a similar unconcern for his own body, leaving it uncouth, unwashed, unexercised, until it reminds him of itself by panting and pain.

It is at the time when the body starts to take its revenge that Luzhin is given a chance to rally. He meets and falls in love with one of those women we find in books of Russian history, women who are philanthropic, ready for self-sacrifice, and often powerfully attracted to superior intellects (Charlotte Brontë and George Eliot were authorities on the subject; Nabokov is one of the very few male writers to treat it sensitively and subtly). Luzhin recognizes her as someone he has been dimly expecting all his life. Her voice bursts through "the usual murk" (*D*, 99) of his rare intervals spent away from the chessboard, creating a clarity that for a long time only chess could give him.

A lover of harmonies, he accepts the fact that she is "not quite as good looking as she might have been" (*D*, 99) because, as the narrator suggests, her face is an invitation to a quest for a harmony that is constantly promised and withheld: "She was not particularly pretty, there was something lacking in her small regular features, as if the last decisive jog that would have made her beautiful—leaving her features the same but endowing them with an ineffable significance—had not been given them by nature. But she was twenty-five, her fashionably bobbed hair was neat and lovely and she had one turn of the head which betrayed a hint of possible harmony, a promise of real beauty that at the last moment remained unfulfilled (*D*, 85).

Luzhin does not know that her features lack "ineffable significance" because her emotional development is incomplete. The "mysterious ability of her soul to apprehend in life only that which had once attracted and tormented her in childhood, the time when the soul's instinct is infallible; to seek out the amusing and the touching; to feel constantly an intolerable, tender pity for the creature whose life is helpless and unhappy" (*D*, 105), is presented as both the most "captivating" thing about her and (as the word "only" suggests) a limitation. It is partly due to this limitation that the relationship which seems to possess the attributes of a protective castling[6] turns out to be the second diversion of the double-rook sacrifice.

There is a chesslike symmetry between the two diversions. Now it is happy married life, which should have been cherished for its own sake, that is used to divert Luzhin from chess. Mrs. Luzhin is guided by pity rather than by understanding; therefore, after her husband breaks down, she takes the advice of a psychiatrist to keep him away from chess. She does not realize that it is not his mind but his body that has failed to withstand the combined strain of courtship and tournament; not his spirit but his physical brain that, as at the match with

[6]See John Updike, "Grandmaster Nabokov," in *Assorted Prose* (New York, 1965), p. 325.

Turati, has "wilted from hitherto unprecedented weariness" (D, 139). Her defense against chess is as unnecessary and ineffectual as Luzhin's defense against life; instead of placing the game in proper perspective, she turns it into a lurking, destructive monster.

Luzhin's experience after his breakdown is thus characterized not by an about-face but by a symmetrical reversal, as though he were again heading to the brink of a breakdown but this time from the lines of a former opponent. The ban on chess creates a void that his bride can "adorn" (D, 176) but not fill. And since nature abhors a vacuum, the emptiness is filled by incipient madness. Accustomed as he is to blind play, Luzhin imagines himself pitted against an invisible competitor as soon as a chess pattern seems to transpire through his experience: "Just as some combination, known from chess problems, can be indistinctly repeated on the board in actual play—so now the consecutive repetition of a familiar pattern was becoming noticeable in his present life" (D, 213–14).

Luzhin's madness is a disease of memory. In the hospital he keeps recollecting his preschool days on his father's estate; on leaving the hospital he seems to reenact his return to St. Petersburg at the end of summer; an encounter with a former classmate evokes troubling memories of school; and a remark of a visitor from Leningrad conjures up the image of his aunt. The tissue that connects these separate moments of the past is part of the "luggage" that Luzhin has lost during his breakdown and that he does not "bother to restore"(D, 160). His whole past seems to have congealed into the moves that make up a chess problem, and when the sequence of memories corresponds to the sequence of the remembered events, he feels as though his present experience is a new chess game. He is pleased when the void in his life is replaced by the sense of harmony so dear to artists and chess players but is then overcome with horror at the thought of the stakes of the game. When he had forgotten to extinguish a match during his competition with Turati, the pain of the burn seemed to reveal "the full horror of the abysmal depths of chess" (D, 139). Now he feels as if blind play were luring him to this abyss.

The game with Turati has another aftermath as well. One of the most common "professional dreams" (A, 359) is that of coming to a crucial test or confrontation unprepared, with one's homework undone. On the eve of his breakdown Luzhin decides that all the unwonted happiness of his love is but a pleasant dream (see D, 132–33); after the breakdown he transfers the features of a professional nightmare to the reality that he takes for this dream of happiness. Having worked hard to construct a defense against Turati's opening, he suddenly feels that he does not have an adequate defense against a blind-play opponent. This feeling contains an element of moral truth: he has indeed failed to do his homework because he has neglected to develop courage and responsibility, the mature qualities that would have rendered him adequate to the strains of adult life.

A madman, it is often believed, can perceive the inner nature of things yet is unable to establish relationships between them. What Luzhin takes for the abyss of chess is, in fact, the revenge of "average reality" for his refusal to give it its due attention.

The abyss is a recurrent motif of Luzhin's life. One of the drawings that he makes after his breakdown represents "a train on a bridge spanning an abyss" (*D*, 208)[7] A picture in Valentinov's office shows a man "hanging by his hands from the ledge of a skyscraper—just about to fall off into the abyss" (*D*, 247). Having decided to "drop out of the game" by committing suicide, Luzhin thrusts himself out of a fifth-story window, coming as close as he can to a plunge over a precipice: "Before letting go he looked down. Some kind of hasty preparations were under way there: the window reflections gathered together and leveled themselves out, the whole chasm was seen to divide into dark and pale squares, and at the instant when Luzhin unclenched his hand, at the instant when icy air gushed into his mouth, he saw exactly what kind of eternity was obligingly and inexorably spread out before him" (*D*, 255–56). In the text of the novel, however, Luzhin never lands on the pavement of Berlin. It seems that the sheet of paper that is supposed to seal his fate becomes transparent and vanishes from the chessboard-patterned tablecloth (the "average reality" of another world) on which Nabokov is writing his chess novel.[8]

[7]The possible symbolism of this drawing is indirectly commented on by the little girl's philosophy in *Ada:* "An individual's life consisted of certain classified things: 'real things' which were unfrequent and priceless, simply 'things' which formed the routine stuff of life; and 'ghost things,' also called 'fogs,' such as fever, toothache, dreadful disappointments, and death. Three or more things occurring at the same time formed a 'tower,' or, if they came in immediate succession, they made a 'bridge' " (*A*, 74). The beginning of Luzhin's married life forms a bridge—over a perilous abyss. The train that moves over this bridge may be associated with (in the order of decreasing probability) Nabokov's toy trains that fell through the ice into the puddles at the Hotel Oranien (*SM*, 27), Anna Karenin's suicide, or the vision of the universe as a steam engine that depresses Carlyle's German scholar in *Sartor Resartus*.
[8]See the photograph following p. 256 of *Speak, Memory*.

The motif of the abyss may be regarded as a thematic reflection of the *en abîme* structure of the novel: "a game of skill" (*D*, 8) seems to be played in a story which itself is a game of skill.⁹ Both games are played for very serious stakes, but neither the novelist's game with the reader nor fate's game with Luzhin is a structured chess match. When the reader tries to distill definite chess patterns from the texture of *The Defense*, he reenacts Luzhin's own mistake of seeking chess patterns where they do not exist. In the foreword Nabokov does mention that "chess effects" can be found "in the basic structure of this attractive novel" (*D*, 9), yet an analysis devoted solely to the discovery of these effects would be tantamount to accepting Nabokov's double-rook sacrifice: superficial chess patterns would divert the reader from the psychological subtlety of the novel and from the complexity of its texture.¹⁰ According to the painter Ardalion in Nabokov's *Despair*, "what the artist perceives is, primarily, the *difference* between things. It is the vulgar who note their resemblance" (*Dp*, 51). The analogies between chess moves and the techniques of *The Defense* are either too esoteric to be understood by the general public or deliberately loose.

⁹The term *mise-en-abîme* for a narrative enclave that reproduces the features of the whole work that contains it was first suggested by André Gide in *Journal 1889–1939* (Paris, 1948), p. 41. In 1929, while writing *The Defense*, Nabokov may already have read Gide's *Les faux-monnayeurs*, which contains clear examples of this technique. The term *mise-en-abîme* is taken from heraldry (in which Nabokov was well versed): a blazon is usually divided into four parts by a cross; the intersection of the vertical and the horizontal lines of the cross is called *l'abîme*, the abyss. Sometimes a miniature of the blazon appears in lieu of this intersection; it is then said to be placed *en abîme* and, presupposing a miniature of itself in its own abyss, etc., it suggests infinite regression. There is no critical consensus as to the limits of the applicability of the term *mise-en-abîme*. Different approaches to the problem are reflected in Lucien Dällenbach, *Le récit spéculaire: Essay sur le mise en abyme* (Paris, 1977); Mieke Bal, "Mise en abyme et iconicité," *Littérature*, 29 (1978), 116–28.

¹⁰A similar point has been made by Fred Moody, who notes that hostile reviewers quote the foreword yet do not notice that some scenes mentioned there do not actually exist in the novel ("Nabokov's Gambit," *Russian Literature Triquarterly*, 14 [1976], 67–70); and by Johnson, who notes that the chess allusions of the foreword are deceptive and send "the reader off on a wild-goose chase looking for castles in the air" (*Worlds in Regression*, p. 91). Thus, this early novel contains reader-entrapment techniques that are more fully developed in Nabokov's subsequent work. A side effect of the wild-goose chase may be found in complaints that the chess content of *The Defense* is not sufficiently interesting: see, e.g., Updike, "Grandmaster Nabokov," p. 326. In hostile criticism—e.g., Strother B. Purdy, "Solus Rex: Nabokov and the Chess Novel," *Modern Fiction Studies*, 14 (Winter 1968–69), 379–95—these complaints turn into the very *Schadenfreude* of which it unfairly accuses Nabokov himself.

My knowledge of chess is, I confess, rudimentary; I read the chess analogies of *The Defense* as a basis for emphasizing the distinction between a chess game and an aesthetic object.

The Defense mimics separate features of both a chess match and a chess problem—this alone is enough to suggest a deliberate inconsistency of its quasi-chesslike structure. Moreover, its chess analogies pertain to the strategies and the psychological reality of the game rather than to specific moves of chess pieces.

III

The features of a chess problem in *The Defense* explore the metaphysical ramifications of the novel's major conflict. They also bear upon the legitimacy with which one can discuss Luzhin's tragedy as the outcome of moral error.

The foreword compares chapters 4, 5, and 6 to a chess problem (D, 9–10). Within a chess problem there is a match between the winning White and the doomed Black. These contestants are apt embodiments of Nabokov's notion of characters as "galley slaves" (*SO*, 95), where "galley" means "the printer's proof of a manuscript" as well as "an ancient rowing vessel."[11] They move the chessmen in accordance with the logic of the game and the exigencies of the situations, yet all the decisions they seem to be making of their own free will are predetermined by the composer of the problem.

Chess problems of the sort referred to in the foreword are to be solved by "retrograde analysis," which is a "back-cast study" (D, 10): that is, "the reconstruction of some part of the hypothetical game that has resulted in the present board position."[12] This relationship between the illusion of free will and retrospective analysis can be regarded as an allegory of the human predicament as described by

---

[11]See Pifer, *Nabokov and the Novel*, p. 11.

[12]Johnson, *Worlds in Regression*, p. 87. Johnson suggests that the reader is invited to reconstruct the events of Luzhin's life between his boyhood and his reappearance, a decade and a half later, in chapter 4. He notes that since these events are practically reconstructed in the subsequent narrative, the reference to chess problems is one of the booby traps laid for the reader in the foreword. I believe, however, that what the reader is invited to reconstruct is not a part of the plot so much as the nature of Luzhin's error, the attitude that would be marked by a disapproving question mark if it were translated into a chess move.

Schopenhauer: "Everyone considers himself *a priori* (i.e., according to his original feeling) free, even in his particular actions, in the sense that in every given case any action is possible to him, and only *a posteriori*, from experience and reflection thereon, does he recognize that his conduct follows with absolute necessity from the coincidence of the character with the motives."[13] Character, according to Novalis, is fate: being what he is, Luzhin cannot escape the sort of tragedy that is tailor-made to fit him. And yet the novel contains references to mistakes and to the ways one "should have played in order to avert disaster" (*D*, 56). The mistakes are, of course, made not by the chessmen but by the players, and though the rules of the game forbid the retraction of a move, players do frequently allow each other to reconsider obviously wrong moves; this happens in at least two unofficial chess games in the novel. Life allows Luzhin such a second chance for happiness, gives him an opportunity to reshape his course after he meets his wife. What the plot of the novel proves to imitate here is not a chess pattern but a human action that could be related to any game of skill: a deliberate breaking of the rules, either in order to allow one's opponent to learn more successful strategies or in order to reject an easy victory in favor of a more challenging confrontation.

If the characters are "galley slaves," their fate is inescapable; yet on rereading the novel one has an experience similar to that of a child who watches the same movie again and again, always hoping that this time the hero will avoid perishing in the end. The hero perishes nevertheless, but the experience of the audience incorporates the knowledge that he never attains. It is thus within the interaction of the movie and the viewer, the book and the reader, that this knowledge is, in principle, attainable and that mistakes are, in principle, avoidable: an analysis of the hero's mistakes *as* mistakes is not a message-hunting fallacy but a duty of the reader. The final words of the novel, "But there was no Aleksandr Ivanovich" (*D*, 256), refer to more than Luzhin's absence from the fifth-floor bathroom through whose window he has made his awkward way to death; as in *Pnin*, they remind the reader that the character is fictional but his experience is real. Freed from the "galley," this experience admits different ways (Borges's "forking paths")[14] of solving the conflict between human commitments and intellectual pursuits.

[13]Schopenhauer, *The World as Will and Representation*, 1:289.
[14]See Borges, "The Garden of Forking Paths," in *Labyrinths*, pp. 19–29. Patricia Merivale compares Nabokov's and Borges's art in "The Flaunting of Artifice in Vladimir Nabokov and Jorge Luis Borges," in Dembo, *Nabokov*, pp. 209–24.

Luzhin never learns to resolve this conflict. Strictly speaking, as a character in the novel he has no power over his fate, but that is not due to the formula of Novalis. The destiny of Nabokov's characters is determined not only by what they are but also by the manner in which they are treated by contingent reality. And if contingent reality had a determinacy of its own, that would not be the determinacy of a chess problem.

In the foreword Nabokov recalls how he "enjoyed taking advantage of this or that image and scene to introduce a fatal pattern into Luzhin's life and to endow the description of a garden, a journey, a sequence of humdrum events, with the semblance of a game of skill, and, especially in the final chapters, with that of a regular chess attack demolishing the innermost elements of the poor fellow's sanity" (*D*, 8). The key word here is "semblance": it is Luzhin who takes the random events of his life for a mysteriously planned chess attack. The nonexistent match that the final chapters resemble is, one should bear in mind, not a match between Nabokov and Luzhin; Luzhin's opponent is neither his creator nor even another character—it is a method of composition. In the novels of Sebastian Knight characters are "methods of composition" (*RLSK*, 95) but not all methods of composition can be personified and turned into characters; it is the deranged Luzhin who flatters a technique by elevating it to the status of a mysterious chess opponent.[15]

It would be too easy to say that what Luzhin takes for a chess attack is in reality a random flow of events. Few things are random in the novelist-reader communication. The seemingly random plot events are actually determined by a specific literary "method of composition." The nature of this method is suggested by a shift in the point of view which takes place only in the English version of the novel and which should be read as an allusion to Flaubert's *Madame Bovary* (on which Nabokov had lectured at Cornell before revising the translation of *The Defense*). The narrator of *The Defense* is omniscient, yet on one occasion he uses the first-person plural, placing himself within the fictional world. As in *Madame Bovary*,[16] this deviation from the general narrative stance occurs in a classroom scene: "When five minutes had

[15] *The Defense* thus initiates a theme that will be of central importance to *Invitation to a Beheading*. Luzhin commits the error into which Cincinnatus C. lapses in his darkest moments: thinking of one's adversaries as real and thus granting them anthropomorphic existence.

[16] Nabokov mentions Flaubert's experimentation with the point of view (see *LL*, 151).

passed after the bell and still no one had come in, there ensued such a premonition of happiness that it seemed the heart would not hold out should the glass door nonetheless now open and the geography teacher, as was his habit, come dashing almost at a run into the room. . . . Our bliss, it seemed, was bound to be realized" (*D*, 47–48).

In his lecture on *Madame Bovary* Nabokov notes that in addition to heredity and environment, the development of a character is also determined by the "unknown agent X" (*LL*, 126). This agent X is the equivalent of the Aubrey McFate who appears in the middle of Lolita's Ramsdale class list. The game of "Aubrey McFate" is an exploration of the "everything that rises must converge" principle for the staging of coincidences. Thus a dog and a driver mentioned earlier in *Lolita* converge in one spot at the moment when Charlotte is frantically running across the street, and they cause an accident that takes the plot out of a blind alley. Were the dog and the car planted in previous episodes by "McFate's" foresight (like the Fatum Insurance Company in *King, Queen, Knave*) in order to soften the impression that Charlotte's accident is a *deus ex machina* device? Or are the fates of Charlotte, Humbert, and Dolly mere side effects of the life of the images? ("On top of everything, I am a slave of images," thinks Nabokov's Krug in another connection: *BS*, 174). In *Lolita* the former is probably the case; yet the latter is largely true in *The Defense*, where the game of skill consists of monitoring recurrent imagery. The development of recurrent imagery is disguised as coincidence, and coincidence is disguised as the intervention of agent X. Luzhin mistakes this intervention for a chess game.

The purpose of the novelist's game of skill is to goad Luzhin into an optimal realization of his potentialities as a character. Agent X seems to intervene when heredity and environment are insufficient to give full play to the tendencies of Luzhin's mind; he enters the story in order to adjust the conditions for the eventual grotesque heightening of the action. However, what looks like an arbitrary or random intervention is always, in fact, part of the network of cross-references formed by the recurrent imagery of the novel. Thus, agent X contrives the funeral of the aunt's old suitor at precisely the moment when the young runaway Luzhin seeks asylum in his aunt's home. Young Luzhin does not attend the funeral (later he will miss the funeral of his father and by the end of the novel will refuse to visit his grave); instead, the boy spends several hours in the cold streets and comes down with a fever. His illness gets the plot out of an impasse, yet it also turns out to be a real-life counterpart of the functional fever that leads to a happy ending in one of his father's sentimental tales. [17] His parents take him to Germany to convalesce, and agent X arranges a chess tournament at their *kurort* (health resort) immediately upon their arrival—which not merely frustrates his parents' wish to keep him away from chess but also initiates the theme of European chess cafés as a setting for Luzhin's life.

As if to reveal a new aspect of Luzhin's character, agent X makes another sort of match for him: in the capacity of a dating service, agent X proves to be a worthy relative of the apprentice fate who, after several miscalculations, brings Fyodor Godunov-Cherdyntsev to meet Zina Mertz in *The Gift*. First, agent X gives Luzhin and his future wife the same geography teacher, the herald of exile (the motif of poorly learned geography is further developed by Luzhin's blind transits through European capitals; by the bright travel folders, too beautiful to be true, that he examines with his wife; and by the fictive "travel tales" of his former classmate Petrishchev). Then agent X sends the girl to play tennis with Luzhin's quiet chess-playing classmate, the one who will eventually lose his arm on a battlefield (in a real-life display of the "militant charging bright force" that Luzhin controls only at the chessboard). Yet these encounters do not lead to Luzhin's meeting the girl, because he keeps aloof from his teachers and fellow students. Finally, X "sends" the heroine to the same *kurort* where Luzhin had once been taken by his parents. This move is successful: when prescribed a vacation where "there is greenery all around" (*D*, 98), Luzhin automatically chooses the familiar location. By now a skillful player (of a game that does not resemble chess), agent X foresees, as it were, Luzhin's in-character move, just as Mr. Sluch anticipates the characteristic moves of Martha at the crisis point of *King, Queen, Knave*.

Now, agent X can let the relationship between the lovers develop its own logic. Disguised as statistical plausibility, he must only arrange the next chess tournament in Berlin, where Luzhin can continue his courtship. After Luzhin's marriage, agent X arranges a few more coincidences: the encounter with a former classmate, the visit of the

[17] This is an element of the "sources" (*Roots III*) technique discussed earlier. An interesting variant of this technique, involving an interpenetration of narrative levels (and the movement of images from fictional "reality" to "fiction within fiction" and vice versa) can be found in Nabokov's *Real Life of Sebastian Knight*. It is discussed, along with other aspects of the novel, in Rimmon, "Problems of Voice," pp. 109–29.

Soviet woman who knows Luzhin's aunt, the reappearance of the ex-impresario Valentinov, the suggestive picture in his office, and his timely exit that permits Luzhin to escape. All these seemingly random moves are in fact links in the strands of imagery that have been woven into the texture of the novel.

Recurrent imagery baffles Luzhin's random defense: as he walks into a store in order to "confuse his opponent," the store turns out to be a ladies' hairdressing salon, a replica of the one in which he had once hidden from the geography teacher. Here again, the development of an image is disguised as coincidence; Luzhin, however, takes it for his opponent's uncannily smart move. Convinced of imminent defeat, he makes his way to the frosted (*matovoye* in Russian, a pun on "checkmating") fifth-story window that has also been duly mentioned in a previous episode. Awkwardly and painfully thrusting himself through its narrow frame, he makes his exit from the world (where "to be born is hardly to be borne") in a manner that makes the image of the abyss converge with the motif of birth; "the Viennese delegation" (D, 10), however, is not invited.

Since the hero's first name is not mentioned until the penultimate sentence of the book, and since the heroine is never named at all, it is only natural that X, "the villain," should also remain incognito. Yet the main reason agent X is neither named nor explicitly referred to is that, unlike Luzhin, he is not only fictional but also nonexistent. Within the world of *The Defense* the moves of agent X are events in the life of the imagery that intertwines with the life of the characters. From the characters' perspective the events are cases of the "chance that mimics choice" (TD, 230); from the perspective of the novelist they are a "game of skill," choices that mimic chance. Upon the onset of madness, Luzhin, like Krug of *Bend Sinister*, appears to be given a glimpse of his creator's mind. There is, after all, a game of skill in which he is inextricably involved.

IV

Luzhin cannot know that the novelist's "game of skill" is played not against him but against (in both senses of the word) "the world." As noted above, a chess problem contains only a semblance of competition between two "galley slaves," the hypothetical White and Black; the real competition is between the composer and the solver. In the case of a novel that borrows the features of a chess problem, the main competition is between the novelist and the reader.

More specifically, the competition is between the reader's search for meaning and the devices through which this search is frustrated. In chess, as Luzhin explains to his prospective father-in-law, there are "strong moves" and "quiet moves": a strong move immediately gives the player an undoubted advantage; a quiet move "implies trickery, subversion, complication" (*D*, 121). The novelist's major "strong move" is the already mentioned complex of deceptive chess allusions that establish loose analogies (like this one) between narrative elements and chess strategies. A quiet move in this game is the handling of repetition.

The "coincidences" of the plot are elements in the patterns of recurrent imagery. A pattern is based on repetition, which, like redundancy in information theory, ensures the perception of meaning. In the final chapters of the novel Luzhin is intensely preoccupied with the search for the "secret meaning" (*D*, 200) of the recent events in his life but can project a meaning on them only when he discovers similar moments in his past; the symmetry, the seeming repetition, helps him to establish a pattern. Luzhin's search for patterns and harmonies is, of course, based on a childishly solipsistic feeling that everything in the surrounding world refers to him. It is not accidental that in "Signs and Symbols" the cousin of the mad boy is a famous chess player; the name of the boy's disease is "referential mania."

The novelist's handling of repetition encourages the reader to conduct his own search for meaning. Pondering repetitions may yield psychological insights. For instance, Luzhin's repeated toying with his fiancée's handbag—the lock shuts badly; she will soon spill everything out (*D*, 73, 83)—turns out to be related to his love of symmetric repetitions: their acquaintance started with the girl's picking up things that had spilled out of Luzhin's pocket; afterward, "dimly and almost unconsciously, he constantly watched to see whether she would drop anything—as if trying to reestablish some secret symmetry" (*D*, 87). But she never does drop anything, so the symmetry is not reestablished.

The relationship is indeed asymmetrical: the childlike Luzhin always remains on the accepting side. Such a symbolic reinterpretation of episodes is another activity in which the novel expects to engage the reader, and again, Luzhin sets the example. Having been vexed by a little boy, probably a beggar, who followed him from the railway station and threw a pebble at him (D, 102), Luzhin suddenly perceives the "secret meaning" of that event. "Consider this footpath," he says to his future mother-in-law. "I was walking along. And just imagine whom I met. Whom did I meet? Out of the myths. Cupid. But not with an arrow—with a pebble. I was struck" (D, 114). It is not made clear whether Luzhin fails to see the analogy between the pebble and the projectiles that in his childhood a group of boys had fired at him from toy pistols, thus heralding his torments at school (see D, 22). Nor can one decide what is more meaningful, the repetition of the pattern (the little boy's pebble likewise announces a new phase in Luzhin's life) or the symbolic reinterpretation of the isolated event. In any case, the "secret meaning" should not eclipse the awkward yet touchingly authentic way in which Luzhin explains that he is in love.

A great number of narrative details in The Defense, however, do not seem either to enter the patterns of recurrent imagery or to submit to symbolic reinterpretation. Here and there a loose chess analogy (in a taxi, for instance, people keep coming into "involuntary contact" like pieces in a closed chessbox: D, 147) or a self-referential pattern (such as the discussion of a novel that seems to be The Defense itself at Mrs. Luzhin's tea table; see D, 232) seems to emerge, yet the incipient patterns soon peter out; scenes from Luzhin's childhood and glimpses of different groups of Russian émigrés in Berlin are, in fact, just what they are—deftly and economically evoked slices of contingent reality. Despite Nabokov's public overstatements of his impatience with "human interest," it is largely for human interest—and for the delicacy with which it is conjured up—that these episodes have to be read. The reader is not supposed to repeat Luzhin's error and turn away from human reality in his pursuit of abstract harmonies and meanings.

And yet the reader's controlled alertness to the possibility of such harmonies, symmetries, and meanings in The Defense has a value of its own. It reenacts the eschatological alertness of Nabokov and of his "favorite character[s]" (BS, 151), the suspicion that there may after all be a cryptographic pattern in what looks like a humdrum flow of events combining novelty with repetition. The novel does not solve the problem of free will versus predetermination, nor does it contain a message about the presence or absence of a pattern of thought that could accommodate the whole of the entropic reality. It suggests, however, that if such a pattern does exist, it is not of human creation and cannot be adequately approximated by what Alfred Tennyson called "our little systems." The search for this pattern, or the pursuit of any intellectual activity that simulates this search, should not divert one's attention from "average reality" and from care for one's neighbor. The name Graalsky, derived from the Russian for Grail, is in this novel given to an old actor, a pleasant but petty, mean, and essentially inconsiderate minor character. The quest for the Holy Grail is often as egotistic as it is beautiful.

The novel also suggests that an unambiguous solution of either metaphysical or ideological problems is not imperative. Mrs. Luzhin is disappointed in both Soviet and émigré newspapers. She eventually relinquishes her search for "a formula, the official embodiment of feeling" in the Soviet press as well as her wish to understand "the complicated struggle between hazy opinions" in émigré newspapers: "If all this was too complex for the mind, then the heart began to grasp one thing quite distinctly: both here and in Russia people tortured, or desired to torture, other people, but there the torture and the desire to torture were a hundred times greater than here and therefore here was better" (*D,* 225–26). With the delicate intuitiveness that adds to the "warmth" of the novel, Mrs. Luzhin understands that ethical conclusions need not be affected by ideological ambiguities. Nor, the book seems to suggest, need they depend on the solution of metaphysical or epistemological mysteries. The complex treatment of the chess patterns in *The Defense* simulates the ambivalence inherent in eschatological alertness, yet this ambivalence brings into relief the novel's insistence on the need for a balance between intellectual pursuits and human commitments. The ethical conclusion is inseparable from an aesthetical one: art and life are not defenses against one another; life enters into the exercise of art, and art is a part of life.

6

Glory: "Good Example of How Metaphysics Can Fool You"

comme ceux qui partent en voyage pour voir de leurs yeux une
cité desirée et s'imaginent qu'on peut goûter dans une realité le
charme du songe.

Marcel Proust, *Du coté de chez Swann*

Nabokov's *Glory* (*Podvig*, 1932), translated into English in
1971 (later than his other Russian novels), is probably the most underrated of his longer narratives. In the thirties, part of the émigré
audience was antagonized by the book's refusal to keep what seemed to
be its promise of a patriotic message;[1] today, readers tend to show an
interest mainly in its autobiographical element (images of the Cambridge life, of the Crimea, of visits to Switzerland) and to wonder at
the relative straightforwardness of its narrative.[2] In fact, however,
Glory is as complex as any of the later works. It is the first novel to
adumbrate Nabokov's cautious metaphysics, a novel that masks eschatological anxiety with apparent simplicity and a lyrical tone.

Glory presents a conflict between the protagonist's version of the
Romantic quest and his commitments to other people. The quest is
explored, and implicitly criticized, through a self-referential use of
recurrent imagery intertwined with the technique of *involution*, the
Möbius-strip-like relationship between the fictional world and the implied author's mind.

For Nabokov, as for his contemporary Jorge Luis Borges (see the
latter's "Circular Ruins" and "A Game of Chess"), the relationship
between the fictional world and its creator is a tentative model for the
solution of "the mystery of the universe," the mystery of the relation-

---

[1]See, e.g., the hostile and troubled review of *Podvig* by V. Varshavskii in *Tchisla*, 7–8
(1933), 266–67.
[2]See, e.g., Field, *Nabokov: His Life in Art*, pp. 118, 123.

88

ship between the humanly cognizable and transcendent worlds. The "creator" in question is not so much the historical author as the creative consciousness, the "involute abode" (*PF*, 63) in which the characters and their worlds are conceived and to which they are ultimately supposed to return. The conventional "omniscience" of this creative consciousness suggests the idea of the "infinite consciousness" (*BS*, 192) that one wishes to attribute to transcendent reality.

In the *The Defense* this model takes the shape of an inchoate *en abîme* pattern; in *Glory* it takes the shape of involution.[3] Involution is a tangling of hierarchies, the erosion of the border between the "inside" and the "outside," between the fictional world and the mind of its author. *The Defense* contains rudiments of this technique: Luzhin's madness is presented almost as a glimpse into the consciousness of his creator. *Glory* develops this hint into a structural principle yet, unlike *Invitation to a Beheading* and *Bend Sinister*, does not lay it bare. Rather, it camouflages involution and thereby deemphasizes its metaphysical probings. The reason for the mask is indirectly suggested in the foreword, in which Nabokov states the specific aim of this novel:

> The book's—certainly very attractive—working title (later discarded in favor of the pithier *Podvig*, "gallant feat," "high deed") was *Romanticheskiy vek*, "romantic times," which I had chosen partly because I had had enough of hearing Western journalists call our era "materialistic," "practical," "utilitarian," etc., but mainly because the purpose of my novel, my only one with a purpose, lay in stressing the thrill and the glamour that my young expatriate finds in the most ordinary pleasures as well as in the seemingly meaningless adventures of a lonely life. [*Gl*, x]

The central explicit concern of *Glory* is, indeed, "the thrill and the glamour" of the humanly cognizable: that is, the beauty of the mask, not the nature of what it conceals. Yet to paraphrase Nabokov's *Bend Sinister*, every mask contains slits for the eyes (see *BS*, 7). The protagonist, Martin Edelweiss, does not probe behind the mask any more than Luzhin does in *The Defense*, but his reason is not Luzhin's fear of the unknown. Martin is one of the Nabokovian characters who are irresistibly attracted to something "that would always remain incom-

---

[3]For *en abîme*, see Chapter 5, n. 9. The term "involution" derives from the adjective "involute," in its literal meaning most frequently used as a geometrical term; figuratively, it occurs in Poe's "Murders in the Rue Morgue" and in John Shade's poem in Nabokov's *Pale Fire*. I have borrowed the word "involution" from Alfred Appel; however, he uses it in a broader sense, referring to signs of the author's control of the fictional universe (see "Nabokov's Puppet Show," pp. 87–93).

prehensible" (*Gl*, 11) but who mistake the nature of their quest. He lacks that intellectual intensity which the better-endowed Luzhin channels away from the surrounding world into surrogate harmonies. Unlike Luzhin, Martin Edelweiss deeply appreciates the world of experience but, finding the Wordsworthian "burthen of the mystery" beyond his endurance, develops a suicidal tendency and a lack of moral considerateness similar to those of Luzhin. *Glory* is in many ways a variation on the theme of *The Defense*, though in different colors and different "nuances of noise" (*LATH*, 118).

The formula that connects what Nabokov would call the "vessel and content" (*PP*, 158) of *Glory* enters into a chiasmic relationship with the structural principle of *The Defense*. Whereas in reading *The Defense* we reenact the error of Luzhin if we turn away from the novel's human interest for the sake of complex chess patterns, in reading *Glory* we reenact the error of Martin Edelweiss if we fail to see the deceptiveness behind the apparent simplicity of the weirdly beautiful tale. Thus, like *The Defense*, *Glory* displays an element of the reader entrapment that will flourish in Nabokov's *Lolita*.

I

What is Martin's quest?

The "glory" of this character is, as Nabokov mentions in an interview, his triumph over fear (see *SO*, 88). The fear in question is not the fear of death but the fear of fear itself: "Martin noticed that on occasion he was so afraid of seeming unmanly, to become known as a coward, that he involuntarily reacted in just the way a coward would—the blood left his face, his legs trembled, and his heart pounded tightly in his chest. Admitting to himself that he was not possessed of genuine, innate *sang-froid*, he nevertheless firmly resolved to behave always as a fearless man would in his place" (*Gl*, 13). Accordingly, what Martin fears is not death but the test of conduct that death would entail:

No matter how poorly Martin might have slept, after bathing he would be permeated with a beneficent vigor. At such times the thought of death, the thought that sometime, maybe soon (who could know?), he would be compelled to surrender and go through what billions and trillions of humans had gone through before him—this thought of an inevitable death accessible to everyone troubled him but slightly. It gained strength only toward evening, and with the coming of night would sometimes swell to monstrous dimensions. The custom of performing executions at dawn seemed charitable to Martin: may the Lord permit it to happen in the morning when a man has control over himself—clears his throat, smiles, then stands straight, spreading his arms.[*Gl*, 182]

Victory over fear is not, moreover, a goal in itself for Martin. This victory, demonstrated by his return to the cliff where he had once almost lost his life (see *Gl*, 169–70), is but a preparatory stage for his fatal ultimate exploit—his expedition to Russia. The purpose of the expedition is apolitical in intent if not in implication: Martin wishes to see the Russian autumn once more in his life. Indirect commentary on this compulsion is provided by the earlier of Nabokov's two poems called "Rasstrel" ("The Execution"), the one dated 1927 and included in a literal translation in his 1970 volume *Poems and Problems*. The lyrical hero imagines himself paying a hard penalty for the chance to revisit the racemosa in bloom:

> On certain nights as soon as I lie down
> my bed starts drifting into Russia,
> and presently I'm led to a ravine,
> to a ravine led to be killed.
>
> I wake—and in the darkness, from a chair
> where watch and matches lie,
> into my eyes, like a gun's steadfast muzzle,
> the glowing dial stares.
>
> .　.　.　.　.
>
> The watch's ticking comes in contact
> with frozen consciousness;
> the fortunate protection
> of my exile I repossess.
>
> But how you would have wished, my heart,
> that *thus* it all had really been:
> Russia, the stars, the night of execution
> and full of racemosas the ravine!
>
> [*PP*, 47]

It must be noted, however, that Martin's nostalgia is different from that expressed in the poem. The imaginary action of the poem is set in spring, the season of the racemosa; Martin's expedition is supposed to take place in autumn. Spring, judging also by the 1920 poem "Not without Tears" ("Ya bez slez ne mogu": *S,* 36), would have been Nabokov's chosen season for an ecstatic reunion with his native land. Most important, however, the lyrical hero of the poem can renounce the racemosa because his longing for it is a natural longing for the unique elements of the ecological niche from which he has been exiled. The nostalgia of Martin Edelweiss is more than that; it leads him into self-sacrifice because it is endowed with a misplaced mysticism.

Indeed, like the characters of Joseph Heller's *We Bombed in New Haven,* Martin seems to have caught glimpses of the script. His early thoughts about death are the involute insight of a doomed "galley slave" (see *SO,* 95) into his creator's mind.

The subliminal awareness of mystery brings Martin's experience close to that of his author. The strong autobiographical element of *Glory* is obliquely commented on in the text: Nabokov seems to have indulged the "writer's covetousness (so akin to the fear of death), . . . that constant state of anxiety compelling one to fix indelibly this or that evanescent trifle" (*Gl,* 60). And yet Martin is not a fictional extension of Nabokov—if only because he is deliberately deprived of artistic talent (see *Gl,* xiii)—and granted an anticipation of death in its stead. Anticipation of death heightens one's perceptiveness, as though familiar objects were about to "break into tragic speech demanding attention before the impending separation" (*Gl,* 179). Martin's response to this demand qualifies him as an appreciative recipient of images from his author's past. It is in its consequences that a "writer's covetousness" is "so akin to the fear of death."

Martin becomes conscious of this almost morbidly keen sensitivity when the doubts concerning his safe return from a clandestine expedition to Russia become too strong to be repressed:

The late afternoon sky was a sunless cheerless blank. The sound of automobile horns now seemed muffled by the mist. An open van passed by drawn by a pair of scrawny horses; upon it enough furniture was heaped to furnish a house: a couch, a chest of drawers, a gilt-framed seascape, and a lot of other melancholy chattels. A woman in mourning crossed the damp-dappled asphalt; she was pushing a pram, and in it sat a blue-eyed attentive infant; on reaching the sidewalk she pushed down the handle forcing the pram to rear. A poodle ran past in pursuit of a black whippet;

the latter stopped and looked back in fear, raising one bent front paw and quivering. "What's the matter, for goodness' sake," thought Martin. "What's all this to me? I know I'm going to return. I must return." [*Gl*, 196][4]

Yet it is the same sensitivity, enhanced by frequent thoughts about death, that makes "everything in the world so strange, so thrillful" (*Gl*, 49) for him long before calling attention to itself. The "thrillfulness" of Martin's world is the aesthetic justification for the mass of descriptive details, objects of the "writer's covetousness," that set *Glory* slightly apart from Nabokov's other novels.

Like the word "romantic" in the discarded title of the novel, the word "thrillfulness" is an allusion to natural supernaturalism, the "thrill" experienced by a Romantic sensibility in the presence of seemingly trivial phenomena.[5] The spirit of Wordsworth presides over the religious feeling that Martin's Anglophile mother wishes to transmit to her son: "She firmly believed in a certain power that bore the same resemblance to God as the house of a man one has never seen, his belongings, his greenhouse and beehives, his distant voice, heard by chance in an open field, bear to their owner. . . . This power had no connection with the Church, and neither absolved nor chastised any sins. It was just that she sometimes felt ashamed in the presence of a tree, of a cloud, of a dog, or of the air itself that bore an ill word just as religiously as a kind one" (*Gl*, 11).

Martin is less conscious of nature as an ethical entity and more capable of a loving attention to particulars, to natural phenomena as well as to man-made things. He appreciates vigorous athletic activities and the gifts of other people's fantasy: "Nothing was wasted on Martin—neither the crunchy English cookies, nor the adventures of King Arthur's knights" (*Gl*, 6). His best Cambridge friend, Darwin, shares this feature of Martin's character to the extent of writing a book of descriptions (of corkscrews and so on) modeled, one could surmise, not so much on Thoreau's *Walden* as on V. Sirin's "Guide to Berlin"

[4]This autumnal scene is reminiscent of the summer scene that creates a wave of unaccountable happiness in both the narrator and the protagonist of "Recruiting"—two characters who are destined to prompt cancellation by the author.

[5]It is noteworthy that the idea of the defamiliarization of the familiar, which is a clue to Nabokov's texture and is generally attributed to Russian formalist criticism, should in fact be traced back at least to Wordsworth's "Preface to *Lyrical Ballads*."

(1925). Moreover, Martin shares Wordsworth's, Nabokov's, and perhaps the fictional Lev Ganin's capacity for poetic memories, yet unlike Ganin he is also capable of finding beauty in the fictional present:

> The splendid autumn he had just seen in Switzerland somehow kept lingering in the background of his first Cambridge impressions. In the morning a delicate haze would enshroud the Alps. A broken cluster of rowan berries lay in the middle of the road, whose ruts were filmed with micalike ice. Despite the absence of wind the bright-yellow birch leafage thinned out with every passing day, and the turquoise sky gazed through it with pensive gaiety. The luxuriant ferns grew reddish; iridescent shreds of spiderweb, which Uncle Henry called "the Virgin's hair," floated about. Martin would look up, thinking that he heard the remote blare of migrating cranes, but no cranes were to be seen. He used to wander around a great deal, as if searching for something; he rode the dilapidated bicycle belonging to one of the menials along the rustling paths, while his mother, seated on a bench beneath a maple, pensively pierced the damp crimson leaves on the brown ground with the point of her walking stick. [*Gl*, 55]

The fragile, evanescent quality of the imagery in this description of the Alpine autumn ("a delicate haze," "filmed with micalike ice," "iridescent shreds of spiderweb") may be compared with Shelley's attempts to arrest "the shadow of an awful power" through reference to indefinable qualities and elusive phenomena; the coloration of *Glory* is pervasively Romantic. Martin Edelweiss, who wanders around "as if searching for something," is troubled by a sense of both the proximity and the elusiveness of the object of his quest: the forests near his uncle's chalet resemble but do not reproduce the Russian landscapes of his childhood—flocks of migrating cranes, for instance, do not fly over the Alps in autumn.[6] On a night after blue butterflies (signs of the involute presence of the author)[7] flutter near his window, Martin seems to reach a conclusion about the cause of his restlessness: hearing the word "Russia" pronounced after one of his uncanny sensations connects the mysterious "beckoning" with thoughts of the lost birth-

---

[6]Cf. Mrs. Bolotov's surprise in *Pnin* at finding southern plants and animals in the New England forest, the "birches and bilberries" of which deceive her "into placing mentally Lake Onkwedo, not on the parallel of, say, Lake Ohrida in the Balkans, where it belong[s], but on that of Lake Onega in northern Russia" (*P*, 120).

[7]One feels entitled to the surmise that these blue Alpine butterflies are related to *Lycaeides samuelis* Nabokov (see Chapter 2, n. 8).

place: "The warm, black night pressed in through window and door. Suddenly Martin raised his head and hearkened as if there were a vague beckoning in this harmony of night and candle flame. 'The last time this patience came out was in Russia,' said Sofia" (*Gl*, 48). Thus Martin mistakes the nature of his Holy Grail—not for a sexual union with an eidolon, as is the case with Albert Albinus and Humbert Humbert,[8] but for the beauty of his native land.

Martin seeks this land not like Antaeus but like a knight-errant who must save it—from wasting behind the glass in the cupboard of his Cambridge professor Archibald Moon. This is why he postpones his expedition to Russia until autumn: in that season he can test Moon's translation of Pushkin's ode "Autumn" against the real landscape. The role of Archibald Moon as a stimulus for Martin's suicide mission is made particularly clear in the English version of the novel. Evading the political discussions of his Cambridge friends, Martin reads them Pushkin's ode, which he considers an expression of the quintessential Russian experience. In the Russian version of the novel he reads the poem in the original, supplying his own gloss and explanations. In the English version, however, it is the translation written by Nabokov for Archibald Moon[9] that Martin offers to his friends:

> O dismal period, visual enchantment!
> Sweet is to me thy farewell loveliness!
> I love the sumptuous withering of nature,
> The woods arrayed in gold and purple dress.
>
> [*Gl*, 57]

This translation, in which the denotational meanings and the prosody are preserved but the inappropriate connotations produce an effect different from that of Pushkin's ode, is entirely in Archibald Moon's character. Moon is engaged at a snail's-pace in writing an English language history of Russia: "one plump volume," an "obvious motto ('A thing of beauty is a joy forever'), ultrathin paper, a soft Morocco binding" (*Gl*, 64). In Nabokov's *Look at the Harlequins!* the line from Keats's *Endymion* is translated into Russian in such a naughty way that upon retranslation into English it turns into "A pretty bauble always

---

[8]See Moynahan, *Vladimir Nabokov*, pp. 25–26.
[9]By the time the English version of *Glory* was prepared, Nabokov had already completed his *literal* translation of *Eugene Onegin*, pursuant to his disapproval of rhyming translations.

gladdens us" (*LATH*, 77). Since Moon's Russia is just such a decorative bauble, the reader can sympathize with Martin's ultimate rejection of Moon, or with his feeling that the "innermost, mysterious something" which, in terms of less esoteric creeds, is the spark of the divine within the human, binds together "the expedition, the love, and Pushkin's ode to autumn" (*Gl*, 189).[10]

II

Yet though the expedition becomes for Martin exactly what Sonya Zilanov means by duty, "the kind of thing which has an inner importance" (*Gl*, 94); and though his role changes from that of "traveling playboy" (*Gl*, 145; *puteshestvuyushchii barchuk: Pd*, 167) to that of knight-errant; and even though in the foreword Nabokov describes him as "the kindest, uprightest, and most touching" of his young men (*Gl*, xi), the novel does not request us to approve of Martin's "high deed." On the contrary, Martin's pursuit of his "duty" is presented as egotistic. Like Ganin in *Mary*, Martin feels no responsibility

[10]Martin Edelweiss can be read as Nabokov's reply to Martin Decoud of Conrad's *Nostromo* (several aspects of the relationship between Nabokov and Conrad are discussed in my article "A Nabokovian Character in Conrad's *Nostromo*"), an expatriate who returns to his native land, risking his life to win the hand of the woman he loves. Both come from patrician families and both flee revolutions; the "Noble White" of Edelweiss's botanical name calls to mind the Blanco party affiliations of Decoud. Conrad's hero undertakes a daring expedition in order to escape a firing squad and shoots himself when he is unable to cope with solitude and silence; Edelweiss, whose expedition is tantamount to suicide, is rumored to have been shot as a spy on the Russian border (*Gl*, 100). In his last days Decoud is unable to think about the people who would be affected by his death—in his solitude he cannot even accept their existence; Edelweiss refuses to consider the misery to which his death would subject his mother. Neither is a genuine patriot like Don José Avellanos of *Nostromo* or Zilanov of *Glory*. Yet Edelweiss rejects a career in journalism, whereas Decoud achieves fame by his articles about Costaguana in the French press as well as by the demagoguery of his Costaguanan gazette. It seems that had Decoud remained abroad, he would have been content with mummifying his country the way Nabokov's Archibald Moon mummifies Russia. In a sense, the flirtatious, fickle, abrasive Sonya Zilanov, "the patriot's daughter," is Antonia Avellanos brought up in a laxer discipline and forced into exile. Sonya is one of Nabokov's wasted women, ranging from Klara in *Mary* to the heroine of "A Russian Beauty." She is a romantic dreamer, like Martin, but unlike Martin she remains staunchly (though not uncomplainingly) attached to her defeated family. It is noteworthy that in the English version Sonya's image is painted in somewhat mellower colors than in the Russian original.

toward the people who surround him; his "duty," unlike Sonya's, is primarily to himself, to his private images of himself and of his native land. The glimpses that the novel gives us of his mother's anguish after he fails to return from Russia (see *Gl,* 74, 100) emphasize his callousness;[11] the feeling of guilt that he bequeaths to Sonya and Darwin without having experienced it himself suggests the cruelty of a child who hurts himself in order to punish his nurse. Martin achieves his "glory" at the expense of human commitments, and we are at liberty to doubt whether the end justifies the means.[12]

Martin's pursuit of an ideal undermines the morality of his decisions. The pursuit itself, moreover, is misdirected. The narrative suggests that he has responded to a call that he has overheard, a call not issued to him: "Thus something happy and languorous lured him from afar, but was not addressed to him" (*Gl,* 46). He keeps finding himself in the wrong places at the wrong times. Arriving at the white Alpine hotel that has mysteriously attracted him, Martin finds nothing of interest—"good example of how metaphysics can fool you" (*Gl,* 76). Leaving the train in pursuit of the mysterious lights that fascinate nocturnal travelers, he lands in a village that cannot be seen from the railroad. Indeed, Martin is not qualified for the quest of mystery; he does not fit into any of the three categories of Nabokovian characters—the lover, the poet, and the madman—who (in accordance with Shakespearean tradition)[13] are granted an awareness of something beyond the ordinary human experience. Martin is untalented and sane, and even his love for Sonya creeps on him unawares, eliding the stage of *Vlyublionnost'* (the "being in love": *LATH,* 25–26) which, in

[11]Nabokov's 1935 short story "Breaking the News" shows the magnitude of the catastrophe that a son's death is for his mother. His 1925 poem "The Mother" (*PP,* 32–33) is devoted to Mary's anguish after Golgotha.

[12]Martin's conduct contrasts with the ostensibly cruel behavior of Kuznetsoff in Nabokov's early play *The Man from the USSR* (*MUSSR,* 32–122). Kuznetsoff is engaged in attempts to overthrow the Communist regime in Russia; he leaves his wife in Berlin and treats her with demonstrative callousness in order to make her stop loving him. Kuznetsoff thinks he is acting with moral courage; since he exposes himself to danger, it is unbearable for him to recognize that his wife is tormentingly worried about him. Instead, he prefers to blacken his image in her eyes—but even this he cannot quite bring himself to do and therefore departs with the knowledge that she is as much a casualty of his exploits as are the friends whom, in a diversionary maneuver, he had sent on to the firing squad. One is forced to wonder whether Kuznetsoff's actions are really motivated by the selfless wish to free Russia from the Bolshevik rule or by a self-emulating imitation of Napoleon's glory.

[13]See the epigraph to Chapter 4.

Nabokov's novels, opens the door on the beyond (see Chapter 4, above). It is therefore not surprising that in addition to misinterpreting the origin of the obscure beckoning, Martin also mistakenly believes that the Russia he yearns for is recoverable otherwise than in memory and imagination.

What is that mysterious something which Martin mistakes for a call of his autumnal Russia?

III

The question must be answered in terms of the relationship between the fictional world and the mind of its creator as a model for the solution of the Mystery. Martin seems to share the "gnostical turpitude" (*IB*, 72) of Cincinnatus C., the vague gnostical self-knowledge that comes to him in his childhood and reaches a peak in adolescence, when he is standing at the edge of a Crimean precipice: "The crickets kept crepitating; from time to time there came a sweet whiff of burning juniper; and above the black alpestrine steppe, above the silken sea, the enormous, all-engulfing sky, dove-gray with stars, made one's head spin, and suddenly Martin again experienced a feeling he had known on more than one occasion as a child: an unbearable intensification of all his senses, a magical and demanding impulse, the presence of something for which alone it was worth living" (*Gl*, 20).

This is mystical experience that somehow misses its peak; and the "demanding impulse" that arises from the "*unbearable* intensification" of the senses is the impulse to *merge* with the "something for which alone it was worth living," not just to feel its presence. Martin is attracted to the "involute abode" of which his soul is a part. Denied the possibility of reaching out to that abode through a leap of creative imagination, he can only merge with it through death, the irreversible sacrifice of identity.

In the fragment "Ultima Thule" (1939–40), the man who claims to have had the Mystery revealed to him maintains that however one may imagine the hereafter, it necessarily involves a dissolution of identities (see *RB*, 176–77). Nabokov's earnest though tentative preoccupation with this idea is evident also in other texts, for example in *Pnin*, a novel that contains the often quoted reflections on life as discreteness (see Chapter 2). If death threatens the discreteness of the soul, then the death of a fictional character is a cancellation of his independent discrete identity, his return to and dissolution in the "involute abode" of the novelist's mind. The "ghost"[14] of the character who is shown dying in the beginning or the middle of the novel may still survive in this involute abode and hover over the remaining portion of the narrative in the guise of recurrent imagery, cross-reference, or even acrostic, as in the end of "The Vane Sisters" (1951). A character's leitmotif may take the place of his or her physical presence in the fictional world. This "haunting" (to extend the metaphor) is one of the techniques of involution used in *Glory* as well as in Nabokov's other works (*Bend Sinister* and *Transparent Things,* in particular). It expresses the author's reluctance to admit that death is annihilation, his reluctance to accept the "inanity of accumulating incalculable treasures of thought and sensation, and thought-behind-thought and sensation-behind-sensation, to lose them all at once and forever in a fit of black nausea followed by infinite nothingness" (*BS,* 99). How can one imagine that the world of man's consciousness can disappear without trace while gross matter is preserved by the law of conservation? Recollecting a speck of dust removed from his eye in childhood, the narrator of *Pnin* wonders where that speck could be after all the intervening years, and notes "the dull, mad fact . . . that it *does* exist somewhere" (*P,* 176).

In his novels Nabokov creates a universe in which the characters do not perish after death. Instead, they return to and become part of the involute abode—the mind of the author, the aesthetic realm, the library of Babel. It is this involute abode which issues the unwarranted call that Martin misinterprets and in which the spirit of his father survives. Martin was therefore not wholly mistaken when, held at gunpoint by a drunkard at the beginning of the novel, he "imagined that perhaps his father was expecting him that night, that perhaps he was making preparations of some kind for their meeting—and here Martin caught himself feeling a strange hostility toward his father, for which he reproached himself for a long time" (*Gl,* 15).

Martin does not know that preparations are being made not by his father but by his author. It is the author who handles the motif of firearms in such a way that the gun collection in the apartment of Martin's father foreshadows both the unloaded gun with which the

---

[14]The presence of "ghosts" in Nabokov's novels is the subject of W. W. Rowe, *Nabokov's Spectral Dimension* (Ann Arbor, Mich., 1981). Rowe's study of recurrent imagery as it relates to Nabokov's characters is valuable, but his understanding of Nabokov's ghosts is too literal.

drunkard threatens Martin and also the "more modern" (*Gl*, 2) and better equipped weapons ready to put an end to his life as he crosses the Russian border. However, we shall see that, contrary to dramatic precept, the gun that hangs on the wall in the "first act" does not fire in the third (nor does it turn into a cigarette lighter, as in *King, Queen, Knave*). The life of Nabokov's images does not follow convention.

It is the author's realism that resembles the "malevolent force obstinately trying to convince [Martin] that life [is] not at all the easy happy thing he [has] imagined" (*Gl*, 102), the author's intention that plays the role of the "inner sentinel" forbidding to Martin's "vocal cords the sounds that [live] in his ears" (*Gl*, 163), and the author's handling of the recurrent imagery that foreshadows Martin's end.

IV

The central element of this imagery is one of Martin's two leitmotifs—the winding path that disappears into a forest. It first appears at the very beginning of the novel:

> On the bright wall above the narrow crib . . . hung a watercolor depicting a dense forest with a winding path disappearing into its depths. Now in one of the English books that his mother used to read to him . . . there was a story about just such a picture with a path in the woods, right above the bed of a little boy, who, one fine night, just as he was, nightshirt and all, went from his bed into the picture, onto the path that disappeared into the woods. His mother, thought Martin anxiously, might notice the resemblance between the watercolor on the wall and the illustration in the book; she would then become alarmed and, according to his calculations, avert the nocturnal journey by removing the picture. Therefore every time he prayed in bed before going to sleep . . . Martin prayed God that she would not notice that tempting path right over his head. When, as a youth, he recalled the past, he would wonder if one night he had not actually hopped from bed to picture, and if this had not been the beginning of the journey, full of joy and anguish, into which his whole life had turned. [*Gl*, 4–5]

Martin follows a forest path in his fantasies and dreams (see *Gl*, 108, 156), and later the path materializes in the vicinity of his uncle's chalet. Yet it is only at the end of the novel that Martin really "hops" into the dream picture that congeals into a reality: the expedition from which

he never returns is supposed to start at the border and continue along
a forest path.[15] Moreover, the novel ends with the image of Darwin
walking along just such a winding path:

> Darwin emerged from the brown depths of the melancholy garden . . .
> and started back along the path through the woods. There he paused to
> light his pipe. . . . It was quiet in the woods, all one could hear was a
> faint gurgle: water was running somewhere under the wet gray snow.
> Darwin listened and for no perceptible reason shook his head. His pipe,
> which had gone out, emitted a helpless sucking sound. He said some-
> thing under his breath, rubbed his cheek pensively, and walked on. The
> air was dingy, here and there tree roots traversed the trail, black fir
> needles now and then brushed against his shoulder, the dark path passed
> between the tree trunks in picturesque and mysterious windings.
> [*GL*, 205]

The last lines seem to depict not only Darwin's experience but also
Martin's after he crosses the Russian border.[16] The Swiss forest in
which Darwin is following a footpath—the author having arranged for
his car to break down—is so similar to a Russian forest that earlier in
the novel Martin has half expected the vegetation to open upon a
Russian village instead of an Alpine slope (see *Gl*, 169). Both Martin
and Darwin thus fulfill Martin's childhood dream of passing to a
different dimension via a picture of a forest path.

This self-referential use of recurrent imagery forms a case of involution, a frame-breaking transition from the fictional world, through
an inset, to the consciousness of the author.[17] The technique is prominent at the end of *Bend Sinister:* the puddle that Krug has seen from a
hospital window turns out to be the puddle that the authorial persona
sees from the window of his room in Cambridge, Massachusetts. The

---

[15]The image of the path links Martin with Isabel, the daughter of the protagonist of
Look at the Harlequins!. Isabel too leaves the West for the Soviet Union. Her one-way
journey, however, is a demonstrative change of allegiance, not so much from one
political system to another as from her father to her husband, whose unstable course
leads her away from her *umnitsa tropka* (*LATH*, 202), the "intelligent trail" (*LATH*,
171) of the poem written in her mismanaged childhood.

[16]See Chapter 1, n. 23.

[17]This is another case of Genette's metalepsis, a transgressional movement from one
narrative level to another (see Chapter 2, n. 4). In *Glory* it takes place in a metaphorical
sense: it is not the character but his image (a "ghost," a leitmotif) that is transferred
from one representation of a forest to another.

picture of the forest on the wall of Martin's nursery, its frame having moved beyond the field of vision, becomes the setting of the novel's last scene.

The sound of the water that Darwin hears in this forest scene is Martin's second leitmotif. Martin is not prepared to give up his morning ablutions "in the sea, in a pond, in a shower, or in [the collapsible rubber] tub" (*Gl*, 182)—one cannot possibly imagine him trapped in the GULAG system. He leaves Russia by sea; he boats in the Cam; in Molignac his favorite job is to conduct the water from the reservoir in the yard to the nurseries; on the night when he is awaiting a sign from the spirit of Sonya Zilanov's dead sister, "the level of silence [keeps] rising, and all at once [pours] over the brim" (*Gl*, 92), bringing Sonya to him as on a wave; and on the night when he awaits a sign from his dead father, he hears the "real" waves, the booming surf of the Black Sea (see *Gl*, 12). The faint gurgle of the water running under the snow in the last scene of the novel may thus suggest that Martin has merged with that involute sphere which is now beckoning to the reluctant Darwin.

V

Darwin does seem to merge with Martin in the same involute forest scene where his cancellation by the novelist becomes final. His ultimate unreality is foreshadowed in the novel, just as is Martin's disappearance into the picture of the forest. In the foreword Nabokov notes that unlike Vadim and Teddy, Darwin is "totally invented" (*Gl*, xi); Sonya refuses to marry him on the grounds that "he isn't a real person" (*Gl*, 113)—words that in the broader context acquire a meaning of which she is not aware. He goes to the ball dressed like an Englishman from a Continental novel and plays this part with gusto. In the end the reader is forced to accept Darwin as a fictional character, an Englishman from a Continental novel, whose identity has been canceled even before the last lines.

Martin likewise ascends to the involute abode through cancellation rather than through physical death. As in the case of Cincinnatus, his death is not recorded in the text. The "open ending" of *Glory* can be interpreted in the following way.

Just before setting out on his expedition, Martin visits a Russian bookstore in Berlin. The owner of the store is familiar to Nabokov's readers from the novella *The Eye*, written just before *Glory*. Like all the insane, or half-insane, characters in Nabokov's fiction, this man is given a glimpse of his creator's mind: in *The Eye* he knows, for instance, that a clandestine expedition is being prepared, though not that it is to take place in another novel. The bookseller is on the constant lookout for Soviet agents; Nabokov, as his short story "The Assistant Producer" (1943) shows, knew that such fears were not ungrounded. It is therefore not improbable that there should be a spy in the world of *Glory;* one may in fact wonder whether Martin is not betrayed by Gruzinov.

Unlike the other patriots Zilanov and Yogolevich, Gruzinov—famous for his illegal shuttling across the Russian border—is securely affluent and inscrutable. His manner to Martin suggests that of a KGB agent who is somehow moved to warn his future victim. Martin confides his plans to Gruzinov under the pretense of trying to help a friend named Nicky (Kolya) and does not recognize his feeling of *déjà vu* as the warning the author adds to that of Gruzinov:

> The two English girls wanted [Gruzinov] to come and have ice cream (he was popular with young ladies, for whose benefit he assumed the character of an easygoing simpleton). "How they like to bother me," Gruzinov said, "I never eat ice cream, anyway." It seemed to Martin for an instant that sometime somewhere the same words had been spoken (as in Blok's play *Incognita*), and that then as now he was perplexed by something, was trying to explain something. "Now here's my advice," said Gruzinov, dexterously rolling up the map and handing it back to Martin. "Tell Nicky to stay at home and find something constructive to do. A nice fellow, I'm sure, and it would be a pity if he lost his way." [*Gl*, 177–78]

Even the allusion to a play in which characters seem to be admitted into the mind of their creator does not deter Martin from his suicide mission. Nor does he recollect that he has indeed already heard the words spoken by Gruzinov (whose name is derived from *gruzin*, the Russian for "Georgian"): once, lying in bed and half expecting a sign from his recently dead father's spirit, Martin had dreamed that he was "sitting in a classroom with his homework not done, while Lida kept idly scratching her shin as she told him that Georgians did not eat ice cream: '*Gruziny ne edyat morozhenogo*' (*Gl*, 12).

Martin, as Nabokov notes in the foreword, is one of those rare people whose "dreams come true" (*Gl*, xii). Not only are many of his wishes granted, but even the shifts in the novel's space and time are often effected in such a way as to trace the transformation of a dream image into "reality" (see *Gl,* 38, 49, 75). What Martin does not know, however, is that such a fulfillment is a danger signal. According to the protagonist-narrator of *The Eye,* "it is frightening when real life suddenly turns out to be a dream, but how much more frightening when that which one had thought a dream—fluid and irresponsible—suddenly starts to congeal into reality" (*E,* 108). As the *déjà vu* in the Gruzinov episode suggests, Martin's wish to "contact" his father is about to be granted.

Significantly, however, it is never definitely established that Gruzinov alerts the Soviet forces of Martin's arrival; in fact, it is not Gruzinov but the author who cancels Martin—just as at the end of *Transparent Things* it is the author who "judiciously" spreads some mysterious combustible liquid over Hugh Person's hotel (*TT,* 103); just as at the end of Gogol's "Portrait" it is the author who "steals" the fateful painting. Martin melts into thin air (like the major characters of Blok's *Incognita*) during his last meeting with Darwin. In a sudden fit of fatigue Darwin lies down and dismisses Martin with the exasperated reluctance of a character from a British (rather than a Continental) novel, a Stephen Guest losing Maggie in *The Mill on the Floss,* or Mr. Rochester losing Jane Eyre:

> Darwin, who lay calmly on the couch, yawned and turned his face to the wall. "So long," said Martin but Darwin did not respond. "So long," Martin repeated. "Nonsense, it can't be true," thought Darwin. He yawned again, and closed his eyes. "He won't leave," thought Darwin and sleepily pulled up one leg. For some time there endured an amusing silence. At last Darwin laughed softly and turned his head. But there was nobody in the room. It seemed impossible that Martin could have left so noiselessly. Perhaps he was hiding behind the furniture. Darwin remained lying a few minutes longer, then glanced warily around the already dimming room, put down his legs and straightened up. "Enough of it, now. Come out," he said as he heard a slight rustle from the baggage recess between the wardrobe and the door. Nobody came out. Darwin went over and glanced into the recess. Nobody. Only a sheet of wrapping paper left over from some purchase. Darwin turned on the light, stood frowning, then opened the door leading into the passage. The passage was long, well lighted, and empty. The evening breeze tried to shut the window. "To hell with him," said Darwin—and was lost in thought again. But suddenly he shook himself up and very deliberately started to change for dinner. [*Gl,* 200–201]

Whether or not Darwin is supposed to have fallen asleep and missed Martin's exit, the latter's physical presence is dissolved in this scene. All that remains of him is the distorted voice on the telephone a page later, several postcards ("the still visible beams of an already extinguished star": *RB*, 38), and images without substance in the memory of the characters and the texture of the closing description. Nabokov spares Martin the final blast by canceling his character before the execution—a finale that can be compared with the ending of *Invitation to a Beheading*, in which it is the setting rather than the character that is canceled at the penultimate moment. It is also analogous to the ending of *Mary*: Lev Ganin's reunion with Mary never takes place because he has not rehearsed it imaginatively; likewise, in his imagination Martin never succeeded in going beyond the preliminaries of his expedition. It is only his dream of disappearing into the forest that, to quote *The Eye*, ultimately "congeals into reality." As at the end of *The Real Life of Sebastian Knight*, when Darwin reenacts Martin's experience on the "intelligent trail" (*LATH*, 171), both seem to rejoin "someone" whom neither of them knows.

A physical death of the kind that the author spares Martin does take place outside this particular script: namely, in the second of Nabokov's two poems bearing the title "Rasstrel" ("The Execution") and dealing with the vision of a firing squad. This poem, dated 1928 (a year later than the one quoted above) is closer to Martin's logical fate. The last thing its lyrical hero sees is not the landscape of his dreams (and Martin's dreams, when fulfilled, are usually slightly yet frustratingly different from their initial form) but a dull fence, a tin in the grass, and the four muzzles of the firing squad. The eschatological alertness of this poem is tempered by a readiness to admit that death is followed by "ruthless darkness" (*neumolimaya t'ma*: *S*, 209). This poem is not included in *Poems and Problems*—evidence, perhaps, that when the English version of *Glory* was published (within a year after *Poems and Problems*) Nabokov may have been more interested in the moral and aesthetic ramifications of Martin's desire for communion with the autumnal beauty of his birthplace than in a Hamlet-like preoccupation with death.

VI

This preoccupation, however, is the spring of the action, the *hubris* that determines Martin's destiny. Since Martin is sane, untalented, and tricked out of Romeo's shock, it is only the heightened awareness of impending death that can make him prophetically responsive to the summons of mystery. Anticipation of death grants him that uncanny metaphysical insight of which he would otherwise have been deprived; his attempts to overcome fear add sublimity to his character. Yet the fact that the anticipation of death and fear of himself, rather than "the secret stir of talent" (D, 25) or a self-effacing heroism, lie at the root of his metaphysical restlessness is frustrating to the reader. Though "fulfillment is the fugal theme of [Martin's] destiny" (Gl, xii), the combination of the sublime and the futile creates the impression that Martin has failed to fulfill an early promise, and this impression is likely to irradiate on the novel itself. Even on close analysis, Martin's character—denied talent and, by way of compensation, granted persistent thoughts of death—may appear to be a rather precarious "method of composition" (RLSK, 95), artificially constructed in order to demonstrate a point and artificially dismantled once his task has been completed.

The sense of futility, however, is a deliberate effect of Glory. In a great number of episodes—the soccer at Cambridge, the scenes with Sonya, and others—the alternation of self-confidence with embarrassment or fear endow Martin's image with a flesh-and-blood solidity. Martin is never as human as when he makes minor mistakes, fights his confusion, or repeats such clichés as "One side is fighting for the ghost of the past and the other for the ghost of the future" (Gl, 67). Perhaps the most valuable aesthetic effect of the novel lies in the reader's regret that this sensitive and pathetically attractive human being should perish—not in a futile Civil War but in a futile pursuit of the ghost of mystery, a ghost that, unlike Hamlet's father, does not even address itself to him. Nabokov achieves the purpose to which he alludes in the foreword, for this regret is tantamount to a reassertion of the thrill and the glory of life, the natural supernaturalism that is no less sublime than the transcendental quest.

7

Laughter in the Dark:
Guinea Pigs and Galley Slaves

> And there is also an art of throwing a wet blanket upon sympathy
> at the very moment it might arise, the result being that the
> situation, though a serious one, is not taken seriously.
>
> Henri Bergson, "Laughter"

The years 1929–32 saw an outburst of creative activity: upon completing *The Defense,* Nabokov wrote a number of shorter works, including *The Eye,* and two novels, *Glory* and *Kamera obscura.* In 1938 his own considerably revised translation of *Kamera obscura* came out in America under the title *Laughter in the Dark.*

There is a close thematic relationship between *Glory* and *Kamera obscura.* Both are devoted to a metaphysical error: their protagonists feel a call, a lure of something inaccessible, and attempt to pursue it in different wrong ways. Whereas Martin Edelweiss of *Glory* mistakes this mysterious beckoning for nostalgia, Bruno Krechmar of *Kamera obscura,* alias Albert Albinus of *Laughter in the Dark,* seeks to capture what Shelley might have called Intellectual Beauty through possession of a sexual eidolon.[1]

An art critic and collector used to owning beautiful things, Albinus forgets that it is the "hopeless sense of loss which makes beauty what it is: a distant tree against golden heavens; ripples of light on the inner curve of a bridge; a thing quite impossible to capture" (*LD,* 10). It is not surprising that some of the pictures in his collection turn out to be fakes. Margot Peters, a vulgar, scheming young girl with whom he becomes infatuated, has only the accidental surface attributes of beauty; in his fixation on her fake loveliness, he half-consciously ignores

[1]Cf. Moynahan, *Vladimir Nabokov,* pp. 25–26.

107

her inner life, brushes aside his own better feelings, stifles his pity for his wife, and allows lust to take control over his life. He cares little for Margot as an individual. For all his abject obedience to her, she becomes an objectification of his desire: when she betrays him, he tries to kill her instead of destroying her image in his consciousness. If in *King, Queen, Knave* Martha's wish for a "dead husband" is a natural sequel of her wish for a "subdued husband," in *Laughter in the Dark* the murderous impulse is an outcome of self-inflicted moral obtuseness. To emphasize, as it were, the relationship between the literal and the metaphoric, the author eventually realizes the metaphor of moral blindness by depriving Albinus of his physical eyesight.

Whereas Albinus turns the object of his pursuit into a potential victim, Hermann, the protagonist of Nabokov's next novel, *Despair* (1934), treats his pseudo-double Felix not as a human being or even as an object but as a dehumanized instrument of his pursuit; and the pursuit is, prophetically, an experiment with murder as a medium of what Hermann considers "art."[2] The idea of experiment is also present in *Laughter in the Dark*, especially in its Russian version. Nabokov's troubled attitude toward this notion may reflect both the experimental attitudes characteristic of contemporary modernist art and the giant social and military experiment that Nazism was preparing to carry out.

The rise of fascism is only obliquely reflected in a brief reference to Mussolini (see *LD*, 138), but the novel complements *King, Queen, Knave* by exploring a psychological phenomenon that makes Nazi crimes possible: the deliberate suppression of sympathy for the suffering of another. Albinus consciously suppresses compassion for his wife; chance lovers shamelessly exploit Margot in her early days; Margot and Axel Rex inflict suffering on others for sheer entertainment. It is this specific theme (rather than the theme of the sexual eidolon, which connects this novel with *Lolita*) that is reflected in the narrative techniques of *Laughter in the Dark*. These techniques, comic and illusionist, systematically counteract the reader's impulses toward sympathy for the protagonist. The suppression of sympathy, both by the

[2]For interesting discussions of *Despair*, see Davydov, *Teksty-Matreshki*, pp. 52–99; Stuart, *Nabokov*, pp. 115–32; Claire Rosenfield, "*Despair* and the Lust for Immortality," in Dembo, *Nabokov*, pp. 66–84; Stephen Suagee, "An Artist's Memory Beats All Other Kinds: An Essay on *Despair*," in Proffer, *Book of Things*, pp. 54–62; and Carl R. Proffer, "From *Otchaianie* to *Despair*," *Slavic Review*, 27 (1968), 258–67.

characters and by the reader, is the structural principle of *Laughter in the Dark*.

I

Kamera obscura, the first version of the novel, opens with a description of a cartoon character invented by Robert Horn (Axel Rex in *Laughter in the Dark*). This rival of Disney's cheerful creatures is a guinea pig called Cheepy, an object of medical experiments. There is a strong whiff of black humor in the pictures where this unfortunate animal appears. Its inventor is a lover of sadistic experiment: "As a child he had poured oil over live mice, set fire to them, and watched them dart about for a few seconds like flaming meteors. And it is best not to inquire into the things he did to cats. Then, in riper years, when his artistic talent developed, he tried in more subtle ways to satiate his curiosity, for it was not anything morbid with a medical name—oh, not at all—just cold, wide-eyed curiosity, just the marginal notes supplied by life to his art" (*LD*, 91). It is with this same curiosity that he watches the suffering of the protagonist, subtly yet inventively augmenting it by the end of the novel. Krechmar/Albinus becomes the human guinea pig of Horn/Rex.

While translating and revising this book for publication in America (*Laughter in the Dark* is, strictly speaking, his first American novel), Nabokov deletes all the traces of the long-suffering guinea pig and replaces its description on the first page with the following prolepsis:

> Once upon a time there lived in Berlin, Germany, a man called Albinus. He was rich, respectable, happy; one day he abandoned his wife for the sake of a youthful mistress; he loved; was not loved; and his life ended in disaster.
>
> This is the whole of the story and we might have left it at that had there not been profit and pleasure in the telling; and although there is plenty of space on a gravestone to contain, bound in moss, the abridged version of a man's life, detail is always welcome. [*LD*, 5]

It is appropriate that the "Americanized" version of the novel should refrain from bringing into relief the motif of experiment, well known to its new audience from, say, Hawthorne's "Birthmark," "Rappaccini's Daughter," "Dr. Heidegger's Experiment," and *The Scarlet Letter* (which, incidentally, ends as *Laughter in the Dark* begins—with a reference to a gravestone). Moreover, emphasis on experiment might have been misleading, since the imaginative procedure at work in *Laughter in the Dark* is not that of experimentation (a movement from cause to effect) but rather that of pondering the data: the reconstruction of the way a given effect has been produced. Indeed, the first paragraphs are strongly reminiscent of the opening of Hawthorne's "Wakefield":

> In some old magazine or newspaper I recollect a story, told as truth, of a man—let us call him Wakefield—who absented himself for a long time from his wife. The fact, thus abstractedly stated, is not very uncommon, nor—without a proper distinction of circumstances—to be condemned either as naughty or nonsensical. . . . The wedded couple lived in London. The man, under pretense of going a journey, took lodgings in the next street to his own house, and there, unheard of by his wife or friends, and without a shadow of a reason for such self-banishment, dwelt upward of twenty years. During that period, he beheld his home every day, and frequently the forlorn Mrs. Wakefield. And after so great a gap in his matrimonial felicity . . . he entered the door one evening, quietly, as from a day's absence, and became a loving spouse till death.
>
> This outline is all that I remember. But the incident, though of the purest originality, unexampled, and probably never to be repeated, is one, I think, which appeals to the generous sympathies of mankind.[3]

Like "Wakefield," *Laughter in the Dark* seems based on a Hawthornean, potentially symbolistic principle: "Whenever any subject so forcibly affects the mind, time is well spent in thinking of it."[4] What is one's mind affected by in *Laughter in the Dark*? Not by a story of marital infidelity; like Albinus's wife Elisabeth, we have all "heard and read that husbands and wives constantly [deceive] each other; indeed, adultery [is] the core of gossip, romantic poetry, funny stories, and famous operas" (*LD*, 45–46). Rather, what justifies the time "spent in thinking of it" is, to borrow Hawthorne's words, the problem of appeal "to the generous sympathies of mankind."

Albinus is not a typical middle-class adulterer. He cannot, for instance, apply certain timeworn safety rules, such as maintaining a

---

[3] *The Complete Novels and Selected Tales of Nathaniel Hawthorne,* ed. Norman Holmes Pearson (New York: 1937), pp. 920–21.

[4] Ibid., p. 921. Cf. Charles Feidelson's remarks on Henry James "ciphering out" a given fictional situation (*Symbolism and American Literature,* [Chicago, 1953], pp. 47–49).

self-protectively callous attitude toward his mistress; his chief claim on
the reader's sympathy is based precisely on his inability to sustain such
an attitude. This inability, however, is caused not by his sympathy or
respect for Margot but by her ascendancy in the power struggle: she
takes full advantage of the hypertrophy of Albinus's desire. The reader's sympathy likewise remains dormant, but this is an effect of the
novel's rhetoric rather than of any features of the characters or the plot.

Albinus is presented, symbolically, as a bungler who cannot do anything with his hands. He bungles his whole life, and yet we are not
really sorry for him. Why? The narrative does not blunt sympathy for
him completely but does reduce it to a bare minimum. The rhetoric of
Laughter in the Dark is indirectly commented on by the far more radical
rhetorical experiment performed by Jerzy Kosinski's *Painted Bird*. In
Kosinski's novel, the sheltered prehistory of a child is abruptly put to
an end when he becomes an unprotected outcast and witness to acts of
cruelty; these acts are presented on a rising scale: the first is staggering
to the reader but is followed by successively more horrifying brutalities
until the sadistic escalation blunts the reader's sense of horror—thus
revealing the mechanism by which one becomes inured to the suffering of another. *The Painted Bird* is a narrative not so much of what was
as of what may be, a narrative that accusingly implicates the reader. In
a much less violent way and in the delicate spirit of aesthetic inquiry,
Laughter in the Dark does the same. The novel implicitly offers two
explanations of what dampens sympathy, one ostensible and one real.

II

The ostensible explanation of the suppression of sympathy is
"poetic justice." If our heart does not go out to Albinus—this pleasant,
kindly, and rather deep-feeling man who is ruthlessly subjected to ever
increasing torments—it is, poetic justice would hold, because "he had
it coming" and because his punishment is not disproportionate to the
crime (his betrayal of his family is responsible for his daughter's
death). Albinus's failure to dissociate his metaphysical quest from carnal lust and his granting of priority to lust over human sympathies
take a variety of easily perceivable external forms. He is not chaste:
before his marriage he was involved in numerous loveless affairs (a
cardinal sin of nineteenth-century fiction). He has an ostrichlike ability
to ignore the suffering of others by turning away from them. His

jealous rage arouses in him an automatic impulse for murder, the worst of all crimes. If we watch his suffering without much pity, is it because we find it justifiable that the man who has inflicted pain on others should, to continue the optical metaphor, give an eye for an eye?

Not really. Poetic justice does not suffice to sabotage pity; if it did, much of the power of *Othello* or *King Lear* would be lost. In his own nontragic genre Nabokov continues the Gogol-Chekhov tradition of bestowing cautious pity on the sordid and the undeserving. He makes the reader feel compassion not only for the gentle Vasili Ivanovich of "Cloud, Castle, Lake" (1937) but even for the obnoxious Koldunov in "Lik" (1939) and for the counterfeiter Romantovski in "The Leonardo" (1933).[5] In order to emphasize that the pain of a little money forger is no less intense than that of a Romantic poet—a forger of a universe (note the root of Romantovski's name)—Nabokov ends "The Leonardo" with a complaint: "My poor Romantovski! And I who believed with them that you were indeed someone exceptional. I believed, let me confess, that you were a remarkable poet whom poverty obliged to dwell in that sinister district. . . . My poor Romantovski! It is all over now. . . . Everything floats away. Harmony and meaning vanish. The world irks me again with its variegated void" (*RB*, 23–24).

Hence it is not because Albinus "deserves to be punished" that the novel is free from melodramatic appeal. Our pity for the protagonist is held in check because our attention is deliberately diverted from matters that invite emotional response.

III

In a circus the conjuror's patter diverts the observer's attention from the real action. The virtuoso techniques that call the reader's attention away from the characters' suffering in *Laughter in the Dark* take the shape of circus tricks: the stage manager combines the skills of *juggling* with a trick known as the *vanishing act*.

Vanishing Act is the title of a novel by one Udo Conrad, a writer who is mentioned at the beginning and who appears at the crucial point of

[5]This story has inspired the pioneering comparison between Hawthorne and Nabokov in Chapel Louise Petty, "A Comparison of Hawthorne's 'Wakefield' and 'The Leonardo': Narrative Commentary and the Struggle of the Literary Artist," *Modern Fiction Studies*, 25 (1979), 499–507.

the American version of the novel (he has also written *Memoirs of a Forgetful Man*, which is a good description of the unreliable narrative of *Despair*). As befits the fictional author of a book "about the old conjurer who spirited himself away at his farewell performance" (*LD*, 5), Udo Conrad performs his own vanishing act in his last lines. Unwittingly, he informs Albinus about Margot's infidelity and, on seeing the effect his remarks have produced, understands that something has gone wrong: " 'I wonder,' muttered Conrad, 'I wonder whether I haven't committed some blunder (...nasty rhyme, that! "*Was* it, I *wonder*, a—*la*, la la—blunder?" Horrible!')" (*LD*, 143). The "nasty rhyme" of "wonder" and "blunder" obtains only in English, whereas Udo Conrad—who would like to address the French audience but is "loath to part with the experience and riches amassed in the course of [his] handling of" his native German (*LD*, 138)—is thinking in German, whose corresponding *wunder* and *Schnitzer* do not rhyme. The situation is logically impossible and therefore cancels itself when subjected to linguistic scrutiny, "spiriting" Udo away as soon as his function in the novel is accomplished. The episode is a self-referential literalization of the "impossible situations" that have fallen to the lot of Albinus.

A similar vanishing act is performed by the actress Dorianna Karenina in her last line. Like all the characters of the novel, she is German, yet when asked by Axel Rex whether she has read Tolstoy, she replies with an unwitting English pun: "Doll's Toy?" (*LD*, 123). The linguistic impossibility is less obvious than in Udo Conrad's act, but the element of the grotesque is highlighted by the notion of a toy possessing a toy. In the Russian original of the novel, the fun is limited to Dorianna Karenina's unfamiliarity with the author of *Anna Karenin*.

Disappearance is one of the most persistent recurrent motifs of the novel. Though as an art connoisseur Albinus wishes to devote himself to the preservation of things of beauty, the "impossible situations" that he cannot control turn his life into a series of vanishing acts. First, his peace of mind disappears when he meets Margot; then his family life is shattered; then his daughter Irma dies. The illusion of his idyllic happiness with Margot is also soon destroyed; then he loses his eyesight and finally his life. Further, the motif of vanishing is an important aspect of the novel's aesthetic theme: beauty cannot be possessed; it vanishes upon appropriation.

The motif of *juggling* is evoked in Axel Rex's feeling that the story of his relationship with Albinus is stage-managed by an "elusive, double, triple, self-reflecting magic Proteus of a phantom, the shadow of many-coloured glass balls flying in a curve, the ghost of a juggler on a shimmering curtain" (*LD*, 118). The "many-coloured glass balls" (reminiscent of the "dome of many-coloured glass" in Shelley's "Adonais") are the recurrent images and motifs in the novel—one of which is the vanishing act.

The anticipatory and recurring visual images and motifs of *Laughter in the Dark* are in fact juggled with consummate skill. The images of the cinema poster and of the movie that Albinus watches when he first meets Margot foreshadow his own future; the screen funeral that he imagines on the day of his daughter's birth foreshadows her funeral, which he does not attend;[6] the scene between Margot, Rex, and Frau Levandovsky foreshadows a later scene between Margot, Rex, and Albinus. Colors, particularly red and blue, come into play with the colorlessness associated with Albinus and Elisabeth as well as with the "darkness" of the title; moral blindness comes into complex interplay with physical blindness, as does movement with stillness, sincerity with hypocrisy, earnestness with cynicism, clothing with nudity, tenderness with cruelty, and so on. Particularly important is the motif of doors, which in this novel (by contrast to *King, Queen, Knave*) are all too often locked fast. On her visit to Albinus's apartment Margot locks him up in his bedroom just as Rex had locked Frau Levandovsky in the lavatory; later she locks the door of the shower between two adjoining hotel rooms in Rouginard in order to pass to Rex's room undetected. Like Martha in *King, Queen, Knave*, Margot and Rex resolutely lock the door on anything beyond sensual gratification; Albinus, in a somewhat loftier although mistaken quest, always seeks out the wrong doors. The door on the Beyond does not come ajar for him as it does for Dreyer, and it is only at the moment of his death that doors symbolically open wide—the doors through which Margot makes her own vanishing act.

The effect of the juggling of motifs is equivalent to the effect of the conjuror's patter; it is a device that diverts us from the characters' suffering. Yet Nabokov does not merely address our intellect, the known enemy of emotion, in order to divide our attention between the subject and the manner of the presentation. That technique would be part of the *skaz* tradition, elements of which, though transformed

---

[6]Accounts of the novel's film imagery can be found in Alfred Appel, Jr., *Nabokov's Dark Cinema* (New York, 1974); and Stuart, *Nabokov*, pp. 87–106.

almost beyond recognition, occur in *Pnin:* the narrator keeps fore-grounding himself, clowning in front of the reader for whose attention he thus competes with the story.[7] In *Laughter in the Dark,* however, the narrator is hardly ever felt; he participates in the author's own "vanishing act." The reader's attention is diverted from Albinus not to the narrator but to the "details" of Albinus's world; not from the subject to the manner of the presentation but from the action to the *mise-en-scène.*

IV

The juggling of imagery in *Laughter in the Dark* is so consummately skillful that the plot may sometimes seem to be a pretext for its display. Yet images are not ornamental vignettes but integral parts of the plot; their selection cancels the difference between the story and the narrative, the subject and the manner of the presentation.

In moments of deep distress, one's eyes are often arrested by a chance detail of the surrounding scene; the detail may then acquire an almost hypnotic power. References to details of the setting, often densely yet elusively meaningful, likewise effectively divert the reader's attention from the force of the character's distress. Whereas in Chekhov's work (as in the work of his fictional fellow writer Trigorin) "the broken bottle glitters on the dam and the mill-wheel casts a black shadow—and there you have the moonlight night,"[8] Nabokov's images in *Laughter in the Dark* do not so much *convey* the atmosphere of the scene as *eclipse* it; Nabokov evokes the hypnotizing detail at the expense of the pain that has caused a character's fixation on it.

Nevertheless, the inferrable relationship between the pain and the symptomatic image endows the latter with symbolic significance. Thus, on finding that Elisabeth has read Margot's letter and left him, Albinus walks into the bedroom and sees a telltale disorder: "His wife's evening gowns lay on the bed. One drawer of the chest was pulled out. The little portrait of his late father-in-law had vanished

[7]See Boris Ejkhenbaum, "Kak sdelana 'Shinel'" Gogolia" ("How Gogol's 'The Overcoat' Is Made") and "Illiuziya Skaza" ("The 'Skaz' Illusion"), in Jurij Striedter, comp., *Texte der Russischen Formalisten* (Munich, 1969), 1:122–58, 160–66.

[8]A. P. Tchehov, *The Sea-Gull,* act 4, in *The Cherry Orchard and Other Plays,* trans. Constance Garnett (London, 1965), p. 223.

from the table. The corner of the rug was turned up" (*LD*, 56). The short sentences convey the fragmentariness of Albinus's consciousness: he has not yet taken in the full impact of the havoc he has wreaked in his life. Elisabeth has taken away what is most precious to her—not the evening gowns but her daughter, her love, the picture of her father (the word "vanish" applied to the picture is significant: when Margot vanishes from the same apartment at the end of the novel, it is the costly miniatures from a cupboard that she carries away). A drawer is open—a secret is out. The corner of the rug is turned up—the underside of Albinus's love life has become visible (the momentary look of genuine anguish in the eyes of Cecilia C. in *Invitation to a Beheading* is similarly compared with the visible lining of a turned up corner of life; see *IB*, 136).

The full power of such images as the turned-up corner of a rug merits a separate phenomenological study, which cannot be undertaken here. It must be noted, however, that a repeated reading of the novel intensifies the force of this particular "glass ball," linking it with a "glass ball" of a different color: the "frozen wave" of the bulging carpet in the scene of Albinus's death (*LD*, 187). During the brief struggle between Albinus and Margot a piece of furniture gets pushed in such a way as to produce an upward crease in the carpet, an almost *en-abîme* image of darkness within darkness. The two carpet positions are expressive traces of, respectively, Elisabeth's outrage and Margot's and Albinus's spasmodic violence. The inference concerning the exact origin of the disorder is an act of the intellect that further deflects the reader's psychic energy from vicarious emotion, enhancing the anaesthetic effect of aesthetic distance.

Aesthetic distance is further increased by dramatic irony and shifts of perspective. Dramatic irony, the difference between the reader's and the protagonist's interpretations of the same set of details, distances Albinus's horror on the morning when he discovers that he has become blind. It does not take us long to understand the meaning of the discrepancy between the daytime sounds of the hospital and the absence of light: Albinus has gone blind. The elaboration of this discrepancy is, in itself, an interesting aesthetic exercise. The pleasure that it produces (at the expense of attention to Albinus's pain) may be related to our subconscious memories of awakenings: hearing is usually the first of the five senses to come alive. For more than a page of the narrative we watch Albinus staving off the truth by attributing the darkness to a series of implausible causes, because the obvious cause is too horrifying. A further irony is achieved by the relative frequency of the wrong and the right causes: blindness is a much rarer phenomenon than, for instance, the noisy though moonless night that Albinus is trying to imagine. He clings to the less logical though more statistically probable explanation rather than to the more logical yet frightfully unusual one. This kind of self-delusion is, in fact, the story of his life.

When the realization of the truth can no longer be delayed, the narrator resorts to a behavioristic description of Albinus's reaction and makes up for its inevitable touch of callousness by using the metaphor of the globe, which suggests the cosmic magnitude of Albinus's pain. Moreover, as if to evade the "emotional danger" lying in that region, the chapter is hastily cut short: 'I... I...' Albinus drew a deep breath which seemed to make his chest swell into some vast monstrous globe full of a whirling roar which presently he let out, lustily, steadily.... And when it had all gone, he started filling up again" (*LD*, 157). The narrative thus reenacts the wariness with which Albinus turns away from his wife's grief upon the death of their child, unwilling to let pity for Elisabeth keep him away from Margot. It turns the tables on Albinus by eventually shifting his own pain to the periphery of the reader's field of vision.

The shifts of perspective in *Laughter in the Dark* frequently amount to turning aesthetic distance into physical distance. Such a monitoring of the "camera eye" is most obvious in the short chapter devoted to Albinus's car accident. The account of the event that causes his blindness is a catalogue of different ways of seeing. The distance between the camera eye and the car increases and begins to decrease only after the accident has taken place; the camera eye never closes up on the accident itself.

In the first sentence of the chapter an old woman is gathering herbs (for medicine or magic?) on a hillside. She sees two cyclists and Albinus's car converging at a sharp bend of the road. The camera eye then rises to look down with the pilot of the mail plane flying over the scene, and then still higher, to a spot from which it can overlook the mountains of Provence and finally the whole "cheek of the earth from Gibraltar to Stockholm" (*LD*, 152).

The camera eye descends over Berlin, and in the ensuing two paragraphs seeing yields to vision. The narrator—or is it Elisabeth?—seems to have a strong visual memory of Irma looking at the ice cream vendor; then Elisabeth notes the symbolmaking contrast between an ice cream vendor's white clothes and her own black ones; finally,

standing on her balcony, Elisabeth becomes aware of a strange ner-
vousness. For the second time in the novel (the first time was after her
brother Paul had run into Albinus and Margot at the stadium) this
bland, habitually absentminded and self-deluding woman turns out to
be capable of a keen intuitive insight (involute insight, one may say,
into her creator's mind). The balcony on which she is standing seems
"to soar higher, higher" (LD, 153), rising over the European cheek of
the earth and descending over Provence, first to the mail plane, then to
the old herb gatherer. The pronoun "she" in the last sentence of the
chapter ("For a whole year at least she would be telling people how she
had seen... what she had seen... " LD, 153) is ambiguous: it is not
clear whether the sentence refers to the actual scene witnessed by the
herb gatherer or the telepathic vision of Elisabeth. Paradoxically,
though this control of distance spares the reader's emotions, it nevertheless presents the accident—and Albinus's ensuing loss of eyesight—
as a cosmic event, no less important than anything else that may be
happening in Europe on that particular morning.

V

The uneasy combination of soberness and awe in the treatment
of Albinus suggests that a touch of callousness is an almost inevitable
result of the comic approach to a melodramatic subject. The comedy
stems from those features of the character that, by themselves, have the
power to reduce his appeal to sympathy. Albinus is a perfect illustration of what Bergson described as a potentially comic character, one
whose emotion is a parasitic growth, rigid and disconnected from the
rest of the soul: "This rigidity may be manifested, when the time
comes, by puppet-like movements, and then it will provoke laughter;
but, before that, it had already alienated our sympathy: how can we
put ourselves in tune with a soul which is not in tune with itself?"[9]
One might say that we can do so if the character is telling his own
story; indeed, part of the troubling effect of Nabokov's first-person
narratives consists precisely in our resentment of the occasional sympathy that the narrators extort from us despite our better judgment.
The third-person narrative of Laughter in the Dark, however, plays
down the attractive features of Albinus and emphasizes the parasitic

[9]Bergson, "Laughter," p. 152.

hypertrophy of the passion that suppresses his concern for Elisabeth, his love for his daughter and feeling of guilt upon her death, his artistic tastes, his judgment. The recurrence of similar situations and patterns of behavior throughout the novel presents Albinus as a "galley slave" (*SO*, 95) at the mercy of his obsession, if not a puppet on the master juggler's strings.

Albinus's disposition forms the ground for the comic; the actual laughter, however, is provoked by the incongruities that stem from his predicament.[10] His desire for Margot as an embodiment of transcendent beauty is incongruous in view of her vulgarity, greed, hypocrisy, and cruelty. This global incongruity yields sundry local errors that also expose Albinus's tendency to commodify art and reify people. The close connection between an aesthetic misprision and a moral flaw is evident in the episode that follows Margot's visit of inspection to Albinus's apartment. Noticing a scarlet patch in the library, Albinus decides that it is the edge of Margot's dress and that she is still hiding behind a bookcase after his family has come back home. During the evening hours he suffers tortures of fear lest she be discovered. However, when his household finally retires his passion for Margot surmounts all caution and propriety. He makes his way to the library not so much to release Margot as to make love to her there and then, with his family sleeping behind the partitions:

> Albinus undid the neck of his pyjamas as he crept along. He was trembling all over. "In a moment—in a moment she will be mine," he thought. Noiselessly he opened the door of the library and turned on the softly shaded light.
>
> "Margot, you mad little thing," he began in a whisper.
>
> But it was only a scarlet silk cushion which he himself had brought there a few days ago, to crouch on while consulting Nonnenmacher's *History of Art*—ten volumes, folio. [*LD*, 44]

The effect of the anecdote is enhanced by the cataloguelike description of the art book: it is characteristic of Albinus to treat the book not just as a source of information but also, perhaps mainly, as a valuable—that is, expensive ("ten volumes, folio")—possession. He wishes to turn Margot, or rather the beauty that he sees in her, into

---

[10]According to Schopenhauer, laughter results "from nothing but the suddenly perceived incongruity between a concept and the real objects that had been thought through it" (*The World as Will and Representation*, 1:59).

such a possession. Moreover, he has expected her to remain motionless for hours behind a bookcase, like an art book on its shelf or a cushion that has tumbled to the floor, waiting patiently for the master's approach. The absurdity of this expectation foreshadows the disappointments that are in store for him, the empty rooms into which he will grope his way in search of his fickle mistress.

The name of the author of the art book can be understood as "a maker of nonnons." In *Invitation to a Beheading*, "nonnons" are strange, grotesque objects that converge to make a picture when they are reflected in a special mirror (see *IB*, 135–36), probably an anamorphoscope (the mirror held up to nature?).[11] As possessions rather than conditions of aesthetic experience, books and objects of art are little more than "nonnons." Creative perception is the anamorphoscope that organizes entropic "average reality" (*SO*, 118) so as to endow it with "harmony and meaning" (*RB*, 24). Albinus and Margot are incapable of authentic perception. They structure their respective world pictures on movieland stereotypes, and as the pervasiveness of the film imagery in the novel suggests, their lives become parodies of film romances and therefore ample sources of the incongruous and grotesque.[12]

VI

"The life of every individual," says Schopenhauer, "viewed as a whole and in general, and when only its most significant features are emphasized, is really a tragedy; but gone through in detail it has the character of a comedy."[13] The "detail" in question is exactly what, according to the second paragraph of *Laughter in the Dark*, "is always welcome."

One of the reasons why the title *Laughter in the Dark* is more appropriate than the earlier *Kamera obscura* is that Daguerre's gadget (see Chapter 1 above) could capture only what is "viewed as a whole and in general, and when only [the] most significant features are emphasized." Though the novel is permeated with visual imagery and veiled references to optical effects, its new title contains a sinister auditory

---

[11]Johnson also interprets the "nonnons" of *Invitation* as an allusion to anamorphic art; see *Worlds in Regression*, pp. 160, 181.

[12]For a detailed discussion of the parodistic element in *Laughter in the Dark*, see Stuart, *Nabokov*, pp. 87–113.

[13]Schopenhauer, *The World as Will and Representation*, 1:322.

image that conveys the prevalently somber coloration ("A title . . . must convey the colour of the book,—not its subject": *RLSK*, 72) of a motley novel haunted by a basic uneasiness: is it right to present human suffering in a way that leaves the reader's sympathy unengaged? Moreover, though explicit references to experimentation have been excluded, the novel does, after all, perform a little experiment of its own—not on human beings but on the limits of the tragicomic. Albinus's life, viewed in detail, does indeed have the features of a comedy, if one forgets its sad ending. Can any person become a comic character, or is a comic character necessarily one that displays a particular sort of flaw?

Nabokov's *Pnin* shows that the answer depends on the sort of laughter the comedy provokes; there, the fun is tempered by the lyrical element. The pathetic Timofey Pnin tends to get so carried away by his memories and research that he forgets average reality; the little mishaps that constantly befall him are the petty revenge of the "here and now." With Pnin, however, no psychological tendency grows beyond an admissible proportion, and there is a great deal of poetry in both his escapes and his returns.

In lectures on *Don Quixote* delivered at Harvard in the spring of 1952 (that is, when the work on *Pnin* had just begun), Nabokov demonstratively dissociated himself from the black humor of Cervantes' contemporary audience (see *LDQ*, 51–57). Accordingly, though history plays ping-pong with Pnin, the author never lets him fall over the edge of farcical catastrophes. On the way to the library, for instance, Pnin totters but does not fall; he breaks a tumbler under the soap suds but not Victor's precious present; he does make it to Cremona in time not only for his lecture but also for dinner; and Isabel Clements is prevented from surprising him, toothless and aghast, in her former room.[14] Pnin's classroom chair emits "an ominous crack," interrupting his story of Pushkin's death, but it does not break—at least not in the text. The narrative tactfully refrains from showing us how Pnin fights his embarrassment; instead, we are given a flashback scene that symbolically summarizes the difference between the practical jokes played on Cervantes' hero and the tests to which the author periodically subjects the resilience of Pnin: "Sometime, somewhere—

---

[14]These and similar episodes are brilliantly discussed by David H. Richter as cases of Nabokov's handling of the "interrupted pratfall" theme in *Pnin*: see "Narrative Entrapment in *Pnin* and 'Signs and Symbols,' " *Papers on Language and Literature*, 20 (1984), 418–30.

Petersburg? Prague?—one of the two musical clowns pulled out the piano stool from under the other, who remained, however, playing on, in a seated, though seatless, position, with his rhapsody unimpaired? Where? Circus Busch, Berlin!" (*P*, 68).

No matter how strenuously Jack Cockerell, the painter Komarov (whose name is derived from the Russian for "mosquito," another prickly nuisance), or the narrator attempt to turn Pnin into a farcical failure, the lyrical strain in Pnin's character remains unimpaired. Moreover, the author seems to be always unobtrusively helping him keep an even score with his tormentors—in much the same way that Don Quixote, according to Nabokov's calculations (see *LDQ*, 89–112), keeps an even score of victories and defeats.

Albinus, however, is no Pnin. The times in which he lives are more sinister than those even of Don Quixote, and the laughter of the novel is not the one of light comedy; it is "laughter in the dark," one of the most sinister sounds that can be produced by a human voice. The gradual loss of all that is dear to Albinus in a series of vanishing acts is a grim inversion of what Bergson calls the snowball effect.[15] It is not surprising that in *Bend Sinister* Nabokov will use the image of a snowball as a metaphor for the historical changes in the course of which human individuality is coldly and callously suppressed by the ruling party's drive toward a systematic undermining of human sympathies. Laughter, according to Bergson, is a social corrective that seeks to check rigidity and parasitic growths,[16] yet it entails—or is made possible by—a suppression of sympathy, a suppression that in itself can develop into a malignant disease. While Nabokov was preparing the American version of the novel, such a disease was rapidly spreading through Europe. Perpetrators of present and future crimes were officially absolved—in advance—of any guilt for carrying out ruthless orders; the *Schadenfreude* of Margot was becoming the order of the day. Like *King, Queen, Knave* with its study of the rejection of spiritual life, *Laughter in the Dark*, with its ill-at-ease atmosphere and its exploration of callousness, is a response to ominous processes on the inner agenda of its decade.

[15]Bergson, "Laughter," p. 113.
[16]Ibid., pp. 73–77.

8

Invitation to a Beheading: "Nameless Existence, Intangible Substance"

The volatile truth of our words should continually betray the inadequacy of the residual statement.

Henry David Thoreau, *Walden*

The first draft of *Invitation to a Beheading* (*Priglashenie na kazn'*, 1935, published in 1938) was written "in one fortnight of wonderful excitement and sustained inspiration" (*SO*, 68). Like most products of a great writer's burst of creative energy, this novel is characterized by a strong element of overdetermination. Cincinnatus C., a citizen of a totalitarian anti-science-fictional dystopia, is accused of an obscure crime called "gnostical turpitude" (*IB*, 72) and described as "opacity" (*IB*, 21). He is imprisoned in a fortress, condemned to death by beheading, and invited to collaborate in his own execution. The Kafkaesque situation lends itself to a variety of complementary readings—political, metaphysical, aesthetic—but in all these readings Cincinnatus emerges as a Nabokovian avatar of the artist in conflict with his environment.

Cincinnatus is not trained for any recognized form of art. What makes him worthy to be called an artist is not even his attempt to produce a written account of his experience; it is his wish to live authentically despite the pressures of the environment on which he depends for the satisfaction of his desires. One by one the objects of his desires fail him, yet their treason also signifies his liberation from commitments and his ultimate freedom to reach out to the transcendent dimension of whose presence he has long been sporadically aware. This is a significant shift in Nabokov's imagination: whereas in his earlier books the people who betrayed human commitments suffered defeat, in *Invitation* a victim of betrayal wins a victory.

123

The shift may be related to the predicament of Russian emigrants in Europe. The life of Russian émigré intellectuals was characterized by their "utter physical dependence on this or that nation, which had coldly granted [them] political refuge" and by "material indigence and intellectual luxury, among perfectly unimportant strangers, spectral Germans and Frenchmen in whose more or less illusory cities" they happened to dwell (*SM*, 276). Yet a sense of "fragile unreality" kept haunting the émigré literature: "The number of titles was more impressive than the number of copies any given work sold, and the names of the publishing houses—Orion, Cosmos, Logos, and so forth—had the hectic, unstable and slightly illegal appearance that firms issuing astrological or facts-of-life literature have" (*SM*, 280). That which seemed real, moreover, would suddenly exchange places with that which seemed illusory. "Quite often in fact," Nabokov recollects in *Speak, Memory*, "the spectral world through which we serenely paraded our sores and our arts would produce a kind of awful convulsion and show us who was the discarnate captive and who the true lord" (*SM*, 276). The shuttling of the sense of unreality between Cincinnatus and his tormentors in *Invitation* may reflect these convulsions, but the tormentors themselves are presented as recognizable philistine Russians rather than "formless and faceless" transparent "aborigines" (*SM*, 276).

In the mid-thirties Nabokov had already lost his hope of ever returning to a "hospitable, remorseful, racemosa-blossoming Russia" (*KQK*, vii). The political realities of Germany were taking a grimly grotesque shape; emigration from Russia had been discontinued; and it was becoming clear that the Russian émigré audience was a doomed enclave. It was then that Nabokov apparently began to consider shifting to another language. One is tempted to regard this crossroads situation as a reason why the overdetermination in *Invitation to a Beheading* combines with a no less pronounced element of indeterminacy: no single component of the novel's multiple meaning is granted supremacy over other components; words constantly reveal the limitations of their power; and the text attempts to compensate for their insufficiency by a number of nonverbal means. Yet indeterminacy need not be considered a reflection of any biographical fact; rather, it is a technique that reflects the novel's deliberate subversion of the distinction between the illusory and the "real."

I

The indeterminacy of *Invitation to a Beheading* is interpretive, lexical, and structural. The interpretive indeterminacy consists in the incompleteness, the noncomprehensiveness, of each layer of significance. The structure of the novel's meaning cannot be described by the conventional pattern of peeling layers. Far from invoking Peer Gynt's onion (with its residual tear), Nabokov devises his own model of relationships between the multiple meanings of his text. This model can be inferred from the following *mise-en-abîme*[1] passage:

> "What a misunderstanding" said Cincinnatus and suddenly burst out laughing. He stood up and took off the dressing gown, the skullcap, the slippers. He took off the linen trousers and shirt. He took off his head like a toupee, took off his collarbones like shoulder straps, took off his rib cage like a hauberk. He took off his hips and his legs, he took off his arms like gauntlets and threw them in a corner. What was left of him gradually dissolved, hardly coloring the air. At first Cincinnatus simply reveled in the coolness; then, fully immersed in his secret medium, he began freely and happily to...
>
> The iron thunderclap of the bolt resounded, and Cincinnatus instantly grew all that he had cast off, the skullcap included. Rodion the jailer brought a dozen yellow plums in a round basket lined with grape leaves, a present from the director's wife.
>
> Cincinnatus, your criminal exercise has refreshed you. [*IB*, 32–33]

The clothes and the parts of the body removed for a blissful respite may be understood as layers of significance that hide "the secret medium" of Cincinnatus, the invisible intangible core that paradoxically produces his illegal "opacity." None of these layers, however, envelops the whole of Cincinnatus. The "philosopher's skullcap" (*IB*, 121) points to the metaphysical allegory of a gnostic imprisoned in the material universe[2] (for many readers it is also a prophetic reminder of the Jewish holocaust). The dressing gown is as ample as the novel's political allegory:[3] the so-called "extrinsic genre"[4] of *Invitation* is that

[1] See Chapter 5, n.9.
[2] For an exhaustive discussion of the significance of gnostic beliefs in *Invitation to a Beheading*, see Moynahan, "A Russian Preface"; and Davydov, *Teksty-Matreshki*, pp. 100–182.
[3] Alter comments on the relationship between the political and aesthetic issues of the novel in "*Invitation to a Beheading*: Nabokov and the Art of Politics," pp. 41–59.
[4] See the discussion of the extrinsic and the intrinsic genre in E. D. Hirsch, *Validity*

of a dystopia; the combination of the Russian and German elements in the setting suggests a caricature of Stalin's and Hitler's regimes; and the name Cincinnatus alludes to an Everyman who is called to leadership from his plough and who returns to the plough when his mission has been accomplished. The other items of clothing and parts of the body may be read as symbols of the oppressiveness of "dead, ready-made art,"[5] of the pressure of bourgeois society on an authentically living individual, of the stifling effect of a consumer audience,[6] of the consciousness of the prison house of language[7] and literary history,[8] or of reading.[9]

Not a single one of these quasi-allegories is comprehensive or definitive; nor is it possible to sustain a one-to-one correspondence between the literal details of Cincinnatus's disrobing and the figurative meanings of his plight—the edges of the allegory soon become blurred. Moreover, each separate image may turn out to be as overdetermined as the conglomerate whole. The episode is of crucial importance to the gnostic allegory, one of the main interpretive planes;[10] through one of Nabokov's "strange loops"[11] it is made to participate in both the embedded and the embedding level of significance.

---

in Interpretation (New Haven, Conn., 1967), pp. 68–110.

[5]Field, Nabokov:His Life in Art, p. 195.

[6]See Ludmila A. Foster, "Nabokov's Gnostic Turpitude: The Surrealistic Vision of Reality in Priglashenie na kazn'," in Baer and Ingham, Mnemozina, pp. 117–29.

[7]See Johnson, Worlds in Regression, pp. 28–46.

[8]Many elements of the novel's setting and external action test and reject products of other people's imagination. Random examples include knocking on the prison wall in Korolenko, secret passages in Dumas, spiders in the kinds of books of which Tom Sawyer remembers too many when he exploits Jim's imprisonment at the end of Huckleberry Finn, the jailer's daughter and the tryst in prison before the execution in Stendhal. Dystopic reality, used up by literary precedent, is thin and threadbare. The parodic element, some aspects of which are discussed in Stuart, Nabokov, pp. 55–85, is thus a means of laying emphasis on the fragility of the "hastily assembled and painted world" (IB, 51) into which Cincinnatus has been thrust. More subtly submerged, less parodistic allusions are studied by Gavriel Shapiro in "Russkie literaturnye alliuzii v romane Nabokova Priglashenie na kazn'," Russian Literature, May 1981, pp. 369–78.

[9]See Dale E. Peterson, "Nabokov's Invitation: Literature as Execution," PMLA, 96 (1981), 824–36.

[10]See the reference to the "disrobing" scene in Davydov, Teksty-Matreshki, p. 121. I do not, however, agree with a number of minor interpretive points made in Davydov's study.

[11]"The 'Strange Loop' phenomenon occurs whenever, by moving upwards (or downwards) through the levels of some hierarchical system, we unexpectedly find ourselves right back where we started" (Douglas R. Hofstadter, Gödel, Escher, Bach: An

For every possible allegorical reading of the novel there are portions of material that fail to fit. For instance, the treatment of Cincinnatus is largely an exploration of a fictional character's predicament: a "galley slave" is imprisoned in his text, doomed to die so that the predatory reader may extract the meaning of his life, and then saved from "execution" as "beheading" by "execution" as "artistic performance."[12] This interpretation, however, leans on a rather small number of episodes and is irrelevant to the understanding of large narrative blocks. Conversely, Cincinnatus stands not only for a character in fiction but also for an artist; the persecution he endures often unmistakably evokes the oppressive demands made on artists by the philistine audience on which they depend for a living. Particularly suggestive here is Pierre's "temptation" speech in chapter 13 (an appropriate number): sell your soul, and you will have it all. Yet Cincinnatus's horror is clearly caused not by moral oppression but by the literal gory details of his imminent beheading. Thus, the material that does not lend support to a specific interpretation either remains neutral or threatens the validity of this interpretation. Another example: Cincinnatus's ultimate achievement of freedom through an effort of imagination and will is a suitable ending to the story of a young gnostic's rebellion, yet it clashes with the political interpretation of the novel: a dissenter in a totalitarian regime can attain neither liberty nor *consolatio philosophiae* through denying the reality of the regime.[13]

Least vulnerable is the metaphysical interpretation: the dystopic fictional universe is the work of a Demiurge; the protagonist's "gnostical turpitude" is his awareness of belonging to a spiritual reality beyond the "hastily assembled and painted world" of matter (*IB*, 51) and of preserving a fragment of that reality within himself. His experience throughout the novel is the accumulation of "Gnosis," the mystical knowledge that is itself salvation. According to Robert Haardt, Gnosis is

> knowledge of the benign acosmic Godhead; his emanations (Aeons); the Realm of Light (Pleroma) and simultaneous knowledge of the private,

---

Eternal Golden Braid [Harmondsworth, 1980], p. 10). In our case the hierarchical system is that of the levels of meaning. The self-referential allegory on the structure of the novel's meaning ought to be the metalevel, but (the hierarchy being tangled) it does not take supremacy over the metaphysical or other levels of interpretation.

[12] For this observation I am indebted to Peterson, "Nabokov's *Invitation*."

[13] The possibility of resisting tyranny by denying its existence in one's private world is treated seriously in Nabokov's 1938 short story "Tyrants Destroyed"; its insufficiency is eventually explored in *Bend Sinister*.

divine spirit-self of man, which has been imprisoned by the world of demons and the creator thereof.

The summons which goes out from the Realm of Light to the Gnostic, plunged into a stupor of self-forgetfulness by the powers which created this world, awakens him out of his erstwhile condition and enables him to realize his own true situation in the world, as well as the pre-history of his existence, and the path of ascent into the Realm of Light.[14]

Cincinnatus's walking away from the scaffold at the end of the novel, a gesture similar to Alice's somewhat retarded realization that her Wonderland enemies are just a pack of cards,[15] is a sign of his complete awakening. Such an interpretation of his story is the easiest to reconcile with most other readings; nevertheless, there are episodes to which it does not apply. The most suggestive is "the moment of truth" at the end of his mother's visit to Cincinnatus in his cell:

[Cincinnatus] suddenly noticed the expression in Cecilia C.'s eyes—just for an instant, an instant—but it was as if something real, unquestionable (in this world, where everything was subject to question), had passed through, as if a corner of this horrible life had curled up, and there was a glimpse of the lining. In his mother's gaze, Cincinnatus suddenly saw that ultimate, secure, all-explaining and from-all-protecting spark that he knew how to discern in himself also. What was this spark so piercingly expressing now? It does not matter what—call it horror, or pity... But rather let us say this: the spark proclaimed such a tumult of truth that Cincinnatus's soul could not help leaping for joy. [IB, 136]

At first glance the "glimpse of the lining" may appear to be a brief vision of the spiritual plane from which man is separated by the wall of his material existence. This reading, however, neglects the central and the most moving issue of the episode: the momentary eruption of authentic maternal anguish in a world where feelings have been replaced by conventional postures, and genuine communication by an exchange of clichés. What is here revealed to Cincinnatus is not transcendent reality but the possibility of authentic relationships in "this world."

[14]Robert Haardt, *Gnosis: Character and Testimony*, trans. J. F. Hendry (Leiden, 1971), pp. 3–4.
[15]The analogy with the ending of *Alice in Wonderland* was, to my knowledge, first commented on by Gleb Struve; see "Notes on Nabokov as a Russian Writer," in Dembo, *Nabokov*, p. 48.

The gnostic cosmology of the novel may turn into a Procrustean matrix if forced to accommodate every portion of the narrative. It frequently functions as a metaphor for the distinction between the fake and the authentic, the stagnant and the creative, rather than as a uniform layer of meaning. Neither the metaphysical nor the moral levels of meaning in *Invitation* can be regarded as the bottom line. If the novel does contain a residual statement, it is that ethics, aesthetics, and metaphysics shade into one another, that borderlines between them do not exist.

The language of Cincinnatus's enemies tends to fizzle out; "matter [is] weary" (*IB*, 43); and the whole "average reality" (*SO*, 118) collapses in the end precisely because, as in the world of Borges's Tlön, it has ceased to be the subject of authentic and hence creative perception. In the world of *Invitation to a Beheading*, authenticity is creativity. Noncreative conventional behavior is expressed in the use of ready-made formulas, which at times Cincinnatus fails to combine in the proper order ("Kind. You. Very," he says in answer to the prison director's speech, feeling that his reply must still be "arranged": *IB*, 15). The prevalence of such behavior turns the world around Cincinnatus into a collection of the "nonnons" with which his mother remembers having played as a child. Nonnons are absurd, "shapeless, mottled, pockmarked, knobby things" (*IB*, 135) that converge into the representation of a definite object when reflected in a special mirror sent over from the factory. The mirror, as noted in the preceding chapter, is obviously an anamorphoscope, and Cecilia's memories are an indirect commentary on the novel that records them—or rather an anticommentary: *Invitation* presents a beautiful account of the "absurd, knobby, pockmarked" figures surrounding Cincinnatus but refuses to supply us with an anamorphoscope. Instead, it challenges us to come up with not one but many anamorphoscopes of our own, because each separate perspective and interpretation is indeterminate, has blurred contours, and leaves some portions of the material outside its scope.

II

The element of lexical indeterminacy in the texture of *Invitation* is related to the ineffability of hypostasis; the spiritual essence, the "secret medium" of Cincinnatus is not available to what Tennyson called "matter-molded forms of speech." Gnosis itself is characterized by a high degree of indefiniteness; it is the approximation of the unknowable frequently achieved *via negationis*.[16] "Nameless existence, intangible substance" says the (eventually erased) writing on the wall of Cincinnatus's cell (*IB*, 26). Aware of the "intangible substance" within himself and beyond his experience, Cincinnatus also becomes aware of its "namelessness," of the catachretic gap in the prison house of language.[17]

This catachretic gap is often made explicit. Cincinnatus is aware of his lack of words to express what he knows: "I know *something*. I know *something*. But expression of it comes so hard! . . . I am frightened—and now I am losing *some* thread, which I held so palpably only a moment ago. Where is it? It has slipped out of my grasp! . . . I repeat: there is *something* I know, there is *something* I know, there is *something*... (*IB*, 91, 95; my italics). A much more tranquil echo of these words can be heard in Nabokov's attempt to answer an interviewer's question about his religious beliefs: "I know more than I can express in words, and the little I can express would not have been expressed, had I not known more" (*SO*, 45).

The word "something," when used by Nabokov to signal a catachretic gap, refers not only to metaphysical insight but also to genuine emotional life. These two kinds of ineffability converge in the Russian word *dusha*, meaning not just "soul" but also something like "emotional warmth." This word is overused in philistine conversation, however, and smacks so strongly of "human humidity" (*KQK*, viii) that Nabokov carefully avoids it. Instead of resorting to the easy if ambiguous label, he chooses the word "something" (more indefinite and less obtrusive than the formulaic *je ne sais quois*) to register his awareness of the unknowable. It is with this word that he pays homage to his Swiss governess Mademoiselle O.:

> Just before the rhythm I hear falters and fades, I catch myself wondering whether, during the years I knew her, I had not kept utterly missing *something* in her that was far more she than her chins or her ways or even her French—*something* perhaps akin to that last glimpse of her, to the

[16]See Davydov, *Teksty-Matreshki*, p. 133.

[17]Catachresis is a notion or a phenomenon that in a given language can be expressed only by a metaphor; see "Catachrèse de métaphore," in Pierre Fontanier, *Les figures du discours* (Paris, 1977), pp. 215–19. "To fall in love," for instance, is catachresis in English; the concept is expressed by one word in most other languages and does not require a metaphorical idiom. Certain meanings, however, cannot be expressed by a word or a conventional formulation in any language. The bridging of these catachretic gaps is what "effing the ineffable" is all about.

radiant deceit she had used in order to have me depart pleased with my own kindness, or to that swan whose agony was so much closer to artistic truth than a drooping dancer's pale arms; *something*, in short, that I could appreciate only after the things and beings that I had most loved in the security of my childhood had been turned to ashes or shot through the heart. [*SM*, 117; my italics]

When the ineffable is the force of Cincinnatus's physical fear, the catachretic gap turns into a black hole: "Still I am afraid! One cannot write it off so easily. Neither is it good that my thoughts keep getting sucked into the *cavity* of the future—I want to think about *something* else, clarify other things... but I write obscurely and limply, like Push-kin's lyrical duelist" (*IB*, 92; my italics).

The novel's repeated references to gaps, cavities, chinks, lacunae are reminders both of Cincinnatus's ability to catch glimpses of the "different dimension" and of the patchiness of his vocabulary, its insufficiency for rendering profound experience. When this experience is of an emotional nature, the novel (especially in the passages ascribed to Cincinnatus) often registers it by aposiopesis, inviting the reader, as if were, to fill the gap nonverbally. For example: "Oh, my anguish —what shall I do with you, with myself? How dare they conceal from me... I, who must pass through an ordeal of supreme pain, I, who, in order to preserve a semblance of dignity (anyway I shall not go beyond silent pallor—I am no hero anyway...), must during that ordeal keep control of all my faculties, I, I... am gradually weakening... the uncertainty is horrible—well, why don't you tell me, do tell me—but no, you have me die anew every morning... " (*IB*, 51).

On two occasions Nabokov uses a structural counterpart of aposiopesis, breaking short (or ending *in medias res*) episodes that promise to lead to momentous revelations. Just as the intrusion of a squirrel in *Pnin* sabotages the maturing of a metaphysical insight (see *P*, 58), so the entrance of Rodion puts an end to the "criminal exercise" of Cincinnatus in the disrobing scene and interrupts the narrator's sentence—and so we never learn what it is that Cincinnatus begins "freely and happily" to do. In another crucial episode Rodion turns off the lights just in time to deny us the account of the young Gnostic's triumph over gravity. Cincinnatus has recollected (or imagined) the day when an aggressive teacher ordered him to get off the windowsill and go to the garden; with somnambulistic yet unconventional compliance, Cincinnatus then took the step which his "matter-molded" common sense would have rejected as suicidal:

> In my sadness, in my abstraction, unconsciously and innocently, instead of descending into the garden by the stairs (the gallery was on the third floor), not thinking what I was doing, but really acting obediently, even submissively, I stepped straight from the window sill onto the elastic air and—feeling nothing more than a half-sensation of barefootedness (even though I had shoes on)—slowly and quite naturally strode forward, still absently sucking and examining the finger in which I had caught a splinter that morning... Suddenly, however, an extraordinary, deafening silence brought me out of my reverie, and I saw below me, like pale daisies, the upturned faces of stupefied children, and the pedagoguette, who seemed to be falling backward; . . . I saw myself, a pink-smocked boy, standing transfixed in mid-air; turning around, I saw, but three aerial paces from me, the window I had just left, and, his hairy arm extended in malevolent amazement, the—"
>
> (Here, unfortunately, the light in the cell went out—Rodion always turned it off exactly at ten.) [IB, 97]

The material reality and the conventional arbitrariness of the language thus block one's access to the essence that is beyond things and words. The trope that often signals the catachretic gap is extended simile. The momentary look in Cecilia C.'s eyes expresses "*Something* real, unquestionable . . . , *as if* a corner of this horrible life had curled up, and there was a glimpse of the lining" (IB, 136; my italics). In trying to explain her experience of what Mircea Eliade would call hierophany,[18] Cecilia uses the more cautious "it seems to me that " as a synonym for "as if": "When I drive across the fields in the little old gig, and see the Strop gleaming, and this hill with the fortress on it, and everything, *it always seems to me* that a marvelous tale is being repeated over and over again, and I either don't have the time to, or am unable to grasp it, and still *somebody* keeps repeating it to me, with such patience!" (IB, 134; my italics).

The description of Cincinnatus's appearance likewise combines extended similes and similes-within-similes with hints at or references to vagueness, elusiveness, ineffability, incompleteness:

[18]Mircea Eliade defines hierophany as "the manifestation of something of a wholly different order, a reality that does not belong to our world, in objects that are an integral part of our natural 'profane' world" (*The Sacred and the Profane* [New York, 1959], p. 11).

The subject will now be the precious quality of Cincinnatus: his fleshy *incompleteness*; the fact that the greater part of him was in a *quite different* place, while only an insignificant portion of it was wandering, *perplexed*, here—a poor, *vague* Cincinnatus, a comparatively stupid Cincinnatus, trusting, feeble and foolish as people are in their sleep. . . . Cincinnatus's face, small and still young despite all the torments, with gliding eyes, *eerie* eyes of *changeable shade*, was, in regard to its expression, *something* absolutely inadmissible by the standards of his surroundings. . . . The open shirt, the black dressing gown that kept flying open, the oversize slippers on his slender feet, the philosopher's skullcap on the top of his head and the *ripple* . . . running through the *transparent* hair on his temples completed a picture, the full indecency of which *it is difficult to put into words*—produced as it was of a thousand *barely noticeable*, overlapping trifles: of the light outline of his lips, *seemingly* not quite fully drawn but touched by a master of masters; of the *fluttering* movements of his empty, *not-yet-shaded-in* hands; of the *dispersing and again gathering rays* in his animated eyes; but even all of this, analyzed and studied, still *could not fully explain* Cincinnatus: it was *as if* one side of his being slid into another dimension, *as* all the complexity of a tree's foliage passes *from shade into radiance*, so that you *cannot distinguish* just where begins the submergence into the *shimmer* of a *different element*. *It seemed as though* at any moment . . . Cincinnatus would step in such a way as to slip naturally and effortlessly through some *chink in the air* into its unknown coulisses to disappear there *with the same easy smoothness with which* the flashing reflection of a *rotated mirror* moves across every object in the room and suddenly vanishes, *as if* beyond the air, in some new *depth of ether*. [*IB*, 120–21; my italics]

The image of Cincinnatus's "fleshy incompleteness" is significant on the (a) metaphysical, (b) political, and (c) aesthetic planes. That "the greater part" of him is in "a quite different place" means that (a) the "secret medium" of Cincinnatus is namelessly present in a transcendent dimension; (b) the jailers have power over his body but not over his spirit; and (c) the unique visual form he takes in the imagination of his author is inaccessible to the reader. The lexical meanings of the words that describe him are types.[19] Hence, words by themselves are powerless to conjure up Nabokov's own Cincinnatus rather than Everyman's Cincinnatus—any small, delicate man with translucent hair and mustache who is forced to become gently and sullenly . . . heroic.

[19]On verbal meaning as type, see Hirsch, *Validity in Interpretation*, pp. 49–67.

A literary artist, however, does not merely depend on words; he commands and combines them so as to obtain compensation for their insufficiency. Catachretic gaps are bridged by tropes such as the extended similes quoted above; the rigidity of meaning as type is reduced by collocation, iconism, synaesthesia—all the things that "one must do for a commonplace word to come alive and to share its neighbor's sheen, heat, shadow, while reflecting itself in its neighbor and renewing the neighboring word in the process, so that the whole line is live iridescence" (*IB*, 93). The word "iridescence" is here used not only in the figurative but also in the literal sense. Nabokov possessed a developed *audition colorée*: that is, he associated sounds with colors. I believe that a study of the polychromatism of his Russian texts, combined with an examination of alliteration, assonance, anagrams, and "ghost words," might reveal subliminal visual effects that extend the power of his language beyond the scope of lexical meaning.[20] His use of alphabetic iconism and the skill with which he endows the graphical shapes of letters (particularly of the Church Slavonic alphabet) with polysemy have already been studied by D. B. Johnson. Johnson also discusses Nabokov's anagrammatic games: for example, the way the words *tut* ("here") and *tam* ("there"), which stand for the two worlds to which Cincinnatus belongs, haunt longer letter sequences in the Russian original of the novel.[21] This is another compensation for the indeterminacy of conventional verbal meanings. Additional emphasis should be placed on the role of ghost words produced by anagrams and puns. In the disrobing episode, for instance, we read that upon Rodion's intrusion Cincinnatus "instantly grew all that he had cast off, the skullcap included" (*IB*, 33). The word "included" translates the Russian *vplot' do* (*Pr*, 45); the word *vplot'*, as a pun on "into flesh" (*v plot'*), smuggles in the not irrelevant associations of birth, incarnation, and the prison house of clay. To retain this effect in the translation would require a linguistic miracle.[22]

Nabokov's conscious awareness of the role of ghost words is already evident in *The Gift*. While composing his poem in the first chapter of

[20]Guidelines for such a study are presented in Johnson, *Worlds in Regression*, pp. 10–27, 43–45.

[21]See ibid., pp. 28–46.

[22]Such a miracle happens in the translation of Nabokov's 1932 short story "Lebeda" ("Orache"). " '*Lebeda*,' " Nabokov notes in his preface to the English version of the story, "is the plant *Atriplex*. Its English name, orache, by a miraculous coincidence, renders in its written form the '*ili beda*,' '*or ache*', suggested by the Russian title" (*DS*, 44).

that novel, Fyodor Godunov-Cherdyntsev notices that the combination of the words *i krylatyi* ("and winged") yields two inappropriate paronomastic ghost words, *ikry* ("calves of legs") and *laty* ("armor"). "Calves. Armor. Where has this Roman come from?" wonders Fyodor and rejects the word "winged" (see *Dar*, 36), unaware of the value of his gesture to modern criticism. The English version of the novel omits this brief episode; in this instance Nabokov failed to coax a parallel wordplay out of the English language.

Nabokov's reliance on what may be called "translexical" devices in *Invitation* is indirectly commented on in *The Gift*. In Godunov-Cherdyntsev's imagination his mysterious rival and friend Koncheev offers him an unofficial diagnosis of some shortcomings of his prose. The first of these is "an excessive trust in words. It sometimes happens that your words in order to introduce the necessary thought have to smuggle it in. The sentence may be excellent, but still it is smuggling, and moreover gratuitous smuggling, since the lawful road is open. But your smugglers under the cover of an obscure style, with all sorts of complicated contrivances, import goods that are duty free anyway" (*G*, 351). Ironically, however, "the excessive trust in words" is its opposite—a dissatisfaction with words as self-contained arbitrary signs and the resulting exploration of their valence and multilevel iconicity for the purpose of adding an unfamiliar dimension to the not always "duty free" goods they import.

III

The structural indeterminacy of *Invitation to a Beheading* consists in recurrent fantastic transformations of characters, situations, and themes; in conflicts between the details of the plot; in logical incompatibility of contiguous scenes. Each case of instability, plurality, or ambiguity has a local rhetorical effect: it redirects the reader's attention and highlights a particular component of the episode's complex meaning. We must examine some examples before discussing the cumulative impact of structural indeterminacy.

When Cincinnatus returns from his trial, Rodion invites him to waltz. They dance around the corridor and glide back into the cell, and then Cincinnatus regrets "that the swoon's friendly embrace [has] been so brief" (*IB*, 14). It is not clear whether "the swoon" has given rise to the hallucinatory dance (Cincinnatus was feeling sick, or rather "seasick," before Rodion's entrance) or whether it has been caused by whirling in the arms of a foul-smelling partner. The ambiguity cannot be resolved on the literal plane, but on the moral plane the episode is univocal: Cincinnatus is still accepting invitations; the surrogate friendliness of the jailers does not yet repel him. The local effect of the ambiguity consists in the redirection of the reader's attention from the literal to the moral meaning of the scene.

When later in the first chapter Cincinnatus is shown leaving prison, walking through the town, coming home, reaching the door of his room, and then entering his prison cell through this door (see *IB*, 18–20), it likewise does not matter whether he is supposed to be awake or asleep and dreaming of the adventure. What matters is the suggestion that his jail is not confined to the fortress on the hill: he is a prisoner in his home, his society, his language, literary history, material existence. An additional reminder of the metaphorical function of the fortress comes in another ambiguous episode. In the hope to get a look through the window of his cell, Cincinnatus moves a table toward it and climbs up, but the view is still inaccessible; the only thing he can see is an inscription made by a previous frustrated prisoner. He is taken down by Rodion, only to find, on trying to move the table for the hundredth time, that "the legs [have] been bolted down for ages" (*IB*, 30). Yet we cannot say that Cincinnatus has dreamed of moving the table, because in a later scene Rodion recounts his doing so to the prison director though he distorts a few details). Again, the contradiction is resolved on the symbolic plane: there are no physical approaches to the view of transcendent reality; if one obstacle is removed, another will take its place.

The same ambiguity likewise makes an indirect comment on *Invitation to a Beheading* as an allegory on reading. The nature of the protagonist's experience takes precedence over its sources. It does not matter whether these sources are fiction or fiction-within-fiction. In Nabokov's 1943 short story "That in Aleppo Once... " the narrator's wife is a compulsive liar, yet her tales evoke the same kind of response in the listeners as if they were truthful. In most cases, however (as in Borges's "Emma Zunz"), her stories are morally true, even though they have never happened. The epistemology of Cincinnatus's moving the table to the window is of minor moment: his despair and anguish are what we recognize as true.

The ambiguity culminates in the last scene of the novel, the purported execution scene. Having already knelt by the block on the scaffold, Cincinnatus gets up and calmly walks away, wrecking the whole routine. The setting then collapses like jerry-built scenery, and all that remains of the fictional world is a jumble of "rags, chips of painted wood, bits of gilded plaster, pasteboard bricks, posters." Amidst this movie-set disaster, Cincinnatus "[makes] his way in that direction where, to judge by the voices, [stand] beings akin to him" (*IB*, 223). Critics have offered conflicting accounts of this ending. Some maintain that it is the soul of the beheaded Cincinnatus making its exit to a different dimension;[23] others note that the execution never takes place;[24] still others acknowledge the ambiguity of the passage.[25]

The ending is indeed ambiguous and at the same time highly over-determined. The ambiguity stems from three sets of conflicting clues.

First, there are *clues with contradictory connotations*. The protagonist's movements away from the block are presented in a concrete visual manner: he stands up, looks around, walks down the steps and away over the debris. In the last sentence of the novel, however, his motions lose their visual quality, and the "voices" that mark his direction seem to have supernatural overtones. Accordingly, the text tells us that Cincinnatus goes toward "beings" (*sushchestva*: *Pr*, 218) rather than "people" akin to him.

Next, there are *doubly directed clues*: that is, clues that can be read in mutually excluding ways. "Come back," cries the jailer after Cincinnatus declines the invitation to his own beheading, "lie down—after all, you were lying down, everything was ready, everything was finished" (*IB*, 223). The words "everything was finished" may be synonymous with "everything was ready" for the beheading, but they may also mean that the beheading has taken place. This alternative meaning is stronger in the Russian "*vsio bylo koncheno*" (*Pr*, 217), a phrase often used to express a sense of finality or loss of hope.

Finally, there are *singly directed clues*: that is, clues that not merely support one hypothesis but also deny its opposite.[26] Thus, when Cin-

[23]E.g., W. W. Rowe, *Nabokov and Others: Patterns in Russian Literature* (Ann Arbor, Mich., 1979), p. 182; and Hyman, "The Handle," p. 61 (this is the only issue on which I disagree with Hyman's essay).

[24]Richard Dillard, "Not Text but Texture: The Novels of Vladimir Nabokov," in R. H. W. Dillard, George Garrett and John Rees Moore, eds., *The Sounder Few: Essays from the Hollins Critic* (Athens, Ga., 1971), p. 143; Morton, *Vladimir Nabokov*, p. 40; Stuart, *Nabokov*, p. 85; Pifer, *Nabokov and the Novel*, pp. 67–68; and Margaret Byrd Boegman, "*Invitation to a Beheading* and the Many Shades of Kafka," in J. E. Rivers and Charles Nicol, eds., *Nabokov's Fifth Arc: Nabokov and Others on His Life's Work* (Austin, Tex., 1982), p. 109.

[25]Khodasevich, "On Sirin," p. 98; Moynahan, "A Russian Preface," p. 15; and Peterson, "Nabokov's *Invitation*," p. 833.

[26]For a discussion of singly and doubly directed clues as causes of ambiguity, see

cinnatus rises from the block, the headsman's hips are still swinging, as if gathering momentum for the blow that has not yet been dealt. At the same time, the pale librarian, whom the reader may suspect of carefully disguising his own "opacity," is vomiting in the audience— suggesting that the gory spectacle has taken place.

What, then, does happen at the end of *Invitation to a Beheading*? To answer this question, one must once again abandon the literal for the figurative. On the moral plane the tormentors of Cincinnatus lose their power over him as soon as he refuses to play by their rules. In the terms of any orthodox religion, "the powers that be" have control over Everyman's body but not over his soul. In the terms of the metaphysics specifically alluded to in the novel, explains Julian Moynahan, "death for a gnostic is always ambiguous. On the one hand, it is the toll he pays to materiality, . . . on the other, it is the only viable release from benightedness and into the 'involute abode.' "[27]

Crucial for placing *Invitation* within the Nabokov cannon is the interpretation of the ending as the climax of the self-referential game in which Cincinnatus emerges not as Everyman but as Every-Fictional-Character.

Lying in bed after one of his frustrated attempts to escape, Cincinnatus cried, "Will no one save me?" As if in answer to this appeal "there fell and bounced on the blanket a large dummy acorn, twice as large as life, splendidly painted a glossy buff, and fitting its cork as snugly as an egg" (*IB*, 125–26). This parody of an acorn falls down from the title oak of the pseudo-realistic novel *Quercus* that Cincinnatus has been reading. Unlike Newton's apple, the acorn is governed not by the law of gravity but by the counterlaw of involution: that is, metaleptic transgression, or the blurring of borderlines between the universe of the author and that of the character.[28] By means of the larger-than-life acorn, the novelist sends Cincinnatus a message promising help. The novelist's other message, often noted, is the beautiful moth that escapes both Rodion and that cellmate spider without which a parody on stories of captivity would be incomplete.

In tune with the artificiality of the acorn, the author's assistance to Cincinnatus takes a frankly *deus ex machina* form. In his lectures

---

Shlomith Rimmon, *The Concept of Ambiguity—The Example of James* (Chicago, 1977), pp. 52–58.

[27]Moynahan, "A Russian Preface," p. 15.

[28]On "metalepsis" and "involution," see Chapter 2, n. 4 and Chapter 6, n. 3.

on James Joyce, Nabokov maintained that the Nighttown scenes of
Ulysses are not the hallucination of either Stephen or Bloom but
the fantasy of the novelist, a "nightmare evolution" of some of the
characters, objects, and themes (*LL*, 350). Something similar occurs
at the end of *Invitation*. Instead of telling us what is supposed to have
happened to Cincinnatus, Nabokov presents a fantastic evolution
of the theme of the protagonist's double. At the beginning of the
novel this double was described as one that "accompanies each of
us—you, and me, and him over there—doing what we would like to
do at that very moment, but cannot" (*IB*, 25). In the fantasy of
the "finale" ("the book itself is dreaming": *LL*, 350) Cincinnatus
merges with this double, this trespassing "gangrel" (*IB*, 25) who
ignores conventions, limitations, and rules. The novelist then dis-
mantles the nightmare setting (thus forestalling the blow of the ax)
and smooths the protagonist's exit to the "involute abode" where
complete novels and their characters properly belong.

This interpretation of the ending (one of at least four that coexist on
different planes of significance) explains but does not resolve the ambiguity. The lexical indeterminacy still remains: who are the "beings"
akin to Cincinnatus, and what is "that direction" from which their
"voices" come? So does the structural indeterminacy: though the
headsman does not seem to have struck, the pale librarian is still vomiting. Here again, however, Nabokov's synaesthetic devices in the Russian original are a partial compensation for the indeterminacy: the
alliteration and assonance in "the pale librarian was vomiting"—
"*ble*val *ble*dnyi bi*bl*iotekar' " (*Pr*, 217; my emphasis)—produce a
comic effect that controls the potentially horrifying implications of the
image. The color values associated with the Russian letters for *b*, *l*, and
e could, perhaps, significantly influence the visual impression of the
flattening and disintegrating dystopia.

The common denominator of the local rhetorical effects of ambiguity in the novel is their redirection of the reader's attention from the
literal to the figurative. The reader is thus made to reenact the protagonist's growing disdain for his material environment as well as his
growing awareness that an infinitely greater significance is shining
through the gaps in the texture of the quotidian. This analogy between
the recurrent element in the protagonist's experience and the reader's
response also extends to the *cumulative effect* of structural indeterminacy.

Cincinnatus makes a self-defeating mistake when he inadvertently
grants reality to his tormentors:

Involuntarily yielding to the temptation of logical development, involuntarily (be careful, Cincinnatus!) forging into a chain all the things that were quite harmless as long as they remained unlinked, he inspired the meaningless with meaning, and the lifeless with life. With the stone darkness for background he now permitted the spotlighted figures of all his usual visitors to appear—it was the very first time that his imagination was so condescending toward them. . . . by evoking them—not believing in them, perhaps, but still evoking them—Cincinnatus allowed them the right to exist, supported them, nourished them with himself. [IB, 155–56]

Cincinnatus ultimately learns that he can escape his predicament by denying that it is real, but the author knows this all along; therefore, he makes constant use of ambiguity to knock the foundations from under the phenomena that to Cincinnatus seem real. "It is frightening," says the narrator of The Eye, "when real life suddenly turns out to be a dream, but how much more frightening when that which one had thought a dream—fluid and irresponsible—suddenly starts to congeal into reality!" (E, 108). The novelist therefore has to prevent the fictional world into which he has thrust Cincinnatus from congealing into a semblance of reality.

This is not an easy task. Despite grotesque imagery and serene absurdities, the social setting of Invitation keeps gaining substance because the reader knows that certain regimes—and not only of times gone by—surpass the gloomiest dystopian fantasies. The strong element of parody on different artistic and pseudoartistic genres suggests, among other things, that Nabokov disowns responsibility for having invented a dystopia. He refuses to compete with the imagination of either Stalin, Hitler, Orwell, or Zamiatin; what he produces is a debunking, a parody on their inventions. Moreover, he knows that the modern reader, who is accustomed to seeing absurd and incredible things actually come to pass in his own world, may, like Cincinnatus, suspend his disbelief too readily, may take the parodies at face value and, "yielding to the temptation of logical development," confuse them with "reality." To prevent this from happening and to render the story as "fluid and irresponsible" as a dream, the author brings an arsenal of local ambiguities and metamorphoses into action. The dreamlike insubstantiality of the fictional world is the cumulative effect of structural indeterminacy.

Whereas classical novelists raised moral problems and supplied readers with systems of values within which they would be invited to formulate solutions, *Invitation* relies on its pervasive indeterminacy to defer a residual statement. Accustomed to look for bottom lines despite discouragement, we will not fail to come away from *Invitation* with neat carry-home conclusions, handy souvenirs of the unpackageable experience of our encounter with the novel. These conclusions will be of our own making, however. In addition to reflecting the theme of deliberate acknowledgment or denial of "reality" to the world into which one has been cast, indeterminacy functions as a rhetorical device: it denies prescriptiveness to the novel's system of values.

"Cincinnatus" is, after all, not "Everyman"; he is an ordinary person in extraordinary circumstances. His definite though not quite intelligible moral and metaphysical victory (particularly appealing to the postwar audience, which has to believe in the ultimate moral victory of the victims of wartime crimes) is made possible by that rare luxury—freedom from commitment. Paradoxically, this luxury is a result of emotional privation and painful loneliness—the losses become compensations for themselves.

No matter how humanly recognizable Cincinnatus's predicament may be, his case is unique and his example not general. The moral freedom that he achieves in the end has the absolute purity of the laboratory experiment. The best commentary on *Invitation* is provided by Nabokov's second major dystopia, *Bend Sinister*, a much less ecstatic and much more sober inquiry into the limits of moral freedom. *Bend Sinister*, however, was written some years after Nabokov had learned exactly what kind of persecution had fallen to the lot of millions and millions of captives in camps and prisons much bigger than the Gothic fortress of Cincinnatus.

9

The Gift:
Models of Infinity

> Nature expects a full-grown man to accept the two black voids, fore and aft, as stolidly as he accepts the extraordinary visions in between. Imagination, the supreme delight of the immortal and the immature, should be limited. In order to enjoy life, we should not enjoy it too much.
> I rebel against this state of affairs.
>
> Vladimir Nabokov, *Speak, Memory*

The Gift, serialized (with the significant omission of its fourth chapter) in 1937–38, is Nabokov's portrait of an artist as a young man. By the end of the novel the protagonist, Fyodor Godunov-Cherdyntsev, is on the threshold of a full-fledged literary career, ready to fulfill his girlfriend's prophecy that he will be "such a writer as has never been before" (*G*, 376). Paradoxically, however, *The Gift* marks the end of its author's career as a Russian writer; through this work Nabokov, who had for some time been polishing his English prose (in 1936 he had translated his *Despair* into English) acknowledged the gift that he had received from Russian literature before bidding it farewell.

The action of the novel is set in the twenties, yet Godunov-Cherdyntsev's disgust with the "native" population of Berlin[1] and a fellow writer's nostalgia for the better days of the émigré literary society (see *G*, 329) suggest an atmosphere more closely reminiscent of the eve of World War II: the sense of an ending has been smuggled

---

[1] In the foreword Nabokov remarks that "Fyodor's attitude toward Germany reflects too typically perhaps the crude and irrational contempt that Russian émigrés had for the 'natives' (in Berlin, Paris or Prague). My young man is moreover influenced by the rise of a nauseous dictatorship belonging to the period when the novel was written and not to the one it patchily reflects" (*G*, x).

into a novel that ostensibly celebrates a beginning. It may be said that the threat of an ending was impossible to keep out without reducing the art of *The Gift* to tenuous artifice. It was therefore incorporated into the novel's main structural idea: the tension between the infinite and the incomplete. The sense of a premature ending, one that leaves things incomplete, is constantly combatted by the models of infinity constructed, with varying success, throughout the novel.

I

Nabokov mentions the years 1935–37 as the period during which he wrote *The Gift*. The writing, however, must have been preceded by the mental composition described in *Strong Opinions* (see, e.g., *SO*, 69, 110–11). The protagonist of *The Gift* seems able to "remember" his future work; if this is also true of Nabokov himself, the "memories" of the yet unwritten novel must have been intense a year earlier, in 1934. That year, however, marks the composition of *Invitation to a Beheading*, the first draft of which was written in a fortnight of miraculous excitement. *Invitation* seems to have got rid of (see *M*, xi) a number of urgent matters whose stronger presence could have disrupted the tremulous design of the projected masterpiece.

First, the contemporary reality had to be got out of the way. The rise of fascism had no place among the motifs of *The Gift*, yet to ignore this uncouth reality would have amounted to following the example of old Luzhin, who attempts to write a wish-fulfilling, wax-figure *Künstlerroman (see D*, 77–78). Nabokov's novel, his castle-in-the-air, does not double as a waxworks gallery because, to continue the metaphor, the edifice is pierced by the winds of contemporary reality—alongside mysterious "drafts" (*SM*, 35) from the other direction. Vapors of the gloomy sociopolitical realities are present in the atmospheric environment of Godunov-Cherdyntsev's emotional life, yet they do not obtrude on *The Gift* too strongly; the main energy of Nabokov's response to them has been channeled into *Invitation*.

Second, hints of the projected shift into another language likewise had to be banned from *The Gift*. Nabokov seems to have been seriously considering that possibility: in 1936, for instance, in addition to translating *Despair* into English, he actually wrote "Mademoiselle O" in French. Yet *The Gift* was supposed to celebrate the resilience of a Russian emigrant writer and his obligation to what was most dear to him in his heritage. It was supposed to be a novel about growth rather than about a drastic change. Therefore it is at the end of *Invitation* rather than in *The Gift* that a kind of breakthrough takes place as the protagonist boldly steps from one reality into another. Margaret Byrd Boegman is probably right in believing that the disproportionate nature of the punishment inflicted on Cincinnatus C. may reflect Nabokov's fears about his survival as a writer in a new language.[2] However, Nabokov had also lived through times when disproportionate punishments were meted out with the most nightmarish matter-of-factness. In 1934 such times were beginning again.

Most important, however, *Invitation* absorbs, like a scavenger, the worst of those tendencies in personal relationships that threaten one's emotional balance, personal freedom, and artistic independence. "Everything has duped me—all this theatrical, pathetic stuff—the promises of a volatile maiden, a mother's moist gaze, the knocking on the wall, a neighbor's friendliness, and, finally, those hills which broke out in a deadly rash," says Cincinnatus near the end of *Invitation* (*IB*, 204–5). Fyodor is not let down in this way; on the contrary, he is staunchly supported by his mother and by the courageous girl with whom he falls in love; he finds genuine friends (though always remaining remote from them), and the presence of sunbathing "natives" does not prevent him from enjoying the forest and lake of Grunewald.

Nevertheless, minor characters of *The Gift* could, upon some densening of the colors, find caricatures of themselves in the world of *Invitation*: Boris Shchyogolev, who interferes with Fyodor's work by dropping in for a chat, would deteriorate into the intrusive M'sieur Pierre; Marianna Nikolayevna's dinners would turn into the meal in the prison director's apartment; Alexander Yakovlevich's tactless practical joke would be debased to Rodrig and Pierre's crude mystifications; Olga Sokratovna Chernyshevski would find her reflection in Marthe, and her student friends in Marthe's incestuous brothers. It is as if the potential darker side of these characters has been dealt with in *Invitation*, so that in *The Gift* they might be treated with mildly humorous exasperation. The grimly comic "mass execution" (cf. *G*, 376) that takes place in the earlier novel has left the coast clear for a more complex and subtle character portrayal in the later work.

[2]See Boegman, "Invitation to a Beheading and the Many Shades of Kafka," pp. 115–18.

The thematic common denominator of *Invitation* and *The Gift* is the relationship of an artist with his environment; the relationship of his aesthetic or metaphysical pursuits with his private life, his commitments. In *The Gift* the treatment of the second term in this relationship is realistic and more tolerant. The novel has been much discussed as an aesthetic battlefield where the Romantic aesthetics of Fyodor is pitted against the utilitarian views of N. G. Chernyshevski. Yet Fyodor Godunov-Cherdyntsev's life is more than a frame for his own and other writers' opinions. Though in the 1962 foreword Nabokov notes that the heroine is "not Zina, but Russian Literature" (*G*, x), one should not forget that the novel is not about the heroine but about the hero, about Fyodor. It is also about literature insofar as literature is the crucial part of his life, in a sense a rival of Zina Merz. Zina knows that at times she will be "wildly unhappy" with Fyodor yet is prepared "to face it" (*G*, 377) because his writing is as important to her as it is to him. The action of the novel is set in Berlin not only because Nabokov knew that city better than, say, Paris, but also because the cheapness of paper in Germany facilitated the publication of émigré books and periodicals. Symptomatically, in *Mary* the disillusioned poet Podtyagin wants to leave for Paris where his niece lives and "where the long crusty loaves and the red wine [are] so cheap" (*M*, 7). He no longer cares about paper.

Fyodor has two problems to solve: what sort of works he wants to write, and what sort of life he must lead. He solves the first by mobilizing the powers of his intellect and imagination and going through a strenuous apprenticeship. The second solves itself through his daily ethical choices.

Fyodor does not find himself in the dystopia of Cincinnatus. The people around Cincinnatus are so thoroughly unwilling to live authentically that they are presented as unselfconscious parodies on sundry genres of popular art. That they cannot create their own worlds is symbolically expressed through their functioning as images in the world of Cincinnatus: for example, the prison director vanishes like a removed slide a few seconds after his first appearance (see *IB*, 15). "To fiction be as to your country true," writes Fyodor in his love poem to Zina (*G*, 168). The appeal is rhetorical, since the strong-willed Zina staunchly refuses to become part of her mother's and stepfather's world; she creates a world ("a fiction") of her own, and only the man she loves is allowed to participate in that creation, just as he allows her to collaborate in the polishing of his book. Like Fyodor's father, the naturalist explorer who would never be influenced by anthropologists in planning his expeditions or by pseudo-patriots in defining his political stand, she is presented as a totally "genuine" personality. Yet Fyodor has learned the art of sympathy even for people whose genuineness is not so complete. His numerous little faults must be forgiven because of the pity he comes to feel for Zina's unprepossessing mother and because of his increasing appreciation of Alexandra Yakovlevna Chernyshevski, whose image is a brilliant and rather underrated achievement of character portrayal.

This woman's name and patronymic are the feminine forms of the name and patronymic of her husband, Alexander Yakovlevich. An identical combination of names for a married couple occurs also in Ilf and Petrov's *Twelve Chairs* (1928), a work that Nabokov admired. Nabokov's bestowing on the Chernyshevskis the names of the "shyly thieving" couple in charge of an old-age home in *The Twelve Chairs* must be considered in conjunction with his bestowing the name of an obnoxious Dostoevsky character (the Luzhin of *Crime and Punishment*) on the pathetic protagonist of *The Defense*. Nabokov reclaims, as it were, the names marred by precursor novels; he obliterates their old connotations and endows them with new ones. Indeed, the reader's attitude towards the Chernyshevski couple changes in the course of the novel, moving away from first impressions. This element of reader's response reenacts the protagonist's emotional maturing, his growing tolerance of people's superficial foibles and his appreciation of their genuine worth.

The image of Alexander Yakovlevich Chernyshevski undergoes a number of transformations: from a man who plays a crude practical joke on Fyodor to one who contritely apologizes for having caused pain; from a deeply suffering bereaved father to a spokesman of tritely elevated conventional liberalism; from a man who seems to be in contact with the other world to a skeptic who denies the hereafter out of sheer self-discipline. The character of his wife is an even more subtle study of the relationship between conventionality of thought and authenticity of intuition combined with an unflinching personal loyalty and a "well-ordered life" (G, 50).

Alexandra Yakovlevna befriends Fyodor because he reminds her of her late son Yasha. At first Fyodor is embarrassed and repelled by the gushing frankness of her shows of grief and by her demands on him, yet these demands eventually slacken—whether because, as Fyodor thinks, she is tired of his unresponsiveness or because she respects his independence. How well Alexandra Yakovlevna comes to understand his character is evident from the vigor with which she addresses his housing problem in chapter 2.

Alexandra Yakovlevna is, to some extent, a cautionary example for Fyodor. Not everything in her soul is "alien" to him (G, 48), but her keen intuition and energy have for a long time been subdued by the conventions of her society. The death of her son has suddenly awakened that plain and indolent forty-five-year-old woman: "She was seized with the fever of activity, with the thirst for an abundant response; her child grew within her and struggled to issue forth; the literary circle newly founded by her husband jointly with Vasiliev, in order to give himself and her something to do, seemed to her the best possible posthumous honor to her poet son" (G, 49). Fyodor does not understand that, by way of compensation, the shattering grief gives Alexandra Yakovlevna a certain distinction, a sense of her own importance which she probably had not had since the days of her pregnancy. The confidence born of grief goes a long way toward releasing her from the conventionality of attitudes and roles. She still submits to middle-class forms, but she is now able to see through them and through her own conformity; she has, for instance, "confessed" to Fyodor that "when she goes shopping in familiar stores she is morally transplanted to a special world where she grows intoxicated from the wine of honesty, from the sweetness of mutual favors, and replies to the salesman's incarnadine smile with a smile of radiant rapture" (G, 17).

Her newly acquired confidence also reveals Alexandra Yakovlevna's excellent literary taste. She is indignant at having to listen to Busch's reading of his play and is sensitive to the minor flaws in Fyodor's poems. If she is indulgently deaf to the flaws in the poems of her late son, it is because they serve her as a means of contact with Yasha himself. Most interesting, however, is her brief remark about her namesake, the famous nineteenth-century writer and critic N. G. Chernyshevski: "Frankly speaking, I myself wouldn't be very interested in resuscitating everything that I felt in this connection when I was a college student in Russia" (G, 209). It seems that, like Fyodor, Alexandra Yakovlevna was disgusted by Chernyshevski's *What to Do?* but did not allow herself to maintain this attitude, because he was a hero of the liberal movement, a long-suffering dissenter persecuted by the regime.

Fyodor, however, does not really need to learn from Alexandra Yakovlevna's negative example of well-meaning conformist self-repression. In matters of artistic judgment he accepts no compromise; he is even somewhat rude to fellow writers when they attempt to draw him into their politics. But this seems to be his only sin against human commitment: he is sufficiently strong not to grudge expenditure of energy on social contacts, friendship, and love. None of the meanings of "getting and spending" are, in fact, among Fyodor's urgent concerns.

The "material indigence and intellectual luxury" (*SM*, 276) that Fyodor shares with many of his fellow emigrants affect the brand of eschatological alertness that allows him to cope with his displaced and disrupted life. Fyodor shares with Cincinnatus "the constant feeling that our days here are only pocket money . . . and that somewhere is stocked the real wealth, from which life should know how to get dividends in the shape of dreams, tears of happiness, distant mountains" (*G*, 176). The "pocket money," to which the bulk of the novel's text is devoted, pertains to the motif of insufficiency and incompleteness, whereas the "dividends," which are interspersed throughout the novel and have to be patiently collected, are tokens of the presence—ever receding—of the infinite. This quaint bookkeeping, the tension between the incomplete and the infinite, is reflected both in the major themes of *The Gift* and in the three main constituents of the novel's structure: the recurrent motifs, the features of perspective, and the self-referential games. The boundary between these techniques is often indistinguishable, as is the difference between structure and thematic content; and the terms in the two oppositions (infinite—incomplete, structure—theme) intertwine, so that the novel both describes and embodies the unfinished quest for the infinite, with the infinite threatening to collapse into the incomplete. As Fyodor notes in another connection, the end reveals a "fatal kinship" (*G*, 237) with the means.

II

The Gift contains numerous samples of Fyodor's work in various states of *incompleteness*. His poems about childhood are supposed to be well-polished miniatures, yet he soon becomes aware of their incidental weak points. His later poems are much more successful, yet he tacitly agrees with Zina that even these are "never quite up to [his] measure" (G, 206). His story about Yasha Chernyshevski remains unwritten, his monograph on his own father's life unfinished. Even the most nearly complete of his writings, the controversial biography of Nikolai Gavrilovich Chernyshevski that forms the fourth chapter of the novel, is referred to as "firing practice" (G, 208): the touch of maliciousness brings in associations with his toy gun that would shoot "a six-inch stick of colored wood, deprived of its rubber suction cup in order to increase the impact" on the target, "making in it a respectable little dent" (G, 26).

Fragments of several other people's writings are incorporated into the text of the novel. Fyodor's correspondence with his mother is presented in fragments that merge with the surrounding discourse. Excerpts from a boring philosophical play are amusingly interpolated in the first chapter. A fragment of a memoir with a reference to the "triple formula of human existence: irrevocability, unrealizability, inevitability" (G, 111) is included in the chapter about Fyodor's father; the whole chapter, in fact, is supposed to consist of bits and pieces of notes, sketches, letters, memoirs, thoughts, and reveries. The biography of Chernyshevski (Yasha's famous namesake) alludes to archival documents, diaries, memoirs, and both actual and spurious monographs. A fragment from Yasha Chernyshevski's notes is likewise used as material for Fyodor's comment.

The motif of fragments brings into relief the relationship between the actual absence and the virtual presence. In "the book of life" crevices, seared edges, and dog-eared corners suggest the presence of things that just happen to be illegible, intangible, unseen. The incomplete is a reminder of the absent, and the absent shades into the infinite.

Fyodor's life is deliberately presented in a fragmentary fashion: long periods are elided; nested texts blend with the master text; and dream is at times allowed to eclipse reality. The texture of Fyodor's humdrum "pocket money" days is punctured by love, memories, and writing, yet when resumed, it consists in the conventional motions through which he is expected to go, surrendering to the expectations and the rules of his environment. Fyodor swerves off mapped paths in order to subvert these rules: he leaves the meetings of the literary society and a funeral service before they end, aborts his first and only "real life" conversation with Koncheev, turns back home in the middle of his ride to a private lesson, neglects to follow up on job offers or to cultivate chance acquaintances. By giving his life an irresponsible fragmentary quality, Fyodor attempts, as it were, to prevent the quotidian from "congeal[ing] into reality" (E, 108).

The element of the fragmentary may account for the mistaken impression that *The Gift* consists of "tenuously connected separate short stories."[3] All the fragments are, in fact, firmly held together by the recurrent motif of eschatological "dividends." Different expressions of this motif comment on each other across intervening stretches of the pocket-money narrative. The fragments, the nested texts that end too soon, do not end completely; they either merge with the framing discourse or are echoed in remoter portions of the narrative; the unfinished thus aspires towards the infinite. People whose lives are made tragically incomplete by a premature short-circuiting—Pushkin, Fyodor's father, Yasha Chernyshevski—likewise continue to haunt the pages of *The Gift* in the shape of recurrent images, allusions, traces of "influence," hallucinations, and dreams.[4]

The sense of incompleteness permeates both structure and subject matter. It is reflected in the ultimate disintegration of two cryptographic designs that the structure of the novel seems to have borrowed from its content: the pattern of five, and the figure of a triangle enclosed in a circle.

The novel contains several sets of five items of which the fifth is problematic, unfinished, unconsummated.

First, before going to the Chernyshevskis' home in chapter 1, Fyodor buys some small Russian pies (*piroshki*), "one with meat, another with cabbage, a third with tapioca, a fourth with rice, a fifth... could

---

[3]Field, *Nabokov: His Life in Art*, p. 241. A similar opinion is expressed in Lee, *Vladimir Nabokov*, pp. 82–83.

[4]Guidelines for the study of the presence of Pushkin in the text and subtext of *The Gift* may be found in Simon Karlinsky, "Vladimir Nabokov's Novel *Dar* as a Work of Literary Criticism: A Structural Analysis," *Slavic and East European Journal*, 7 (1963), 284–90; Hyde, *Vladimir Nabokov*, pp. 21–23; and Johnson, *Worlds in Regression*, pp. 100–101. Some motifs related to the character of Fyodor's father are surveyed in Rowe, *Nabokov's Spectral Dimension*, pp. 33–39. The story of Yasha Chernyshevski is discussed in Douglas Fowler, *Reading Nabokov* (Ithaca, 1974), pp. 80–90. Fowler notes that part of the information presented in that story cannot be firsthand: "The narrator's voice has become that of an omniscient, creative deity"(p. 88), which is strongly reminiscent of the technique of *Pnin*. As in the latter novel, the first-person narrator uses the "sources" technique, augmenting the density of the story's setting by projecting into it elements of his own experience: e.g., the architect Stockschmeisser who promenades in Grunewald with his dog on the day of Yasha's suicide in chapter 1 (see G, 59–60) as well as after the crash of a small airplane in chapter 5 (see G, 343). However, the recurrence of motifs related to Yasha's character in the other parts of the novel still awaits investigation.

not afford a fifth" (G, 42). It seems that Fyodor's hunger will not be satisfied.

Second, trying to guess who wrote the favorable review of his poems, Fyodor thinks of several critics: "This one was scrupulous but untalented; that one, dishonest but gifted; a third wrote only about prose; a fourth only about his friends; a fifth... and Fyodor's imagination conjured up this fifth one"—the ever inaccessible Koncheev (G, 42). Upon arriving at the Chernyshevskis', Fyodor learns that the supposed review is the host's April-Fool joke.

Third, in the first of his two imaginary conversations with Koncheev, Fyodor mentions five Russian poets whose names begin with B, "the five senses of the new Russian poetry"—and Koncheev wonders "which of the five represents taste" (G, 86). Who might the five be? Blok, Briusov, Bunin, Balmont, and . . . Andrey Belyi? or perhaps Baltrushaitis? The problem of taste remains unsettled.

Fourth, *The Gift* consists of five chapters, the last of which effects the novel's "return-upon-itself." Indeed, the last paragraph of the novel is a poem that "mimics an Onegin Stanza" (G, xi).[5] *Eugene Onegin* is mentioned within the text of the poem: "Onegin from his knees will rise—but his creator strolls away" (G, 378). This is an allusion to the

---

[5]*Eugene Onegin* is written in stanzas of fourteen iambic tetrameter lines with an *abab ccdd effe gg* rhyme scheme. The last paragraph of *The Gift* (in both Russian and English) can be easily rearranged to suit this pattern:

> Good-by, my book! Like mortal eyes,
> Imagined ones must close some day.
> Onegin from his knees will rise—
> But his creator strolls away.
> And yet the ear cannot right now
> Part with the music and allow
> The tale to fade; the chords of fate
> Itself continue to vibrate;
> And no obstruction for the sage
> Exists where I have put The End:
> The shadows of my world extend
> Beyond the skyline of the page,
> Blue as tomorrow's morning haze—
> Nor does this terminate the phrase.

The End

Chapter 3 of *The Gift* also contains hidden poems. Anna Maria Salehar was, to my knowledge, the first to detect them and to quote them in lineated form. Her valuable study "Nabokov's *Gift*: An Apprenticeship in Creativity," in Proffer, *Book of Things*, pp. 70–83, presents a detailed discussion of their imagery and the manner of their composition. One may, however, argue with Salehar concerning the exact

in medias res ending of Pushkin's novel in verse: the curtain falls when Onegin is rejected by Tatiana; a "clink of spurs" is heard (*EO* 1. 307). and her husband appears. A metaphorical reading of this "clink of spurs" is given in Nabokov's Commentary to *Eugene Onegin*: the sound "might have heralded the appearance of the Chief of Police, Count Benkendorf (Benckendorff), whose shadow caused Pushkin to interrupt his novel" (*EO* 3.243). *The Gift* likewise reinterprets the "clink of spurs": the author is strolling away in his riding boots (Pegasus is saddled for a new venture), leaving his hero "at an unkind minute for him" (*EO* 1. 307). "Nor does this terminate the phrase," asserts the last sentence of the novel (*G*, 378) even though, ironically, it is followed by the required full stop. An "unkind minute" is in store for Fyodor, and the movielike final words "The End," which Nabokov "revised into" the English version, will not hinder the reader from picturing it to himself. Fyodor's keys have been stolen; Zina's keys seem to have been left inside the apartment.[6] Will the lovers, finally alone together, find themselves locked out?

We are not to know, since the author is strolling away—and not without a chuckle: "I wonder how far the imagination of the reader will follow the young lovers after they have been dismissed" (*G*, x). Fyodor has not witnessed the dialogue between Zina and her mother, so he does not know that her keys are locked inside. But has that dialogue really taken place? Fyodor is the focal character of the novel; the scene at which he has not been present may be understood as his fearful imagination—one way in which fate could revenge itself for his flippant remarks about it (see *G*, 375). On the other hand the dialogue may be a postdated projection of information obtained after the finale. In any case, Fyodor and Zina never get to the apartment, because the novel ends while they are still in the street. Here the reader has a choice of recollections: of the unattainable goals depicted on Keats's Grecian Urn or, closer to home, of a statement made *á propos de rien* by a character in *The Real Life of Sebastian Knight*: "I'll be disappointed in your book if it all ends in bed" (*RLSK*, 170). *The Gift* certainly does not end in bed. It does not, in fact, end at all; rather, it "winds up": a

---

limits of the poem: what she considers its fourth part ("She always unexpectedly appeared . . . ": *G*, 189) seems to me a case of the flesh of prose and the specter of translucent poetry (cf. *G*, 21); this likewise seems to apply to the penultimate paragraph of the novel, which Salehar regards as a tonic poem.

[6]The theme of the keys in *The Gift* is extensively discussed in Johnson, *Worlds in Regression*, pp. 93–106.

mislaid key, the wrong key, a forgotten key form one of the most significant recurring motifs of chapter 1.

Finally, the number five is disrupted by addition and subtraction. Chapter 5 acquaints us with six rather than five reviews of Fyodor's monograph—actual reviews that replace the wish-fulfilling supposed one of chapter 1. Koncheev's favorable review is the fourth; slot number five is reserved for an angry article in a monarchistic newspaper. Curiously, its author is not mistaken in remarking that Fyodor "goes wholly over to the side of his sorry, but pernicious hero as soon as the long-suffering Russian Tsar finally has him safely tucked away" (G, 320). Further, in chapter 5 the five-member Committee of the society of Russian Writers in Germany is shown disintegrating. Its venerable chairman Vasiliev announces his resignation, and there seem to be no suitable replacements for the dishonest three of the remaining four committee members—who, incidentally, are not even writers. The pattern of five breaks down.

So does the pattern of the triangle enclosed in a circle. This figure is first introduced in chapter 1, where it describes the relationship of three young people: Yasha Chernyshevski has conceived a passion for Rudolf Baumann, who is in love with Olya G., who in turn falls in love with Yasha; the circle of their common friendship gradually erodes. In chapter 4 the same figure applies to the Hegelian thesis-antithesis-synthesis triad (Nabokov seems to have preferred Schopenhauer to Hegel) on which the fictional historian Strannolyubski ("Mr. Strangelove," whose remarks in the spurious quotation marks serve to bring into relief Fyodor's own strikingly formulated thoughts) makes the following comment: "There lies concealed in the triad . . . a vague image of the circumference controlling all life of the mind, and the mind is confined inescapably within it. This is truth's merry-go-round, for truth is always round; consequently, in the development of life's forms a certain pardonable curvature is possible: the hump of truth; but no more" (G, 256).

The "development of life's forms" accepts patterns only on sufferance, as hints at a possibility. Circles imposed on life by the mind erode, leaving here and there only a "hump of truth." Imagination seeks to complete the circle that is suggested by its humplike fragment but succeeds only on the borderline between the transience of insight in one's mind and its immortality "in the flesh" of an aesthetic object.[7]

[7] A sensitive discussion of the significance that patterns and the incompleteness

In chapter 3 the encircled triangle is suggested but fails to take shape in the Fyodor-Zina-Koncheev triangle. The description of Zina's mysterious fiancé, whom she leaves for Fyodor, fits Koncheev in every detail except age: Koncheev is younger than Fyodor, whereas the ex-fiancé is supposed to have been about twelve years older than Zina, which would make him Fyodor's senior by about four years. The fact that Zina has for a long time been collecting clippings with Fyodor's and Koncheev's poems is evidence of her literary taste rather than an element of the pattern.

The same figure seems to emerge in the contrasts between three young writers in the novel: Fyodor Godunov-Cherdyntsev (whose monograph on Chernyshevski foreshadows Nabokov's monograph on Gogol, written several years after *The Gift*); the novelist Vladimirov, who briefly appears in chapter 5; and the poet Koncheev. Different elements of Nabokov's personality and views are distributed among these three characters.

The most significant triangle enclosed in a circle emerges in chapter 2. It is the "triple formula of human existence: irrevocability, unrealizability, inevitability," which, according to the memoirist Suhoshchokov, was known to Pushkin (G, 111). Death signifies the ultimate erosion of the circle. Throughout the novel, however, the protagonist and the author keep trying to disrupt not the circumference but the triangle. The spurious memoirs are a text within an unwritten text (the biography of Fyodor's father) within a text: the formula loses some of its authoritativeness by being placed in such a complicated perspective. The novel offers a whole catalogue of models of infinity that are meant to refute the finality of the irrecoverable, the unrealizable, and the unavoidable. These models range from failures farcical through failures noble to failures barely distinguishable from success. The first are based on the crude workings of conscious reason and produce gross, slapdash models of infinity; the last are miraculously spontaneous gifts of life and "inspiration."[8] They are still failures insofar as they are qualified by the doubt that their nature may be psychological rather than spiritual. Yasha Chernyshevski attempts to sublimate his homosexual passion by persuading himself that he is in

---

of patterns hold for Nabokov's characters can be found in Morton, *Vladimir Nabokov*, pp. 10–12.

[8]Incidentally, Nabokov's essay "Inspiration" quotes an extract from the fourth canto of John Shade's "Pale Fire" but, like chapters 3 and 5 of *The Gift*, prints it as a prose passage (see *SO*, 311).

love with Rudolf's soul. Conversely, the modern reader tends to reduce creativity to the workings of the libidinous subconscious. Neither extreme is endorsed in a Nabokovian context where skepticism is a dialectical counterpart of mystical insight. Since Fyodor prefers the latter, his skepticism is deflected to himself, reduced to an attitude of self-irony and thus made innocuous. This complex position is conveyed in a wavelike prose, subtly modified in its tone and its branching hues.

III

The Irrecoverable: To recover the irrecoverable—the past, the childhood, the exile's birthplace, the dead father—would amount to canceling time. A return to Russia is as impossible for Fyodor as a return to childhood or as his father's return from the dead. Only in the mental activities that make up his inner world can the bans be broken.

One of these activities is the result of an accurate visual memory. Fyodor and his mother can simultaneously imagine that they are walking in the same direction on their Leshino estate: "And suddenly, in the middle of this silent walk being performed by two minds, using according to the rules of the game the rate of a human footstep . . . both stopped and said where they had got to, and when it turned out, as it often did, that neither had outpaced the other, having halted in the same coppice, the same smile flashed upon mother and son and shone through their common tear" (G, 101).

Yet deliberate recollection is only a "habit interpreted by memory."[9] A habit fades when discontinued; and Fyodor has to admit to himself that "it is already difficult . . . to gather all the parts of the past; already [he is] beginning to forget relationships and connections between objects that still thrive in [his] memory, objects [he] thereby condemn[s] to extinction" (G, 30).[10]

[9]See Henri Bergson, *Matter and Memory*, trans. Nancy Margaret Paul and W. Scott Palmer (London, 1929), p. 95. Echoes of Bergson are particularly distinct in the remarks attributed to Koncheev during Fyodor's second imaginary dialogue with this mysterious poet: cf. G, 354; and *Matter and Memory*, pp. 48, 88.

[10]Cf. SM, 135–36: "The struggle that had gone on since my grandfather's time to keep the park from reverting to the wild state always fell short of complete success. . . . The disintegrating process continues still, in a different sense, for when, nowadays, I attempt to follow in memory the winding paths from one given point to another, I notice with alarm that there are many gaps, due to oblivion or ignorance, akin to the

Triumph over oblivion is not granted when solicited. Memory becomes a successful model of infinity only when it is joined to something independent of conscious will. This happens in the case of spontaneous recollection, which, as Bergson has observed, imagines rather than repeats and is "as capricious in reproducing as it is faithful in preserving."[11] In Nabokov's novels, as well as in his autobiography, spontaneous recollection is combined with the artistic transformation of an image into a work of art that exists in a sort of limbo until captured in a medium.

"To call up the past in the form of an image," wrote Bergson in *Matter and Memory*, "we must be able to withdraw ourselves from the action of the moment, we must have the power to value the useless, we must have the will to dream."[12] Never does Fyodor recapture moments of the past with greater vividness than when he slips into doing precisely what he considers useless and inappropriate (see G, 151): namely, into diluting with his own life the biography of his father that he attempts to write. It is then that a commonplace object turns into a focus of infinite symbolic significance. This happens, for instance, when Fyodor recollects ("with incredible vividness": G, 137) the day of his father's last return from an expedition. The recollection becomes a reliving of the past, a return from a rented room in Berlin to "that world which was as natural to him as snow to the white hare or water to Ophelia" (G, 137).

In preparation for the scene the narrative pace slows down, conveying the sense of "inflated, exaggerated time" (G, 137). Fyodor's mother has gone to the railway station to meet his father, and Fyodor is "loaf[ing] about the manor, feeling the weight and pain of his agitation, and envying the way the others [get] through these big, empty minutes." Meanwhile, his sister Tanya is "swinging enthusiastically and powerfully on the swing in the garden, standing on the seat" (G, 138). A little later Fyodor runs to meet his father's carriage but somehow takes the wrong road. The first thing he sees when he retraces his steps is "the abandoned swing . . . still quivering in the garden": Tanya is already hanging on their father's neck, and the father has "taken a watch from his pocket with his free hand . . . for he always liked to know how fast he had got home from the station" (G, 139).

---

terra-incognita blanks map makers of old used to call 'sleeping beauties.' "
[11] See Bergson, *Matter and Memory*, p. 93, 102.
[12] Ibid., p. 94.

The glance at the watch arrests the moment but not the movement of the still quivering abandoned swing. This residual yet unending oscillation is Fyodor's—and Nabokov's—model of *perpetuum mobile;* it foreshadows the theme of the perpetual motion machine that Fyodor will trace in his biography of Chernyshevski (who, of course, justified his search for a model of infinity by utilitarian considerations, hoping that it would be a source of cheap energy). The vision ends abruptly, as with the click of a chronometer, and the whole of the ensuing year is condensed into one paragraph.

Notably, the episode is presented in the third person, which means that it is not Fyodor's written narrative. Fyodor does not wish to tell the story of his own emotions in the scholarly monograph about his father. The memory overwhelms him unsolicited and is captured by the author in the kind of prose that Fyodor's own pen is not yet ready to produce.

Later, confessing his inability to complete the monograph, Fyodor tells his mother that the period of research and recollections has given him intense happiness: "All these months while I was making my research, taking notes, recollecting and thinking, I was blissfully happy: I was certain that something unprecedentedly beautiful was being created, that my notes were merely small props for the work, trail-marks, pegs, and that the most important thing was developing and being created of itself, but now I see, like waking up on the floor, that besides these pitiful notes there is nothing" (*G*, 150–51).

Fyodor cannot give material substance to the images that have arisen in his mind, but he fails as a craftsman rather than as an artist. "Something unprecedentedly beautiful" has indeed been created "of itself": not only the story of a brave naturalist (written by Nabokov instead of Fyodor) but also, and in tune with the tentative metaphysics of the novel, a model of contact with irrecoverable time.

Fyodor's notes on works by and about his father are confused and almost unintelligible: like "the irritating sham of a caryatid, a hanger-on and not a support" (*G*, 16), they cling to his work but do not promote it. (The experience gives him a technical lesson in note-taking that he later puts to use during his work on Chernyshevski). The notes are the crudest model of resistance to oblivion; more "fanciful and rare" (*G*, 168) are the solicited recollections, as in the game Fyodor plays with his mother. At the top of the scale are feats of spontaneous recollection that seem to cancel time and, when transformed into a work of art, save the images from (no longer unavoidable) effacement.

Even so, the images, are on the near side of the newly erected "verbal fence" (G, 24); the past is on the far side. It remains irrecoverable because aesthetic distance replaces rather than reduces distance in time and space.

The Unavoidable: Notes and diaries also belong to the coarser models of the contest against the unavoidable, the end, the full stop, death. Diaries, however, interfere with the winnowing action of memory; meant to salvage one's life from oblivion, they devaluate genuine experience by blending grain with chaff.[13] The diary of Chernyshevski, for instance, preserves for the prying historian much of what probably ought to have been forgotten. Chernyshevski also supplies another crude model of infinity, the projected perpetual motion machine meant to avoid the inevitable exhaustion of energy in a closed system. That such a machine is impossible makes the very idea as counterproductive as the idea of a diary: both divert creative energy into blind alleys.

Another approach to the idea of endlessness is made, with due reference to Pascal, in the fragment of a philosophical novel of Herman Ivanovich Busch, an aimiable graphomaniac who eventually helps Fyodor to publish his biography of Chernyshevski. Busch's model, rather than dabbling at infinite mechanical extension, aims to probe depth through an interplay of the microcosm and the macrocosm: "The universe is but the final fraction of one, I think, central atom, of those it consists of. It's not easy to understand, but if you understand this you will understand everything. Out of the prison of mathematics! The whole is equal to the smallest part of the whole, the sum of the parts is equal to one part of the sum" (G, 222).

The philosopher who says these words in Busch's novel is addressing "a cutie, his lady friend" (G, 222): this narrative situation is an *en abîme* parody on Fyodor's discussions of his work with Zina. Moreover, the "game of worlds" described in the fragment is an *en abîme* parody on two other models of infinity found in the novel: the Möbius strip, and the infinitely receding spiral.

---

[13]Forgetting is often no less important than remembering. *The Gift* makes an elaborate allusion to Pushkin's poem "The Three Springs" ("Tri klyucha"—the Russian for "a key" also means "a spring," and the pun is fruitfully exploited in the novel; see Johnson, *Worlds in Regression*, pp. 100–101): the spring of youth, the Castalian spring of inspiration, and the spring of oblivion. The last seems to be as sweet as the fountain of the muses.

The motif of the Möbius strip is related to that of the "miracle of the lemniscate" mentioned in *Pale Fire*.[14] The lemniscate, a figure eight gone to sleep, the mathematical symbol of infinity, could serve as a two-dimensional graphical symbol of the Möbius strip. In *The Gift*, as in *Pale Fire*, it is traced by the tire of a bicycle. Fyodor's early poem about learning to ride a bicycle mentions the "weavers and wavers in an alley": that is, lemniscates drawn on the sand by a still unsteady rider. "Drozhan'ye i vily v alleye" in the Russian text of the novel (*Dar*, 33, 41–42) makes use of the sounds "vil" which the noun *vily* ("pitchforks") shares with the verb *viliat'*, indicating a wavery, swerving, unsteady movement. The result is an inept pun—Fyodor has to agree with his friends that the expression is "doubtful" (*G*, 46)—as are, in fact, most models of infinity in the novel.

The figure-eight shape of the lemniscate recurs at the end of the evening at the Chernyshevskis'. The departure of the tired guests is depicted as the waning of their faces in one's memory: "And now they all began gradually to grow less distinct, to ripple with the random agitation of a fog, and then to vanish altogether; their outlines, weaving in figure-eight patterns, were evaporating" (*G*, 64). The use of the verb "weave" in the English version echoes the bicycle theme, thus compensating for the lost association with a bicycle wheel in disrepair that is evoked by the Russian word *vos'miorka* (*Dar*, 62), translated as "figure-eight pattern." The image self-referentially describes the gradual cancellation of the hypotyposis: the faces and the bodies of the people wane into two circles connected by a narrow neck, just as in Maurits Escher's drawings birds or fish gradually turn into triangles. At the same time, the pattern of the lemniscate suggests that through that very text the characters have attained their own eternity.

The number eight soon recurs in a seemingly unrelated context: Fyodor buys himself a pair of shoes after the salesgirl brings him an *eighth* pair to try on (*G*, 76). The X-ray view of his foot in the shoe store gives him an impulse to start composing a poem about stepping ashore ("with this": that is, with his skeleton foot) from Charon's ferry (*G*, 76). The river, he notes, "is not the Lethe but rather the Styx" (*G*, 87): eternity can be free from oblivion. One recollects the shoes (they

---

[14]The significance of the image of the lemniscate in *Pale Fire* has been observed by Robert Alter, "Nabokov's Game of Worlds," in *Partial Magic* (Berkeley, Calif., 1975), pp. 189–90.

are supposed to fit but are too tight) when Zina tells Fyodor that he should write in a different genre because his poems are "a size too small" for him. The shoes seem to stretch together with the growth of Fyodor's creative experience.[15]

The lemniscate is referred to again as "the Dunlop stripe left by Tanya's bicycle, dividing into two waves at the turn" (G, 97), and once more, indirectly, at the end of chapter 2, as "the rounded shape of eternity" with which Fyodor tends to endow a stretch of granted time (G, 152). This wish to arrest the infinite within the finite is also obvious in one of the main structural peculiarities of the novel: namely, the subversion of the ending.

The structure of the novel has been compared to the Möbius strip[16] (of which, as already noted, the lemniscate is a simplified two-dimensional projection) mainly because at the end Fyodor decides to write a novel that would be "built up, curtained, surrounded by dense life—[his] life, [his] professional passions and cares" (G, 376). In a letter to his mother he mentions his wish to write "a classical novel, with 'types,' love, fate, conversations . . . and with descriptions of nature" (G, 361)—which rather aptly describes The Gift. Moreover, in chapter 1 Fyodor passes by a square to which the narrative refers as the one "where we dined" (G, 65), yet the dinner in question takes place at the end of chapter 5.[17] The narrative future has already taken place, so that by the time Fyodor plans to write his novel, it seems to have been written for him already.

And yet the text does not quite support the analogy between the Möbius strip and the structure of The Gift. Fyodor overrules Zina's objection that his novel may "result in an autobiography with mass executions of good acquaintances"; he says: "Well, let's suppose that I so shuffle, twist, mix, rechew and rebelch everything, add such spices of my own and impregnate things so much with myself that nothing remains of the autobiography but dust—the kind of dust, of course, which makes the most orange of skies" (G, 376).

---

[15]Sergei Davydov, "The Gift: Nabokov's Aesthetic Exorcism of Chernyshevskii," Canadian-American Slavic Studies, 19 (1985), 357–74, discusses, among other things, different ramifications of the theme of shoes.

[16]See Davydov, Teksty-Matreshki, pp. 183–99. A Möbius strip may be obtained by cutting a narrow length of paper, twisting one of its ends, and attaching it to the other end. The resulting ringlike structure will turn out to have only one edge and only one surface in which the outside merges with the inside.

[17]For this observation I am indebted to Johnson, Worlds in Regression, p. 97.

Given this transformation, the novel that Fyodor is going to write will not contain an exact account of his experience as recounted in the master text. And if what we have just read is in fact Fyodor's novel, then the experience it describes has already been "shuffled, twisted, and mixed." In other words, not only does the story of *The Gift* differ from the supposed "real" experience of the narrator, but the novel that the narrator is planning to write must also differ from his experience. And if in the end the hero of that projected novel likewise decides to write a novel, it will likewise have shuffled, twisted, and mixed the loop that preceded it. The figure that emerges from this relationship is that of a receding spiral: its narrowing gyres are not closed circles—according to Nabokov, circles are always vicious (see *NG*, 149). Such a spiral may continue *ad infinitum*; it may be imagined as a wedge that is stuck through the familiar material universe into the world of "infinite consciousness" (*BS*, 192).

In his biography of Chernyshevski, Fyodor has to content himself with a finite spiral: "There must be a single uninterrupted progression of thought. I must peel my apple in a single strip, without removing the knife" (*G*, 212). The tip of the peeling contains the first part (the octet) of the sonnet whose end (the sestet) appears at the very beginning. Therefore, the end of the peeling easily joins its starting point, forming a Möbius strip; the necessary twist consists in the change in the narrator's attitude to Chernyshevski after his arrest (ironically, as noted above, it is a hostile reactionary reviewer who notices this twist). Upon passing the twist of a Möbius strip, one repeats one's previous trajectory yet has, in fact, a new experience because the path is a continuation rather than a repetition of the surface covered before. Thus, whereas on first reading the biography one is mainly conscious of Fyodor's mercilessly iconoclastic mocking criticism of Chernyshevski, with repeated reading one senses that Fyodor is treating his ideological adversary with suppressed admiration and that under his surface maliciousness there is a fascination with the ways in which destiny imitates poetic justice. Such a reinterpretation of the biography is facilitated by the scholarly review noting that the biographer Strannolyubski ("Strangelove") is spurious. In a repeated reading, moving along the inner surface of the Möbius strip, we are much better aware of Fyodor's strange love for the problematic revolutionary whose utilitarian views on art may have misled generations of critics and writers yet, by the same token, helped Fyodor to resist their influence. Thus it is chapter 4 that has the form of the Möbius strip; the narrative as a whole imitates a never-ending spiral.

Fyodor's purpose in writing his projected novel is to sabotage the unavoidable and thus preserve and immortalize that which is passing away. This can be done, he feels, not by diary records or by willed exertions of the memory but by the most successful model of infinity—the mysterious "royal experiment" of transforming gifts of life into art:

> [Fyodor] recalled how he had met [Alexandra Yakovlevna] this spring— for the last time—after her husband's death, and the strange sensation that overwhelmed him when looking at her lowered face with its unworldly frown, as if he had never really seen her before and was now making out on her face the resemblance to her deceased husband. . . . A day later she went away to some relatives in Riga, and already her face, the stories about her son, the literary evenings at her house, and Alexander Yakov-levich's mental illness—all this that had served its time—now rolled up of its own accord and came to an end, like a bundle of life tied up crosswise, which will long be kept but which will never again be untied by our lazy, procrastinating, ungrateful hands. He was seized by a panicky desire not to allow it to close and get lost in a corner of his soul's lumber room, a desire to apply all this to himself, to his eternity, to his truth, so as to enable it to sprout up in a new way. There is a way—the only way. [G, 349]

A finished work, "a thing of beauty" is not "a pretty bauble" that "always gladdens us" (LATH, 77); nor is it a record of definite experience, a "bundle of life tied up crosswise."[18] Rather, it is an evocation of what the bundle has "sprouted" into in "the other dimension." When composing literary works or chess problems, Fyodor (see G, 182–84) and Nabokov himself have the feeling that the result sought already exists in some "now transparent, now dimming, dimension" (SO, 69). When at the beginning of the first chapter Fyodor observes a moving van in front of his new lodgings, he thinks that one day he must "use such a scene to start a good, thick old-fashioned novel. The fleeting thought was touched with a careless irony; an irony, however, that was quite unnecessary, because somebody within him, on his behalf, independently from him, had absorbed all this, recorded it, and filed it away" (G, 16).

---

[18]The image of the "bundle tied crosswise" likewise has the connotations of a gift, especially since it forms a contrast to the boxed gifts that frustrated Fyodor and his sister in their childhood (see G, 25).

This passage is most often read in its self-referential meaning: at the moment Fyodor does not know that a thick (though not quite old-fashioned) novel, *The Gift*, which opens with the scene he is witnessing, has already been written. But the remark also has a meaning within the provisionally self-contained fictional world: the "somebody within" Fyodor is precisely that which makes Cincinnatus (in *Invitation to a Beheading*) opaque. It is his contact with that "other dimension" where a latent work of art sprouts from the seed of possibility, waiting for Fyodor or Nabokov or some other artist to "take it down."

The moments when this "taking it down" is carried into effect are the most tormenting and yet the happiest in Fyodor's life; it is then that he seems to be in touch with real immortality. And this immortality is not synonymous with either posthumous fame or the appreciation of his work by the contemporary world "in the person of a few hundred lovers of literature who had left St. Petersburg, Moscow and Kiev" (G, 21). The story of Fyodor's composition of the poem "Thank You, My Land" in chapter 1 is a pertinent example: a sudden impulse, the emergence of a prosodic matrix in which words and rhyming endings alternate with gaps, the tortuous filling-in of the gaps, the rejection of sound clusters that draw inappropriate associations (again, this is more obvious in the Russian than in the English text), the discovery of the meaning in the words that have just been found, and the approval of this meaning. Miraculously, a meaning exactly appropriate to Fyodor's concerns at the time of composition seems to be generated spontaneously, without being planned.[19] Fyodor eventually falls out of love with most of his old poems; his belief in his gift is based not on the volume of his completed production but on those moments when he seems to become a medium between quotidian reality and the "involute abode," the aesthetic realm.

---

[19]This seems to be an answer to Salehar's question of why the poet creates—"because he desires to express 'something' or because he is driven to write by the power of the word, i.e., rhythm and rhyme" ("Nabokov's *Gift*," p. 71). The poet's conscious efforts are directed toward fitting appropriate words into the rhythmic matrix that springs out of unexpected rhymes between morphologically different items that would hardly be paired in any conventional dictionary of rhyme. The secret, irrational workings of the imagination behind the filling of the mold result in unpremeditated "expression." A painstaking filling of the mold is recorded (partly) only in chapter 1. In chapter 3 it takes place behind the curtain of the text, while the curtain itself contains a flashback account of Fyodor's apprenticeship in the writing of poetry (see G, 160–68). When the curtain rises, the reader is presented with a finished poem.

Significantly, Fyodor hardly ever courts inspiration. It overtakes him spontaneously and often at the wrong moments, as when he is dressing for a ball that Zina has been eagerly anticipating. By analogy, the clockwork Malayan nightingale of his childhood (another model) does not sing when wound up but starts its trills unexpectedly, awakened by a "mysterious tremor" of a floorboard when someone accidentally walks past the toy bird's "lofty wardrobe-top perch" (G, 24). The mystery of inspiration may, if one so wishes, be reduced from a spiritual to a psychological phenomenon, however imperfectly investigated: for a movie director in *Ada*, infinity is reduced to "the farthest point from the camera which is still in fair focus" (A, 333). Throughout *The Gift* the infinite persistently threatens to collapse into the unfinished. A doubt lurks, for instance, even behind the exhilaration of the poem "Thank You, My Land."

Ostensibly, the poem deals with Fyodor's belief in his gift, with the gift of his land to him, and with his persistence as a poet despite the lack of public recognition. His only audience is himself:

> Thank you, my land; for your remotest
> Most cruel mist my thanks are due.
> By you possessed, by you unnoticed,
> Unto myself I speak of you.

The word "mist," which at first glance seems to be a *pis aller* translation of the Russian *dal'* ("distance"), is in fact an appropriate reference (though veiled, or "curtained," to use the vocabulary of the novel) to the "noises" in the channel of communication with that aesthetic realm where his poem has already "sprouted." Yet in the second quatrain he cannot help wondering whether his poem is a token of that realm's autonomous existence or whether it is the product of a psychological idiosyncrasy:

> And in these talks between somnambules
> My inmost being hardly knows
> If it's my demency that rambles
> Or your own melody that grows.
>   [G, 68]

The doubt, in its turn, is balanced by the suggestion (pervasive in Nabokov's work) that "demency" may be a glimpse of the Mystery.

This suggestion is most explicit in the "Ultima Thule" fragment[20] (written within a year or two after *The Gift*, during the abortive return to Russian-language prose that followed Nabokov's completion of *The Real Life of Sebastian Knight*). The fragment explores the impossibility of determining whether Mr. Falter's "solution of the mystery of the universe" (which he obstinately withholds from the protagonist, pretending to protect him from a heart attack) is the cause or a symptom of his insanity.

Fyodor's poem, however, is a "writing exercise," just as his biography of Chernyshevski is "shooting practice." Both seem to be rehearsals for a work whose composition would really bring him in touch with his own immortality. Like all more or less successful model approximations of infinity, this writing apprenticeship finds a parody on itself in the "writing exercises" of young N. G. Chernyshevski: for example, copying into his notebook Feuerbach's maxim "Man is what he eats" (*G*, 226). In the Russian text this copying is ironically referred to as *propis'* (*Dar*, 241), which means exercises to improve one's handwriting (the "art of writing well"?), usually performed by an endless copying of adages, miniature models of eternal truths.

Fyodor's ironic reference to handwriting exercises may evoke Gogol's image of the pathetically inarticulate master calligrapher in "The Overcoat"; Chernyshevski's examination of pictures in shop windows and the economies of his ascetic student days as described in Fyodor's monograph are likewise reminiscent, however vaguely, of Gogol's Akaky Akakievich. Between the unfinished biography of his father and the conception of Chernyshevski's biography, Fyodor moves to new lodgings: "the distance from the old residence to the new [is] about the same as, somewhere in Russia, that from Pushkin Avenue to Gogol Street" (*G*, 157).

The Unrealizable: The motif of the unrealizable is closely connected with the theme of Fyodor's father; it involves the inaccessibility of information about the father's death, the impossibility of establishing contact with him, and the unattainability of the mystical knowledge that Fyodor believes his father to have possessed.

The impasse that Fyodor shares with historians is metaphorically described in the sestet of the sonnet that frames Fyodor's biography of Chernyshevski:

[20]The central theme of this fragment is examined in Johnson, *Worlds in Regression*, pp. 206–19.

Alas! In vain historians pry and probe:
The same wind blows, and in the same live robe
Truth bends her head to fingers curved cupwise;

And with a woman's smile and a child's care
Examines something she is holding there
Concealed by her own shoulder from our eyes.

[G, 224]

The image of truth as a half-woman, half-child holding something in "fingers curved cupwise" foreshadows Krug's memories of a young girl carefully carrying a large hawk moth in her hands in *Bend Sinister*. *Psyche*, the Greek for "butterfly," also means "soul": for all the probings of a historian, the soul of a person and the essence of a past event remain hidden behind the shoulder of truth. Standard history, like the volumes that N. G. Chernyshevski is translating (not quite closely) in his last years, is a coarser model of the quest for the inaccessible. Another coarse model is likewise mentioned in chapter 4: the "table-turning," an attempt, made by the credulous rather than by the imaginative, to achieve contact with the souls of the dead. Chernyshevski writes to his father about this "new fad," and both agree that it is "all gullibility and fraud" (G, 231).

The reference to the theme of spiritualism in the father-son correspondence is less important for the portrait of Chernyshevski than it is for the spectrum of motifs around another father-son relationship. The table-turning belongs to the same cluster of motifs as the diary, the perpetual motion machine, and other attempts to build models of the infinite out of materials close at hand. Somewhat higher on the scale of success are the purely mental efforts to probe the darkness, such as Fyodor's strenuous and painful surmises about the way his father may have met his death:

Oh, how did he die? From illness? From exposure? From thirst? By the hand of man? . . . Did he return their fire for a long time? Did he save a last bullet for himself? Was he taken alive? Did they bring him to the parlor car at the railway headquarters of some punitive detachment (I can see its hideous locomotive stoked with dried fish), having suspected him of being a White spy? . . . Did they shoot him in the ladies' room of some godforsaken station (broken looking glass, tattered plush), or did they lead him out into some kitchen garden one dark night and wait for the moon to peep out? How did he wait with them in the dark? With a smile of disdain? And if a whitish moth had hovered among the shadowy burdocks he would, even at that moment, I *know* have followed it with that same glance of encouragement with which . . . he used to greet the pink hawks sampling our lilacs. [G, 149]

Having thus worked through the literary variants of the death of a hero, Fyodor hits upon the image of a hawk moth, which renders the imagined scene of his father's death morally, if not historically, correct.

The reader, and Fyodor himself, may doubt whether any of his guesses reflect what may really have happened. One can also doubt whether Fyodor succeeds in recapturing the father's experience when he describes one of his journeys in the first person. Yet it may be that at some other moments he does unknowingly reenact the experience of his father, whether in his dream about their reunion ("His heart was bursting like that of a man before execution, but at the same time this execution was such a joy that life faded before it": G, 366), or in the flow of unsolicited memories that bring back the pain he felt after seeing his father off on the last journey:

Fyodor walked across the park, opened the tuneful wicket gate and cut across the road where the thick tires had just imprinted their tracks. A familiar black-and-white beauty rose smoothly off the ground and de-scribed a wide circle, also taking part in the seeing-off. He turned into the trees and came by way of a shady path, where golden flies hung aquiver in transversal sunbeams, to his favorite clearing, boggy, bloom-ing, moistly glistening in the hot sun. The divine meaning of this wood meadow was expressed in its butterflies. Everyone might have found something here. The holidaymaker might have rested on a stump. The artist might have screwed up his eyes. But its *truth* would have been *probed* somewhat deeper by knowledge-amplified love: by its "wide-open orbs"—to paraphrase Pushkin. [G, 144; my italics]

It is not without significance that in the sestet quoted above the motif of probing the truth likewise precedes an indirect reference to a butterfly. A glimpse of the truth—the most successful rebellion against the finality of the inaccessible—is granted when not consciously sought. Fyodor surrenders to the flow of his memories and, as in the episode of his father's last return, blends a moment of the present with a moment of the past. Now, however, the crumbling of time has an additional suggestion: it is also a blend of the experience of the father and the son.[21] A communion between them is embodied in the ensuing description of butterflies in the meadow. Here is the end of the page-long paragraph:

A small hummingbird moth with a bumblebee's body and glasslike wings, beating invisibly, tried from the air a flower with its long proboscis, darted to another and then to a third. All this fascinating life, by whose present blend one could infallibly tell both the age of the summer (with an accuracy almost to within one day), the geographical location of the area, and the vegetal composition of the clearing—all this that was living, genuine and eternally dear to him, Fyodor perceived in a flash, with one penetrating and experienced glance. Suddenly he placed a fist against the trunk of a birch tree and leaning on it, burst into tears. [G, 145]

It is hard to say what narrative convention Nabokov is using in the episode. Does the scene arise spontaneously, "in a flash" in Fyodor's memory? Or is it a direct account of a past event ostensibly shaped as a recollection? Or a requiem for Fyodor's lepidopterist father?

This structural indeterminacy reflects the tentativeness of the meaning behind the scene. Fyodor's father had taught him entomology, and therefore the father's perception of the meadow (perhaps on a previous day—which would make the parenthetic remark about the accuracy in determining the season particularly important) could have been the same as his own. In fact, Fyodor's landscape may be an exact reproduction of his father's experience, just as Darwin's walk along a winding path in a Swiss forest may be a reenactment of Martin Edelweiss's last walk in a forest near the Soviet border. The possible clairvoyance is suggested by a childhood episode in which the sick Fyodor, in a kind of waking dream, perceived what later turned out to be the exact

---

[21]Minute sense perception—whether actual, as in the case of Proust's *madeleine*, or re-created—seems to cancel the intervening years. "I like to fold my magic carpet, after use, in such a way," writes Nabokov (*SM*, 139), "as to superimpose one part of the pattern upon another"—time disappears in the fold. When "fancy's rear-vision mirror" takes Nabokov from the New England winter to a cold winter of his childhood Russia, "the snow is real," and as he scoops up a handful, "sixty years crumble to glittering frost-dust between [his] fingers" (*SM*, 100). When this experience is related to the haunts of butterflies, its mystical coloration is enhanced: "This is ecstasy, and behind the ecstasy is something else, which is hard to explain. It is like a momentary vacuum into which rushes all that I love. A sense of oneness with sun and stone. A thrill of gratitude to whom it may concern—to the contrapuntal genius of human fate or to tender ghosts humoring a lucky mortal" (*SM*, 139).

motions of his mother buying him a once-coveted gift. Fyodor thinks that this "clairvoyant spell" is the only one he has ever experienced (*G*, 34–36), in fact, it is the only one whose correctness has been explicitly confirmed.

Likewise tentative is Fyodor's suggestion that his father was capable of mystical insight:

> In and around my father, around this clear and direct strength, there was something difficult to convey in words, a haze, a mystery, an enigmatic reserve which made itself felt sometimes more, sometimes less. It was as if this genuine, very genuine man possessed an aura of something still unknown but which was perhaps the most genuine of all. . . . I cannot track down a name for his secret, but I only know that that was the source of that special—neither glad nor morose, having indeed no connection with the outward appearance of human emotions—solitude to which neither my mother nor all the entomologists of the world had any admittance. And strange: perhaps the estate watchman, a crooked old man who had twice been singed by night lightning, . . . who frankly and with no fear or surprise considered that my father knew a thing or two that nobody else knew, was in his own way right. [*G*, 126–27]

Images and circumlocutions "something difficult to convey in words, a haze, a mystery, an enigmatic reserve"; "an aura of something still unknown"; "I cannot track down a name for his secret"—echo the tentative approaches to the "other dimension" in *Invitation to a Beheading*. This, according to Fyodor, is a genuine, no matter how elusive, realization of the unrealizable. Only a little less genuine, and therefore more transient, is the revolutionary ardor, the mysterious charisma of N. G. Chernyshevski: "That mysterious 'something' which Steklov talks about in spite of his Marxism, and which was extinguished in Siberia (although 'learning' and 'logic' and even 'implacability' remained), undoubtedly existed in Chernyshevski and manifested itself with unusual strength just before his banishment to Siberia. Magnetic and dangerous, it was this that frightened the government far more than any proclamations" (*G*, 276). It is therefore not surprising that some of the motifs in *Invitation to a Beheading*—an idealistic prisoner, a fortress, a treacherous fellow prisoner, an unfaithful wife—seem to be nightmare transformations of motifs from Chernyshevski's biography.

Like all the approximations of Mystery in *The Gift*, contact with transcendent reality finds a caricature of itself in the crude model of an optical illusion. The flat blue letters on the side of the yellow van are "shaded laterally with black paint: a dishonest attempt to climb into the next dimension" (G, 15). Significantly, the combination of blue and yellow recurs in the first chapter. The dress of Fyodor's landlady is pale yellow with bluish tulips; the wallpaper of his room has the same design, and Fyodor's imagination will have trouble transforming it into "a distant steppe" (G, 20). When he recollects the images that flowed before his eyes during his childhood illnesses, he includes among them what may be a telepathic glimpse (in similar colors) of his father, who was at that time away on one of his journeys: "[Mother] unhurriedly shakes the thermometer and slips it back into its case, looking at me as if not quite recognizing me, while my father rides his horse at a walk across a vernal plain all blue with irises" (G, 33).

It is in this rented room, some time after the publication of Fyodor's monograph, that his reunion with his father takes place in his dream (chapter 5). One of the most touching things about the dream is the sense of the father's approval. Since Fyodor refers to dreams as dividends from a mysterious transcendent capital of infinite happiness (see G, 176), one may wonder whether the dream could signify a moment of contact with the other dimension. In his waking life Fyodor fails to imagine this reunion, partly because of his horror at the thought of the possible changes in his father if, despite the rumors of his death, he has miraculously survived. His troubled remark in the monograph that it might have been better for Chernyshevski if instead of suffering a symbolic civil execution he had been really executed rather than compelled to go through long years of decline in exile, may thus bear a personal relevance. At the same time, part of his fear may be attributed to memories of his father's anger at Fyodor's childhood failings and to the anxiety that his father might disapprove of his idleness (cf. G, 126). The fear could be a muted expression of the vague doubts that sometimes threaten to undermine Fyodor's belief in his gift.

This surmise, suggested but not sanctioned by the text, brings into relief the psychological subtext that threatens to demystify what to Fyodor is most sacred. The passage that deals with the halo of mystery surrounding his father is written in the first person, explicitly denoting Fyodor's, rather than the author's, attempt to idealize the father, to turn him into a hero capable of walking with the gods. Yet Fyodor's is an unreliable point of view. At the beginning of chapter 2 he says that once his father, "climbing a hill after a storm, inadvertently entered the base of a rainbow—the rarest occurrence!—and found himself in colored air, in a play of light as if in paradise. He took one more step—and left paradise" (*G*, 89). Only in fairytales is it possible to enter the base of a rainbow: a rainbow recedes as one approaches it. What the passage contains is yet another model for realizing the unrealizable, and its striking inadequacy is a subversive comment on the other models constructed in the text.

Even without the evidence of this broader context, there are traces of repressed doubt in Fyodor's account of his father's mysteriousnes: "I have no means of explaining the impression his face made on me when I looked through his study window from outside and saw how, having suddenly forgotten his work, . . . he sat for a minute without moving. It sometimes seems to me nowadays that—who knows—he might go off on his journeys not so much to seek something as to flee something, and that on returning, he would realize that it was still with him, inside him, unriddable, inexhaustible" (*G*, 126–27).

The "something" that Konstantin Kirillovich would try to flee might be either the gnostical "itch of being" (*Gl*, xiii) or memories of some past experience. Here, the impossibility of Fyodor's consciously understanding ("probing") his father's contact with the "infinite consciousness" combines with the impossibility of retrieving information ("prying") about his early life. Thus, once again, the infinite threatens to collapse into the unfinished. Even the portrait of the estate watchman who believes in his master's mystical knowledge is shot through with irony: he has all by himself learned to catch and kill a butterfly without mangling it, yet he persists in his mistaken belief that butterflies grow in size from spring to summer (see *G*, 127).

IV

The tug-of-war between the motifs of the finite and the infinite, death and immortality, agnostic skepticism and mystical insight, continues throughout the novel. Neither religion nor atheism are of any help. "Religion," in Fyodor's rendering of the thoughts of the dying Alexander Yakovlevich, "has the same relation to man's heavenly condition that mathematics has to his earthly one: both the one and the other are merely the rules of the game. Belief in God and belief in numbers: local truth and the truth of location" (*G*, 321). Both mathematics and religion contain promises of the infinite, yet both are felt to be insufficient. The "mathematical universe expanding endlessly" appears in the delirium of Fyodor's childhood fevers and therefore "sheds an odd light on the macrocosmic theories of today's physicists" (G, 34), whereas the overpopulated "hereafter" of "popular faiths" (G, 322) repels Alexander Yakovlevich in his last illness. The very quest for the infinite is subjected to irony in the thoughts that Fyodor projects upon Chernyshevski's agony: "Somehow simpler. Somehow at once! One effort—and I'll understand all. The search for God: the longing of any hound for a master; give me a boss and I shall kneel at his enormous feet. All this is earthly. Father, headmaster, rector, president of the board, tsar, God. Numbers, numbers—and one wants so much to find the biggest number, so that all the rest may mean something and climb somewhere. No, that way you end up in padded dead ends—and everything ceases to be interesting"(G, 322–23).

The "padding" of the dead end (an asylum cell?) is a veiled reference to the mental illness that Alexander Yakovlevich developed after his son's suicide. Until the onset of his agony he seemed to be in touch with his son's spirit, saw his son entering the room or leaving it, disappearing through the door that led not to the adjoining bedroom but to a world which, in the literal translation of the Russian *potustoronnyi*, is "on the other side." The image of the door, which in *King, Queen, Knave* and *Look at the Harlequins!* is associated with the motif of "the Beyond," is also prominent in Fyodor's dream of the reunion with his father. Yet the door is always a part of "this" world: "I know that death in itself is in no way connected with the topography of the hereafter, for a door is merely the exit from the house and not a part of its surroundings, like a tree or a hill. One has to get out somehow, 'but I refuse to see in a door more than a hole, and a carpenter's job' (*Delalande, Discours sur les ombres*, p. 45)" (G, 321–22).[22]

Until "a given time" the door is closed, but, as the passage goes on to say, "air comes in through the cracks" (G, 322). These gusts of air from "the other side" are spontaneous gifts of memory, creative transformation, and quaint parapsychological phenomena. In *Speak, Memory*, continuing to use the imagery of gaps and doors, Nabokov refers to the phenomenon of synaesthesia, or *audition colorée*, as "leakings and drafts" (*SM*, 35).

[22]Delalande (literally, "of the faraway land") is the fictional philosopher responsible for the somewhat ambiguous epigraph to *Invitation to a Beheading:* "Comme un foux se croit Dieux, nous nous croyons mortels."

It is not clear whether the apparitions of Yasha's ghost are a reward or merely a symptom of his father's insanity. Moreover, it is not clear whether Yasha's ghost does indeed haunt anything but the narrative itself: "perhaps," thinks Fyodor, "perhaps, this is all wrong, perhaps he . . . is not imagining his dead son at all right now as I imagine him doing" (G, 47). Indeed, just before dying, Alexander Yakovlevich denies the very existence of anything on "the other side":

> The following day he died, but before that he had a moment of lucidity, complaining of pains and then saying (it was darkish in the room because of the lowered blinds): "What nonsense. Of course there is nothing afterwards." He sighed, listened to the trickling and drumming outside the window and repeated with extreme distinctnesss: "There is nothing. It is as clear as the fact that it is raining."
>
> And meanwhile outside the spring sun was playing on the roof tiles, the sky was dreamy and cloudless, the tenant upstairs was watering the flowers on the edge of her balcony, and the water trickled down with a drummy sound. [G, 324]

The fact that the sound of the rain turns out to be the sound of something else undermines the validity of the dying man's insight, even though his being wrong about the weather does not automatically mean that he is wrong about life after death. The ambivalence of the passage is further supported by an unexpected development: coming from a Jewish family that had converted to the Russian Orthodox church, Alexander Yakovlevich ultimately turns out to be a Lutheran—his beliefs do not seem to be stable. Besides, whereas almost the whole of the novel's material is filtered through the consciousness of Fyodor, the deathbed scene takes place on a day "following" the one on which Fyodor has been admitted to the then unconscious and silent Alexander Yakovlevich. The narrator deliberately neglects to inform us how the account of the scene reached Fyodor: here, as in *Pnin*, Nabokov endows the very structure of the narrative with cognitive unreliability in order to suggest that Fyodor may be projecting his own persistent but not unqualified skepticism on his dying friend.

With its tentative promise of reunions, the idea of life after death or of the infinity of consciousness is a great comfort to the bereaved— which is precisely why it is never allowed to turn into a sentimentally wish-fulfilling, bottom-line conclusion. Both Alexander Yakovlevich and Fyodor accept the grim possibility of annihilation along with the powerlessness of rational thought. This acceptance is akin to Yasha

Chernyshevski's attitude toward his own suicide: "that honesty of spirit that imparts to the most reckless act an almost everyday simplicity" (G, 59). In Fyodor's monograph the same quality is exhibited by N. G. Chernyshevski when he hastily yet undemonstratively swallows the papers that could incriminate his friends and behaves with unobtrusive matter-of-factness during his absurd civil execution.

The simplicity and the matter-of-factness might, however, be a cutain drawn over a "multifaceted thought" (G, 176). Fyodor's thought process balances between earnestness and self-refutation. Man is not what he eats; he is what he thinks—that is, the content of his consciousness. His worth depends not on birth and not on past achievement but on his sense of the present gift. Reminders of his own unique gift are summoned just in time to stifle Fyodor's incipient depression, yet having served their purpose, they are ironically refuted; like Rabelais's Pantagruel, Fyodor repeatedly changes his size:

> It would have been pleasant to look down from above on the gliding street ennobled by perspective, if it were not for the everlasting, chilly thought: there he is, a special, rare and as yet undescribed and unnamed variant of man, and he is occupied with God knows what, rushing from lesson to lesson, wasting his youth on a boring and empty task, on the mediocre teaching of foreign languages—when he has his own language, out of which he can make anything he likes—a midge, a mammoth, a thousand different clouds. What he should be really teaching was that mysterious and refined thing which he alone . . . knew how to teach: for example—multilevel thinking: you look at a person and you see him as clearly as if he were fashioned of glass and you were the glass blower, while at the same time without in the least impinging upon that clarity you notice some trifle on the side. . . . .Or: a piercing pity—for the tin box in a waste patch, for the cigarette card from the series National Costumes trampled in the mud, for the poor, stray word repeated by the kind-hearted, weak, loving creature who has just been scolded for nothing—for all the trash of life which by means of a momentary alchemic distillation—the "royal experiment"—is turned into something valuable and eternal. Or else: the constant feeling that our days here are only pocket money . . . and that somewhere is stocked the real wealth. . . . And at the same time he found it amusing to refute himself: all this was nonsense, the shadows of nonsense, presumptuous dreams. I am simply a poor young Russian selling the surplus from a gentleman's upbringing, while scribbling verses in my spare time, that's the total of my little immortality. But even this shade of multifaceted thought, this play of the mind with its own self, had no prospective pupils. [G, 175–76]

This wholesome control of one's flow of thoughts would later produce the miraculous resilience of Pnin.

The habit of self-refutation finds its reflection in Fyodor's aesthetics. "The spirit of parody always goes along with genuine poetry," as he comments on his poem about a toy clown (*G*, 24). The target of the parody is not only the work of precursors but also, and mainly, one's own endeavor. At the outset of his work on Chernyshevski's biography, Fyodor formulates his approach: "I want to keep everything as it were on the very brink of parody. You know those idiotic *'biographies romancées'* where Byron is coolly slipped a dream extracted from one of his own poems? And there must be on the other hand an abyss of seriousness, and I must make my way along this narrow ridge between my own truth and a caricature of it" (*G*, 212).

The "abyss of seriousness" finds a parody on itself in the strident tones of the novel *The Hoary Abyss* by Shirin. The element of parody, on the other hand, is kept from lapsing into tastelessness: upon reading about the tsar's police firing into people at the station of Bezdna, Fyodor resists the temptation "to regard the further fate of Russia's rulers as the run between the stations Bezdna (Bottomless) and Dno (Bottom)" (*G*, 215).

The technique of balancing between truth and parody, between the infinite and the incomplete, reflects the tentativeness of the novel's metaphysics. The excursus into the subject of doors and drafts is supposed to reflect the thoughts of the dying Alexander Yakovlevich and therefore ends on a note of tired resignation: "But all this is only symbols—symbols which become a burden to the mind as soon as it takes a close look at them" (*G*, 322). The novel itself seems to be likewise unsure about the metaphysical position suggested by its imagery. However, it deflects its skepticism from the existence of the hereafter toward human ability to solve the Mystery. In the words that Fyodor attributes to Koncheev, "the attempt to comprehend the world is reduced to an attempt to comprehend that which we ourselves have deliberately made incomprehensible. The absurdity at which searching thought arrives is only a natural, generic sign of its belonging to man, and striving to obtain an answer is the same as demanding of chicken broth that it begin to cluck" (*G*, 354). Thus within but a few lines even the seriousness of skepticism yields to a parody on itself.

" 'You will understand when you are big,' those are really the wisest words that I know" (*G*, 354). Second best are, perhaps, the grammar-book sentences used as the epigraph to *The Gift*: "An oak is a tree. A rose is a flower. A deer is an animal. A sparrow is a bird. Russia is our fatherland. Death is inevitable." The rhythmical repetition of the grammatical pattern distracts our notice from the fact that the last sentence is somewhat out of line: its complement is an adjective rather than a noun. When we recognize this anomaly, it calls our attention to the fact that within the pattern of the novel's motifs, this statement is also less obvious than the preceding ones. Each of the sentences of the epigraph, then, seems to be a fragment of a shadow syllogism whose conclusion may vary from an adage suitable for "writing exercises" to the "absolute formula" (G, 221), which, as a paramathematical phenomenon, can only be a rule of the game.

10

Bend Sinister:
The "Inner" Problem

He that hath Wife and Children, hath given Hostages to Fortune.
                    Francis Bacon, "Of Marriage and Single Life"

The inmates of my cottage, all at rest,
Have left me to that solitude, which suits
Abstruser musings: save that at my side
My cradled infant slumbers peacefully.
                    . . . . . .
My babe so beautiful! it thrills my heart
With tender gladness, thus to look at thee,
And think that thou shalt learn far other lore,
And in far other scenes!
                    Samuel Taylor Coleridge, "Frost at Midnight"

Bend Sinister was written five or six years after Nabokov's immigration to the United States in 1940; it was published in 1947. In the 1963 foreword, Nabokov notes that it was composed "at a particularly cloudless and vigorous period" of his life, yet he calls its main characters his "whims and megrims" (*BS*, v, viii). The reference to "whims" should remind the reader of the deliberate overstatement with which Emerson proclaimed his wish to write *Whim* "on the lintels of the doorpost."[1] "Megrims" is an ironic understatement: the time is winter and spring 1945–46; reports of the scale of recent disasters are filtering across the Atlantic. "Much as one might want to hide in one's little ivory tower," Nabokov will write to his sister in June 1946, "there are things that torment too deeply, e.g., the German vilenesses, the burning of children in ovens,—children as funny and as

---

[1]Emerson, "Self-Reliance," in *The Complete Works,* 2:51.

178   Nabokov

strongly loved as our children"(PS, 41; my translation).[2]

It is not surprising that the tormented Adam Krug takes a long time to separate from the fictionalized extension of his creator.[3] The houses that Krug sees through the hospital window in chapter 1 are those seen through the window of the "novelist's" apartment in his dactylic "comparative paradise" (BS, 241) of the last chapter. Krug's thoughts about time in chapter 2 seem to be so close to "the novelist's" own thoughts that by the middle of the chapter the novelist has to remind the reader that the protagonist ("Krug—for it was still he—": BS, 13) has already assumed a discrete identity of his own.

The world into which this Adam has been cast is a dystopia. Because of his wife's surgery and death, Krug has failed to notice the frightening shape that the regime in his country has taken after a very recent revolution. The power has been seized by Krug's former classmate Paduk, alias "the Toad" (the Shakespearean "paddock"). In their schooldays Krug had bullied Paduk, sat on his face, or ignored him. Now Paduk wishes to force Krug, a world famous philosopher, to collaborate with the regime. He can no longer be ignored; he arrests Krug's friends, surrounds him with spies, and finally tries to take advantage of Krug's love for his eight-year-old son David. Upon capture, the child is not held hostage in safety but sent, by mistake, to an institution for juvenile delinquents, where he is murdered—a human sacrifice in a grisly psychological experiment. Krug loses his sanity and his life the day after he learns about his son's fate.

One of the rejected titles for Bend Sinister was "A Person from Porlock," a reference to Coleridge's famous story of having composed a long poem in his sleep; on awakening the poet started transcribing it on paper but was interrupted by a person on business from Porlock; afterward, he found he had forgotten the rest of the poem, and so "Kubla Khan" remained unfinished.

The intrusion of a person from Porlock is reenacted at the end of Bend Sinister. After a long period of grieving for his wife, Krug feels a reawakening of inspiration. He bids his son goodnight in order to pursue his "abstruser musings" but is interrupted by the lascivous maid Mariette; the lovemaking is, in its turn, interrupted by the po-

[2]Nabokov's younger brother Sergei was killed in a Nazi camp.
[3]The subtle links between the text of Bend Sinister and Nabokov's biography (and autobiography) are discussed, brilliantly if not always convincingly, in David I. Sheidlower, "Reading Between the Lines and the Squares," Modern Fiction Studies, 25 (1979), 413–25.

lice, who come to arrest Krug and his son; Krug's swan-song essay remains unwritten.

On a different level, however, the role of the person from Porlock is played not by the intruding characters but by what Nabokov calls "an anthropomorphic deity impersonated by me"(*BS*, xii). It is the omnipotent novelist who, time and again, cancels the illusion of reality or signals his own presence to Krug and the reader[4]; in the end he unambiguously assumes the responsibility for the *coup de grâce* madness of the protagonist: "It was at that moment, just after Krug had fallen through the bottom of a confused dream and sat up on the straw with a gasp—and just before his reality, his remembered hideous misfortune could pounce upon him—it was then that I felt a pang of pity for Adam and slid towards him along an inclined beam of pale light— causing instantaneous madness, but at least saving him from the senseless agony of his logical fate"(*BS*, 233). The avatar of the person from Porlock in *Bend Sinister* thus forestalls Krug's memories of what is, in fact, Nabokov's own nightmare fantasy.

Why, then, did Nabokov reject a title so suitable as "A Person from Porlock"? Perhaps because it would have deemphasized the novel's concern with Krug's love for his son and wife and with the torment that this love causes him (see *BS*, 187-88: "what agony . . ."), especially when the attachment to the child proves to be the "handle" by means of which Paduk can get hold of Krug: in addition to bearing the heraldic meaning of "the wrong turn taken by life" (*BS*, vi), "Bend Sinister" also stands for the curvature of this handle—*Krug* being not only the Russian for "circle" but also the German for "pitcher ."[5]

On his way to an interview with Paduk, Krug is shown a room where several physicians are listening to the beating of Paduk's heart transmitted through the radio: "Thump-ah, thump-ah, thump-ah, went the machine, and every now and then there was an additional systole, causing a slight break in the rhythm" (*BS*, 142). The scene is a parodistic realization of the central metaphor of the novel, the beating

---

[4]The episodes in which Nabokov reminds us of the fictionality of the tale are discussed in e.g., Richard F. Patteson, "Nabokov's *Bend Sinister*: The Narrator as God," *Studies in American Fiction*, 5 (1977), 241–53. See also Johnson, *Worlds in Regression*, pp. 190–93.

[5]This interpetation of the title was first suggested in Hyman, "The Handle," pp. 60–71. For Nabokov's approving response, see *SO*, 287. The significance of Krug's and other names and words in *Bend Sinister* is discussed in Johnson, *Worlds in Regression*, pp. 195–202.

of a heart—not that of Paduk but that of Adam Krug. "The main theme of *Bend Sinister*," says Nabokov in the foreword, "is the beating of Krug's loving heart, the torture an intense tenderness is subjected to—and it is for the sake of the pages about David and his father that the book was written and should be read." Two other themes, he continues, "accompany the main one: the theme of dim-brained brutality which thwarts its own purpose by destroying the right child and keeping the wrong one; and the theme of Krug's blessed madness when he suddenly perceives the simple reality of things and knows but cannot express in the words of his world that he and his son and his wife and everybody else are merely my whims and megrims"(*BS*, viii). Though the development of these two themes occupies a much larger textual surface space, it is the main theme—the agony of Krug's love for Olga and David, the ebb and flow of his emotions, the fluctuations of his attention and intensity—that forms the organizing principle of the novel and accounts for its peculiar tonal iridescence. The two "accompanying themes" are subordinated to this central concern.

I

The main theme is seldom presented directly; its effect might have been shattering for both the novelist and the reader. The "beating of Krug's loving heart" is signaled at very frequent intervals, but it is only in repeated reading that one can identify these signals and understand their meaning.

The narrative abounds in metaphorical references to the somewhat uneven systole-diastole rhythm of experience: the movement of a nurse's face and her speech, inaudible to the grief-stricken Krug, are described as "pulsation"(*BS*, 5); trees are "pulsating rhythmically with countless fireflies" in a remote jungle (*BS*, 79); "the individual atom . . . pulsates "(*BS*, 158); the hospital in which Olga died stands beyond old tenement houses "unseen but throbbingly present"(*BS*, 189); "frames of reference pulsate with Fitz-Gerald contractions"(*BS*, 172); and among the "nocturnal sounds" of a great prison one can distinguish "the heartbeats of younger men noiselessly digging an underground passage to freedom and recapture"(*BS*, 233). Krug's own heart "pounds" when he is frantically looking for David around a provincial police station (*BS*, 103) and "thumps" when he is trying to suppress his desire for Mariette (*BS*, 196).

The changes in the texture of *Bend Sinister* parallel the systole-diastole-pause rhythm. The narrative "pulsates" as passages conveying or signaling Krug's emotions (systole) alternate with those recording the thoughts or events that temporarily divert him (diastole) and those supplying background information and thus effecting "camera-stopping" breaks (pause) in the represented time.[6]

One of the clearest examples of a violent systole is the description of Krug's panic on losing sight of David near the police station:

> "I want my little boy," said Krug (another Krug, horribly handicapped by a spasm in the throat and a pounding heart). . . . I must not lose my head, thought Adam the Ninth—for by now there were quite a number of these serial Krugs: turning this way and that like the baffled buffeted seeker in a game of blindman's buff: battering with imaginary fists a cardboard police station to pulp; running through nightmare tunnels; half-hiding together with Olga behind a tree to watch David warily tiptoe around another, his whole body ready for a little shiver of glee; searching an intricate dungeon where, somewhere, a shrieking child was being tortured by experienced hands; hugging the boots of a uniformed brute; strangling the brute amid a chaos of overturned furniture; finding a small skeleton in a dark cellar.
>
> At this point it may be mentioned that David wore on the fourth finger of his left hand a child's enamelled ring. [*BS*, 103–4]

The sequence of parallel constructions reenacts the stages of the spasm: fright yields to violence, then to hope (at the thought of the happy endings in games of hide-and-seek), then to unmitigated horror. An abyss opens in the last sentence of the passage, which is, ironically, couched in dry academic language: it is left for the reader to imagine what makes Krug recollect David's ring, another circle, "at this point."

Krug's unconventional acts, like his refusal to keep his dead wife's comb and other mementos, show that his pain has not yet yielded to what Emily Dickinson called "a formal feeling." Systoles are signaled by his spasmodic weeping on the night of Olga's death and his out-bursts of helpless violence on the night of David's ordeal. A systole is also registered by a metaphoric allusion to Krug's "heart" following

---

[6]Robert Alter uses the "camera-stopping" metaphor to describe Fielding's technique of freezing the action of a scene into a tableau and providing the narrative commentary in lieu of a legend; see *Fielding and the Nature of the Novel* (Cambridge, Mass., 1968), p. 194. The space allotted to this commentary need not correspond to the represented time that is supposed to elapse between the interruption and the resumption of the scene.

the description of his bulky physical presence (pause) at Professor Azureus's emergency meeting (diastole):

> Under this visible surface, a silk shirt enveloped his robust torso and tired hips. . . . Under this was the warm white skin. Out of the dark an ant trail, a narrow capillary caravan, went up the middle of his abdomen to end at the brink of his navel; and a blacker and denser growth was spread-eagled upon his chest.
> Under this was a dead wife and a sleeping child. [*BS*, 47]

Among the devices that signal the systoles of the text are *multilingual word games*. Russian words occur at moments replete with the most intimate emotion.[7] Thus Krug explodes with "*Stoy, chort* [Stop, curse you]" (*BS*, 17) when a farcical grocer's gyrations on the bridge remind him of his child.

The multilingual games are frequently accompanied by paronomastic translations that are probably best described as cases of "tralatition," which, according to an eccentric writer in *Transparent Things*, is "a perfectly respectable synonym of the word 'metaphor ' " (*TT*, 69). The play of the intellect that tralatitions represent enters into a tug-of-war with the emotion whose presence they signal and whose intensity they seek to reduce. They also compensate for catachretic gaps: like the synaesthetic devices of *Invitation to a Beheading*, they are among the means of "effing the ineffable." Frequently combined with cross-referential recurrent imagery, they produce branching rhetorical effects. For example, when Krug, in response to Maximov's warnings, irresponsibly reduces political reality to word play, the word play immediately conjures up another reality, that of his inner world: "*Yer un dah* [stuff and nonsense]," he says. "[Paduk] will go on licking my hand in the dark. I am invulnerable. Invulnerable—the rumbling sea wave [*volna*] rolling the rabble of pebbles as it recedes. Nothing can happen to Krug the Rock"(*BS*, 89). The "average reality," the "here and now" (*hier und da* in German) is "stuff and nonsense" (*yerunda* in Russian) for the flippant Krug. Yet as the multilingual punning continues, the Russian ghost word *volna* ("wave") is heard in "in-vulnerable": a wave of Krug's emotion that belies his invulnerability is ominously followed by the rolling "r" in the "rabble of pebbles": the

[7]Some aspects of the use of non-English words are discussed in Antonina Filonov Gove, "Multilingualism and Ranges of Tone in Nabokov's *Bend Sinister*," *Slavic Review*, 32 (1973), 79–90.

"grating roar" of Matthew Arnold's "Dover Beach." In the kind of experiment in group dynamics during which David will be killed, the torture starts with a pebble being spat into a child's credulously opened mouth (see *BS*, 219).

In the capacity of defense mechanisms ("transfer" is another "respectable synonym" for metaphor), tralatitions are the only possible way of describing Krug's reaction to the sight of his murdered child:

> *Tut pocherk zhizni stanovitsa kraĭne nerazborchivym* [here the long hand of life becomes extremely illegible]. *Ochevidtzy, sredi kotorykh byl i evo vnutrenniĭ sogliadataĭ* [witnesses among whom was his own something or other ("inner spy?" "private detective?" The sense is not at all clear)] *potom govorili* [afterwards said] *shto evo prishlos' sviazat'* [that he had to be tied]. *Mezhdu tem* [among the themes? (Perhaps: among the subjects of his dreamlike state)] *Kristalsen, nevozmutimo dymia sigaroĭ* [Crystalsen calmly smoking his cigar], *sobral ves' shtat v aktovom zale* [called a meeting of the whole staff in the assembly hall]. [*BS*, 225]

The conglomerate of transliteration, translation, and tralatition is a means of rendering "life out of focus"—but more about that later. *Soglyadatai* ("inner spy," "private detective") alludes to Nabokov's short novel *The Eye (Soglyadatai)*. The "eye" of that novel is akin to the inner "double" of Krug, the observing part of the self that maintains a distance from the acting, feeling, and erring "I" and that probably staves off Krug's insanity.

Mezhdu tem is the Russian for "meanwhile." Yet the word *tem*, apart from being the singular instrumental case of *to* ("that")—the meaning in which it is used in the idiom above—is also the plural genitive of *tema* ("theme"). The tralatition "between themes" echoes the recurrent motifs of *The Eye* and *Invitation to a Beheading*. In *The Eye* the protagonist convinces himself that all the events of his life following what he deems a successful suicide attempt are but dreamlike images evoked by his fancy. In *Invitation to a Beheading* the author wishes to convince the protagonist that all his oppressors are, in the language of *Bend Sinister*, his "whims and megrims." The sense of unreality (the "dreamlike state") is another defense mechanism that staves off Krug's insanity until the morning in prison when insanity proves to be the only possible defense against pain.

One should add that the name of the cool Crystalsen (*Kristalsen* in the Russian transliteration) evokes associations with *Kristallnacht*, the pogrom of 1938 that gave the first unambiguous signal for massive persecution of the Jews in Nazi Germany.

Whereas tralatitions signal Krug's systoles and reduce their intensity for both Krug and the reader, other devices register the pain against which Krug has no ready defense. These are *"semantic transparencies yielding layers of receding or welling sense"* (*BS*, x; my italics): that is, references to fleeting memories, conscious thoughts, and dream images of Olga, unwittingly tactless references to her made by Beuret, contact with or memory of objects associated with her. "Sense wells," for instance, when in Peter Quist's shop Krug notices a plate representing an ocellated hawk moth (see *BS*, 181): it is with such a moth in her carefully cupped hands that Olga seems to have first appeared to Krug, and it is in the shape of this moth that she knocks at "Nabokov's" window on the last page of the novel.

In a first reading we cannot register the flow and ebb of Krug's emotions precisely because it is impossible to recognize some of the textual details as referring to Olga. For example, when Krug accuses police agents of having stolen Ember's porcelain owl, we do not know that Olga bought this owl for Ember and, as it turns out later, never gave it to him. Repeated reading also makes it clear that Krug's pain is egotistic: it dulls his consciousness of Ember's plight. Ember is being arrested and will probably suffer mistreatment as a result of Krug's rudeness to the captors. One begins to understand the difference between Krug's imagining the word "loyalty" as "a golden fork lying in the sun on a smooth spread of pale yellow silk" (*BS*, 87) and Maximov's less sophisticated but more upright rejection of any but the dictionary meaning of this word.

Semantic trasparencies *register* rather than *render* moments of acute pain. Less mediated expressions of emotion are cautiously infrequent in *Bend Sinister*—and not only because "Nabokov" cannot "afford to suffer" with his character. The evasion is a symptom of the skepticism that *Bend Sinister* has carried over from "Ultima Thule": consciousness is as mysterious as outer space and transcendent reality. Courting recalcitrant inspiration, Krug wonders "what is more important to solve: the 'outer' problem (space, time, matter, the unknown without) or the 'inner' one (life, thought, love, the unknown within) or again their point of contact (death)"; and the author seems to join him in adding, self-referentially, "for we agree, do we not, that problems *as* problems do exist even if the world be something made of nothing within nothing made of something"*(BS*, 173–74).

As Nabokov stated in "Anniversary Notes," *Bend Sinister* and *Invitation to a Beheading* are "bookends" between which all his other novels "tightly huddle"*(SO, 287). Invitation* deals with the "outer" problem: since human commitments fail Cincinnatus, he is free to pursue his quest of "nameless existence, intangible substance"*(IB, 26),* defy the limitations of the material world into which he is cast,[8] and break through the weary matter to the "unknown without." *Bend Sinister* deals rather with the "inner problem," which is also, however, a problem of "nameless existence": both Nabokov and his "favorite character" Krug *(BS, 151)* recognize the impossibility of tackling the mystery of consciousness through ready-made lexical tools, and so both content themselves with model approximations: "In this preliminary report on infinite consciousness a certain scumbling of the essential outline is unavoidable. We have to discuss sight without being able to see. The knowledge we may acquire in the course of such a discussion will necessarily stand in the same relation to the truth as the black peacock spot produced intraoptically by pressure on the palpebra does in regard to a garden path brindled with genuine sunlight"*(BS, 192).* The theatrical framework over whose ruins the liberated prisoner of *Invitation to a Beheading* steps on the way toward "beings akin to him" *(IB, 223)* is an apt model for his gnostical monster world. No such model is available for approximating the "inner" problem, the problem of authentic feeling for another human being.

The narrative of *Bend Sinister* comes closest to the verbal expression of the inexpressible when Krug is shown falling asleep in prison on the day of his son's death. His love for David and an admixture of the feeling of guilt are then rendered through the use of synaesthetic imagery and lyrical undulations:

All he felt was a slow sinking, a concentration of darkness and tenderness, a gradual growth of sweet warmth. His head and Olga's head, cheek to cheek, two heads held together by a pair of small experimenting hands which stretched up from a dim bed, were (or was—for the two heads formed one) going down, down, down towards a third point, towards a silently laughing face. There was a soft chuckle just as his and her lips reached the child's cool brow and hot cheek, but the descent did not stop there and Krug continued to sink into the heart-rending softness, into the black dazzling depths of a belated but—never mind—eternal caress. *[BS, 232]*

[8]See also Hyman, "The Handle," pp. 63–64.

The barriers of identity break down in death, and the infinite consciousness is suffused with tenderness. The passage transforms the three balls of Krug's schooldays, the three shapes in the pattern of the stone parapet, and the three birthmarks on David's face into three heads[9]—of the child and of the parents—converging in love and death. The pattern of three is thus one of the "semantic transparencies" that signal the systoles of the text.

II

The relative inconspicuousness of the text's systoles in a first reading is also the result of the novelist's use of perspective, particularly the illusion of three-dimensionality, to monitor the attention of the reader. Unlike the settings of Kafka's novels or that of *Invitation to a Beheading*, the dystopic setting of *Bend Sinister* possesses spatial depth, and its main characters are endowed with a strong physical presence.

The latter effect is a response to a challenge: Nabokov was facing a new audience and could not rely on characters who would be "transparent to the eye of the era"*(KQK*, viii).[10] *Invitation to a Beheading* emphasized the elusive, spiritual, transparent quality of Cincinnatus; *Bend Sinister*, in which physical death plays a far more prominent part, emphasizes the sense of the main characters' presence (or absence) in the flesh, infusing their physical bulk with very physical, mortal, vulnerable tenderness. Krug, Olga, David, and even Ember and Mariette may still be Nabokov's "galley slaves" but unlike the characters of *Sebastian Knight* they are no longer ephemeral "methods of composition."

Conversely, a method of composition is actually personified and turned into a minor character, an obscure dissident student by the name of Phokus: he is referred to twice (see *BS*, 95, 177). In Russian, *focus* has not only the familiar optical meaning but also the related meaning of "magic trick," to which several of Nabokov's recurrent

[9]For a detailed analysis of these images and their significance, see Susan Fromberg Schaeffer, "*Bend Sinister* and the Novelist as Anthropomorphic Deity," *Centennial Review*, 17 (1973), 128–35.

[10]For more on this subject, see my "Between Allusion and Coincidence: Nabokov, Dickens, and Others," *HSLA*, 12 (1984), 188–92.

techniques bear an affinity; for instance, his chains of homogeneous parts of long sentences often function like a conjuror's patter, making one crucial detail inconspicuous (the stuffed squirrel in *Pnin*, or the sanitary pads that Humbert buys for Dolly after their first night together). The prominent technique of *Bend Sinister* can be traced to the snapshot-viewing episode in *Mary*: it consists of a selective focusing (or phokusing) of the reader's attention. "Phokus" is a method of putting things together (composing) in such a way to as to achieve (an) aesthetic distance through remoteness in space.

The world of *Bend Sinister* is presented visually with the selective focus of the camera eye.[11] The selectiveness produces an impression of spatial depth; this becomes particularly obvious if one compares the exhaustively described cell in *Invitation to a Beheading* with Ember's bedroom, which is never described, in *Bend Sinister*. The workings of Paduk's regime—exemplified in the behavior of the guards on the bridge, the periodical arrivals of Linda Bachofen, the slips of Peter Quist's tongue—burst into the foreground from the background of the fictional world with growing frequency as the spiderweb closes in on Krug. Presented scenically, these grotesque intrusions occupy much more narrative space than Krug's feelings. The feelings, being authentic, "real," defiant of verbal expression, are treated with wary indirectness.

The philosopher Krug is much less capable of "multilevel thinking" (*G*, 175) than the artist Godunov-Cherdyntsev. Like Pnin, he controls his attention by channeling it to intellectual matters and disconnecting it from the emotional substratum. The record of his experience, therefore, contains extensive passages of discourse that are free not only from roller-coaster plunges into emotion but even from the more gentle "semantic transparencies." In one of the most brilliant episodes of the novel the narrator joins forces with Krug's friend Ember in helping Krug "phokus" his attention away from his grief. This is the essence of the Nabokovian variety of "foregrounding."[12] Whereas in Gogol

---

[11]Discussing perspective in *Bend Sinister* in terms of the camera eye is particularly appropriate because, like *Laughter in the Dark*, this novel is permeated with film imagery; see Beverly Gray Bienstock, "Focus Pocus: Film Imagery in *Bend Sinister*," in Rivers and Nicol, *Fifth Arc*, pp. 125–38. On the relationship between cinema and Nabokov's novels, see Appel, *Nabokov's Dark Cinema*.

[12]"Foregrounding" is the emphasis on the narrative itself rather than on the narrated events. Western criticism has taken over this term from Ejkhenbaum's work on Gogol, "Kak sdelana 'Shinel' ' Gogolia," and "Illiuziya Skaza."

the manner of presentation may compete with the content for the reader's attention, here one component of the content (the play of the intellect) is moved to the fore so that it might keep another (the potentially devastating emotion) out of sight. Whatever gets said in the episode is an alibi for not talking about Olga or dwelling on other regions fraught with "emotional dangers":

> Krug will not speak of her, will not even inquire about her ashes; and Ember, who feels the shame of death too, does not know what to say. . . . Krug, semi-intentionally, keeps out of reach. He is a difficult person. Describe the bedroom. Allude to Ember's bright brown eyes. Hot punch and a touch of fever. His strong shining blue-veined nose and the bracelet on his hairy wrist. Say something. Ask about David. Relate the horror of those rehearsals.
>
> "David is also laid up with a cold [*ist auk beterkeltet*] but that is not why we had to come back [*zueruk*]. What [*shto bish*] were you saying about these rehearsals [*repetitia*]?"
>
> Ember gratefully adopts the subject selected. He might have asked: "why then?" He will learn the reason a little later. Vaguely he perceives emotional dangers in that dim region. So he prefers to talk shop. Last chance of describing the bedroom.
>
> Too late. Ember gushes. He exaggerates his own gushing manner.
> [*BS*, 106–7]

The tralatition *repetitia* (the Russian for "a rehearsal") is here used for its connotation of "repeating." It foreshadows the repetition of the arrests of Krug's friends. *Shto bish,* an old-fashioned Russian familiar way of inquiring about something that has been mentioned, sounds like a tribute to the Maximovs, the most recognizably Russian of the novel's characters, who have already been arrested and are to be shortly followed by Ember and Hedron.

The bits of advice to "describe the bedroom," "allude to Ember's bright brown eyes," and the like, stand for the narrator's self-conscious search for ways to fill in pauses in the characters' conversation. The narrator likewise seems to be groping for an excuse not to talk about the things that really matter. The sentences "Say something. Ask about David. Relate the horror of those rehearsals" render the thoughts of Ember, thoughts running in the same roundabout channel as the narrator's own. Just as Krug points Ember in the safest direction by asking about his *Hamlet* rehearsals, so Ember, by readily "gushing" forth, seems to provide such a direction for the narrator. The narrator's missing his "last chance to describe the bedroom" has a double effect: on the one hand it divides (phokuses) the reader's attention between the painful scene (the undercurrent of pain is conveyed through spasmodically short sentences and "tralatitions") and the author's artistic choices in rendering it; on the other hand, it suggests that the choices are dictated by what takes place independently of the narrator, in a reality that has taken over and escaped control.

As if to relinquish his creative prerogative, the narrator bestows his ingeniousness, wit, and intellectual brilliance on Ember, whose para-Shakespearean exercise in the main part of the scene enters into competition with the library chapter of Joyce's *Ulysses* and also in a sense with its "Oxen-in-the-Sun" chapter, in which a stylistic exercise occupies the representational time spanning a difficult childbirth. Ember's language game, however, is completely free from the element of callousness that Joyce's text neglects to avoid; it is played out of sympathy, and its aim is to rechannel the flow of psychic energy that would otherwise have fueled Krug's grief.

Thus, the reason Krug's emotional fluctuations seem to occupy comparatively little space in the narrative is that they mainly take place not in the foreground but in the third dimension of the novel, along the depth axis. The method of composition (Phokus) of *Bend Sinister* offers marked contrast to that of *Invitation to a Beheading*, in which this third dimension—unlike the metaphysical fourth one—does not exist. As soon as the characters exit from the foreground of *Invitation,* they cease to exist. One cannot imagine the presence of any parts of the fictional world away from the limelight; there is nothing behind the stage except, perhaps, the theatrical props. Cincinnatus is the subject of experience rather than a fully realized character. Moreover, whereas conventional novels about political prisoners usually create an almost paranoid sense of conspiracy or of the impersonal workings of the bureaucratic machine behind the hero's back, nothing of this kind goes on behind the back of Cincinnatus. All the characters of whom Cincinnatus inquires the date of his execution are strangely disconcerted; not only do they have no answer, but the question itself is illegitimate because, there being no fictional background, no action behind the coulisses, the date of the execution is determined only by the involute author and not by somebody within the fictional world.

In *Invitation to a Beheading* very few scenes imply more information than they present. One that does so is the scene in which the prison director follows the librarian out of the cell and returns carrying the librarian's scarf and nursing a broken fingernail; M'sieur Pierre tactfully pretends that nothing has happened, and the reader is invited to infer that the director has tortured the librarian behind the stage. This is exactly the kind of thing that keeps happening in the world of *Bend Sinister*, where bloodstained shoes or cufflinks in the street are traces of police brutality. Martin Edelweiss is never shot in the world of *Glory*, and Cincinnatus C. is never beheaded in the world of *Invitation to a Beheading*; the former novel cancels the character and the latter cancels the setting just in time to sabotage the protagonist's "logical fate"(*BS*, 233). By contrast, there is no doubt that David Krug is tortured to death in the world of *Bend Sinister*—not in the foreground but, mercifully, in the background of the action, between two paragraphs or, to continue Nabokov's bilingual word play, "between themes." Political prisoners are arrested, tortured, and killed outside the range of the camera eye; spies hover on the fringes of the picture; and Krug's heart contracts at the thought of his wife and son in the emotional background of the text.

III

One of Nabokov's two "accompanying themes" in *Bend Sinister* is that of the "dim-brained brutality which thwarts its own purpose by destroying the right child and keeping the wrong one." What is the relationship between this theme and the main theme of the novel?

The "dim-brained" inexperience of Paduk's regime—its trial-and-error tactics—provides the interval of time necessary for a full display of Krug's character, his grief, his recklessness, his concern for his child and Coleridgean wish to see him in "far other scenes," his growing uneasiness, the dormancy and the awakening of inspiration. In chapter 2, Krug is caught between the obtuse illiterate soldiers on one side of the bridge and the cheerful para-academic lovers of bureaucracy on the other side—the sluggish, potentially violent *mouzhiks* and sleek careerist Nazis? This is a *mise-en-abîme* episode: suspended between legal brutality and its bungled implementation, Krug has ample time to oscillate between emotion and intellect (grief for Olga and attempts to cope with it), never completely bridging the gap.

Krug represses his emotions by maintaining a Schopenhauerian split between his active-feeling and passive-observing selves[13] and by iden-

---

[13]See Schopenhauer, *The World as Will and Representation*, 1:85.

tifying with the latter, the one (in the language of "Frost at Midnight")
that makes "a toy of thought":

> As usual he discriminated between the throbbing one and the one that
> looked on: looked on with concern, with sympathy, with a sigh, or with
> bland surprise. This was the last stronghold of the dualism he abhorred.
> The square root of I is I. Footnotes, forget-me-nots. The stranger quietly
> watching the torrents of local grief from an abstract bank. A familiar
> figure, albeit anonymous and aloof. He saw me crying when I was ten
> and led me to a looking glass in an unused room . . . so that I might
> study my dissolving face. He has listened to me with raised eyebrows
> when I said things which I had no business to say. In every mask I tried
> on, there were slits for his eyes. Even at the very moment when I was
> rocked by the convulsion men value most. My savior. My witness.
> [*BS*, 7]

This division of personality (in a sense a model of the relationship
between Krug and his creator) temporarily allays Krug's heartache, yet
it ultimately turns out to be his *hubris*. Krug tragically fails to achieve
that unity of emotion and thought which Coleridge celebrates at the
end of "Frost at Midnight." Reenacting the pulsation of his heart, he
oscillates from the throbbing to the observing man and dissociates
himself from the one as he identifies with the other. This is the essence
of the dualism that he "abhors." His intellect is not attuned to his
emotions and fails to foresee a possible link between the child, the
object of his tenderness, and the web woven around him by Paduk. To
the reader, however, the link is made clear by the "tralatition" in
Paduk's speech, which Krug hears on the radio: "The most popular
photograph which appeared in *all* capitalist newspapers of that period
was a picture of two rare butterflies glittering *vsemi tzvetami radugi*
[with all the hues of the rainbow]. But not a word about the strike of
the textile workers!"(*BS*, 167).

In Nabokov's work, especially in *Lolita* and *The Gift*, the motif of
the rainbow is associated with children and parent-child relationships.
Raduga moya ("my rainbow")—instead of the more common Russian
radost' moya) ("my joy")—are Krug's tender words of address to his
son. Krug fails to read Paduk's random dart as a danger signal, just as
in a later episode he does not see the meaning of David's stepping into
a puddle:

> "Didn't you have any rubbers?"
> "Uh-uh."

"Then give me your hand. And if you walk into a puddle but once..."

"And if I do it by chance [*nechaianno*]?"

"I shall see to that. Come, *raduga moya* [my rainbow], give me your hand and let us be moving."

"Billy brought a bone today. Gee whizz—some bone. I want to bring one, too."

"Is it the dark Billy or the little fellow with the glasses?"

"The glasses. He said my mother was dead. Look, look, a woman chimney sweep."

(These had recently appeared owing to some obscure shift or rift or sift or drift in the economics of the State—and much to the delight of the children.) Krug was silent. David went on talking.

"*That* was your fault, not mine. My left shoe is full of water, Daddy!"

"Yes."

"My left shoe is full of water."

"Yes. I'm sorry. Let's walk a little faster. What did you answer?"

"When?"

"When Billy said that stupid thing about your mother." [*BS*, 160–61]

The image of a puddle, part of both a landscape and an acoustic "inscape," occurs in the first sentence of the novel. The puddle looks like "a fancy footprint filled to the brim with quicksilver; like a spatulate hole through which you can see the nether sky"(*BS*, 1). The "nether sky" is both the reflection of the sky in Cambridge, Massachusetts—the "comparative paradise" where the novel is being written—and the sky of the nether world into which Krug is about to be cast.[14] In the last paragraph of the novel, after the nether (never?) world has been canceled, "Nabokov" catches one more glimpse of this puddle, "the one Krug had somehow perceived through the layer of his own life" (*BS*, 241). The puddle is thus a kind of gateway from Krug's world to that of the novelist. Therefore, David's stepping into the puddle foreshadows his death (his passage to another world?) at the end of the novel.[15]

Significantly, it is Krug himself who, having lost his equanimity on hearing the allusion to Olga's death, leads David into a puddle. "*That* was your fault, not mine," says the boy: like most of Nabokov's

[14]More about the "nether sky" in Toker, "Between Allusion and Coincidence," 184–86.

[15]See also Johnson's discussion of the image of the puddle, *Worlds in Regression*, pp. 194–96.

doomed characters (including even the policeman Mac, who quite inexplicably hits upon Mariette's nickname; see *BS*, 207), he seems to be given a prophetic glimpse of his creator's mind. Indeed, at a crucial moment Krug is unable to reason with the people who come to arrest him. His violently emotional active self takes over; the controlling observing self is suppressed; and his irrational behavior largely leads to the "mistake" that his captors make with David. David himself, on the other hand, is heard "trying to reason with his impossible visitors" (*BS*, 201). Krug fails to follow his example, just as he has failed to perceive the ominous significance in the cryptographic recurrences of the pattern of three, of the shoe-shaped puddles, of stains that imitate the form of Lake Malheur, and other danger signals sent him by the "anthropomorphic deity" impersonated by "Nabokov."[16]

More surprisingly, for a long time Krug takes no heed of Maximov's warnings, of his friends' arrests, of the badly trained spies around him, of Mariette's phone calls, and the oddities in the behavior of Peter Quist (who blushes on realizing that David is the handle by which the regime can get hold of Krug). The episodes that thus describe the workings of Paduk's regime effect the "diastoles" of the text: Krug is unable to see the connection between the sinister bend of politics and his private world, his *"mirok"*[17] (*BS*, 8); therefore the encounters with Paduk and his agents divert him not only from his inner life, "turn[ing] the torrent away"(*BS*, 11), but also from the possibility of having to concede his child to the threatening larger world, the circle (*krug*) without a circle. Krug has not found a working solution for the "inner problem." Incidentally, under no circumstances is it a good idea to make a habit of sitting on anybody's face during or after one's schooldays.

The obtuseness of the regime is not an arbitrary means of retarding the climax of Krug's tragedy of errors. In Paduk's "Ekwilist" society a "little human creature" is "of no value to the community" (*BS*, 218); no one is irreplaceable; and the citizens are promised that their "groping individualities will become interchangeable and, instead of crouching in the prison cell on an illegal ego, the naked soul will be in

---

[16]See also Shaeffer, "*Bend Sinister* and the Novelist as Anthropomorphic Deity," pp. 128–35.

[17]*Mirok*, the tralatition for which is "[small pink potato]," is the diminutive of the Russian *mir*—"world." Asking a salesman for a soccer ball, Pnin describes with his hand a "portable world" (*P*, 99); proportionately, a little world, *mirok*, would assume the dimensions of a potato.

contact with that of every other man in this land" (*BS*, 97). It is quite natural, therefore, that the ideologist of practical Ekwilism should for a long time fail to realize the force of Krug's love for a "disposable" little human creature.

It is not for a police state to understand the agony of the physical blended with the spiritual in a father's love for a child. Discrete physical life is a "prism or prison" of finite consciousness (*BS*, 171) in which "infinite consciousness"—call it Shelley's "white radiance of eternity"—is refracted into a breathtaking rainbow. In this great prison of physical life "younger men [are] noiselessly digging an underground passage to freedom and recapture"(*BS*, 233). So long as physical life continues, moments of transcendent freedom will be followed by recapture. Only death is the final escape into infinite consciousness, the perfect knowledge, the fulfillment of "the attempt of a point in space and time to identify itself with every other point" (*BS*, 175). This is a much more pleasing variant of death than that other hypothesis, the "absolute nothingness, *nichto*" (*BS*, 175); all the same, as in Shakespeare's famous sonnet, to die is to leave one's love alone. Whereas in Nabokov's novels sexual love (especially the magical state of "being in love") opens a door to transcendent reality, tenderness (especially that of parental love) promotes the acceptance of the prison of so-called material reality and fosters the love of this rainbow world despite its "endless waves of pain" (*ND*, 67).

It is noteworthy that Nabokov did not manage to dam the waves of pain by writing *Bend Sinister;* they spill into "Signs and Symbols," written within a year after the publication of this novel. Like *Bend Sinister,* "Signs and Symbols" is devoted to "the incalculable amount of tenderness contained in the world" and to "the fate of this tenderness, which is either crushed, or wasted, or transformed into madness" (*ND*, 67).

The somewhat Kafkaesque, *outré* treatment of the sinister regime that exposes tenderness to torture is deliberately nonrealistic in *Bend Sinister.* The mechanical absentminded predictability of the conduct of its servants is used for comic relief, following, as it were, Bergson's prescriptions for the creation of the laughable[18] because the humor could not be spontaneous. As noted above, Nabokov does not have to invent a dystopia; others have done it, with different degrees of success, before him. His Padugrad is economically built of narrative de-

---

[18]See Bergson, "Laughter," pp. 117–43.

tails whose amount barely suffices to give "Nabokov" something to destroy by canceling the dramatic illusion in the last pages of the book: "He saw the Toad crouching at the foot of the wall, shaking, dissolving, speeding up his shrill incantations, protecting his dimming face with his transparent arm, and Krug ran towards him, and just a fraction of an instant before another and better bullet hit him, he shouted again: You, you—and the wall vanished, like a rapidly withdrawn slide, and I stretched myself and got up from among the chaos of written and rewritten pages, to investigate the sudden twang that something had made in striking the wire netting of my window" (*BS*, 240).

This involute cleanup (the "epilogical mopping up": *A*, 528) is possible only if there exists some dystopia, at least a "hastily assembled" one (*IB*, 51), to remove. The theme of the totalitarian regime is thus subservient not only to the main theme of the novel but also to the second "accompanying" theme: "Krug's blessed madness," during which—like the hero of Borges's "Circular Ruins"—Krug understands that he is an invention of someone else.

IV

Just as the accounts of Paduk and his regime (the first accompanying theme) do not form a political allegory as such, so the account of Krug's madness and return to the bosom of the "anthropomorphic deity impersonated by" his maker (the second accompanying theme) does not form a full-fledged cosmogonal allegory. Krug's madness and the "mopping up" associated with it belong to the complex of self-referential devices scattered throughout the novel.[19] These devices remind the reader of the fictionality of the tale and function as the kind of reassurance that we offer frightened children ("There, there, this is only a story"). Yet such reassurance is not unreserved: Nabokov insists that his story is essentially true. Even after canceling the dramatic illusion by suggesting variants of Krug's interview with Paduk, he makes a "definitive" statement: "Did Krug really glance at the prepared speech? And if he did, was it really as silly as that? He did; it was.

---

[19]The self-referential aspect of *Bend Sinister* is exhaustively discussed in Johnson, *Worlds in Regression*, pp. 187–205; Patteson, "Nabokov's *Bend Sinister*"; and Schaeffer, "*Bend Sinister* and the Novelist as Anthropomorphic Deity."

The seedy tyrant or the president of the State, or the dictator, or whoever he was—the man Paduk in a word, the Toad in another—did hand my favorite character a mysterious batch of neatly typed pages" (*BS*, 151). The sentence must be read figuratively: we all know how tyrants in this or "forking" worlds (Marianne Moore's "real toads" in real or imaginary gardens) demand that the great minds and talents of the age surrender their intellectual integrity. One may wonder which historical personages, between the collaborating Heidegger and the defiant Gumilyov, were in the back of Nabokov's mind during his work on *Bend Sinister*. Nor are hostage situations like David's an invention of Nabokov. The experience of which Krug is an exponent represents both Hawthorne's "truth of the human heart" and the historical truth; only its outer trappings are fictional, changeable, disposable—and disposed of by the dense self-referentiality of the text.

It is not only that Nabokov, like Ember during Krug's visit, chooses to "talk shop" in order to rechannel part of the reader's attention from shared pain to the writer's craft. His cavalier dismantling of the fictional world cancels not just the setting but also the plot, including, among other things, what seems to have been Krug's major mistake. The novel discourages such reflections as "If only Krug had done this or that, David would have been saved, and everything would have been fine, you see." When Krug is ready to take Paduk's dictation in order to get his son back, the guards produce "the wrong child," Arvid Krug, whom they have obviously been mistreating. This boy, to quote Nabokov's letter to his sister, is perhaps "just as funny and as strongly loved" as David: whatever Krug does or does not do, one of these two children (and there have been at least two million of them) will suffer a terrible fate. There are no solutions to Krug's predicament within his own world; "Nabokov," at least, knows better than to offer one. Among the sound that Krug hears in his giant prison there is "the cautious crackling of a page which had been viciously crumpled and thrown into the wastebasket and was making a pitiful effort to uncrumple itself and live just a little longer"(*BS*, 233–34). This may be the sheet of paper on which "Nabokov," in the "comparative paradise" of his workshop, wrote a provisional plot solution (different from that of the fair copy) and, feeling it inadequacy, "viciously crumpled" it and threw it out. There are no solutions—even Adam Krug's timely choice of death would not have saved either David or Arvid Krug—in the world where even a discarded sheet of paper wishes to "live just a little longer."

Tragic or near-tragic novels often create extreme situations in which ultimate questions can receive no solutions. One could say that in *Bend Sinister* Nabokov provides no solution (short of the wish-fulfilling cancellation of the dystopia), because the extreme situation that he has created admits of none. Yet it seems that he has created the extreme situation precisely for the purpose of denying his novel the right to propose a definite moral or political solution. In life, by contrast to tragic fiction, partial solutions are welcome: the bombing of Auschwitz would have helped and individual acts of heroism did help to save individual universes before the major dystopia of the present century was canceled by the allied armies. *Bend Sinister* is not a propagandistic call for action. It is a muted call for attention and empathy. In an imaginary dystopia it seeks out the real vulnerable tenderness that has always been caught and harassed between recurrent epidemics of brutality and never ending, beautifully sterile abstruse research.

11

"Reader! *Bruder!*": Broodings on the Rhetoric of *Lolita*

> What a strange couple to go on their rambles together!
> Nathaniel Hawthorne, "Little Annie's Ramble"

A novel that deals with a broken sexual taboo is suspected either of sensationalism or of a defiantly callous aestheticism that promotes insensitivity to crime and suffering. It is no longer necessary to defend *Lolita* from the former imputation; yet Nabokov's much-quoted remarks about the priority of "aesthetic bliss" may still leave him exposed to the latter charge. What all too often remains unnoticed, however, is that these remarks contain unmistakable moral connotations: "aesthetic bliss" is "a sense of being somehow, somewhere, connected with other states of being where art (curiosity, tenderness, kindness, ecstasy) is the norm" (*L*, 316–17). In the humdrum states of being on this side of an aesthetic object, curiosity, tenderness, kindness, and ecstasy are "fanciful and rare" (*G*, 168); the norm is set by "average reality" and one's daily efforts to stave off its disintegration. It is not for nothing that throughout Humbert's most touching last interview with Dolly, her husband is patiently fixing wires near a neighbor's shack.

But to return to the "fanciful and rare." Nabokov's brand of "aesthetic bliss" is, to a large extent, a Schopenhauerian notion. It is as if he had drawn the conclusion about the ennobling effect of art from Schopenhauer's belief in the power of aesthetic enjoyment to put to sleep the insistent urgings of the malevolent will. If Nabokov's novels are not *littérature engageé* (see *SO*, 33), neither are they "art for art's sake." Aesthetic experience is disinterested, yet, as Marianne Moore observed in "Poetry," it is also "useful," especially when it produces a cathartic effect.

The foreword to Humbert's memoirs, signed by one John Ray, ends in a comically well-meaning cliché: " 'Lolita' should make all of us—parents, social workers, educators—apply ourselves with still greater vigilance and vision to the task of bringing up a better generation in a safer world" (*L*, 8). A cliché is a statement that has lost its efficacy but not necessarily its validity; one should recollect Tess Durbeyfield's indignant "What all women say some women may feel."[1] *Lolita* does, in a sense, improve one's "vigilance and vision," yet it does not merely call upon "parents, teachers, and social workers" to instill more solid values into the younger generation and protect it from prowlers. The desired "better generation" is not even the moldable younger generation; it is the current generation of the readers themselves. The "vigilance" is, or should be, introspective, directed to the potential vulnerability of the reader's own system of values.

The rhetoric of *Lolita* is the rhetoric of reader entrapment: like many classical novelists before him, Nabokov reads the reader, revealing in him or her attitudes parallel to the ones that threaten the "safety" within the fictional world. The nonvicarious tribulations that make us reassess the attitudes involved in our reading process constitute the cathartic element of the novel; the narrative promotes and then purges certain tendencies in the reader's response. This cathartic element is generally limited to the first reading; in repeated readings it yields to serener aesthetic enjoyment and to a more active participation in constructing the fictional world. Yet these two aspects of the reader's response are also endowed with a specific moral significance.

I

Nabokov's road to the achievement of a balance between aesthesis and catharsis was not easy. The theme of child molestation first appeared in his novella *The Enchanter (Volshebnik)*, written in 1939. Nabokov read it to a group of friends but did not then publish it because he "was not pleased with the thing" (*L*, 314). Pedophilia being "so distant" from his own "emotional life" (*SO*, 15), he knew that the right approach to the subject was still eluding him. It took several years, as well as the freedom from the anxiety of his protracted stay in prewar France, the release of certain tensions through *Bend Sinister*,

---

[1] Thomas Hardy, *Tess of the d'Urbervilles* (Harmondsworth, 1982), p. 125.

and a fascination with the new linguistic medium, to allow him to
explore the whole complexity of the "strange couple" theme. The
impact of *Lolita* made him change his mind about *The Enchanter;* yet
it was only the aesthetic quality of the novella's texture that he com-
mended in a letter to the president of G. P. Putnam's Sons in 1959,
describing the ten-year-old manuscript as "a beautiful piece of Russian
prose, precise and lucid" and adding that "with a little care [it] could
be done into English by the Nabokovs"(*En,* 16). Eventually, however,
instead of having *The Enchanter* translated into English, Nabokov
translated *Lolita* into Russian.

The Enchanter has appeared posthumously in an English translation
by Dmitri Nabokov. It is the story of a man in his forties, a pedo-
philiac who focuses his obsession on a pretty twelve-year-old girl he
meets in the park. The girl, symptomatically, is always roller-skating
out of the field of vision or otherwise moving away; her loveliness is
a shadow of Platonic beauty that no one should presume to capture.
Yet in the words of the *Knickerbocker* debate, most of Nabokov's tragic
villains confuse "metaphysics with chowder."[2] In order to gain access
to the girl, the so-called "enchanter" marries her terminally sick
mother. After the mother's death he attempts to consummate his passion in a hotel room; when the girl's screams awaken the neighbors, he
throws himself under the wheels of a car.

The Enchanter makes good reading, but it is much more limited in
scope than *Lolita*. The books differ in length, setting, and tone. Moreover, unlike *The Enchanter, Lolita* produces a cathartic effect. It lulls us
into long spans of sympathy for Humbert and then punishes us for our
temporary suspension of judgment, whereas *The Enchanter* fails to
"enchant" us out of our consistent disapproval of the protagonist, a
disapproval punctured by only brief touches of compassion.

The protagonist of *The Enchanter* is shown to be capable of considerateness and occasional pity for the mother, who is "pregnant . . .
with her own death" (*En,* 59) and for the daughter, who is being
brought up by friends of the family in "a home without caresses,"
with "strict order, symptoms of fatigue, a favor for a friend grown

---

[2]One wonders what "Knickerbocker" it is that Nabokov has in mind when he uses
the name to explain how the "bo" in his own name should be pronounced (*SO*, 51);
given his interest in Melville, it may allude to the New York literary journal of the
mid-nineteenth century. On "metaphysics and chowder," see Perry Miller, *The Raven
and the Whale: The War of Words and Wits in the Era of Poe and Melville* (New York, 1956),
pp. 59–68.

burdensome" (*En*, 36). However, we are seldom allowed to forget his role of a mad wolf in "Granny's night-cap" (*En*, 67). The scholarly Humbert turns out to be a far better magician. Humbert, of course, is allowed to tell his own story, whereas *The Enchanter* is written in the third person. Although not directly censorious, the novella's third-person narrator is clearly critical of the protagonist's carnal designs upon the little girl's unselfconscious beauty. Such a narrative stance is not conducive to the kind of sympathetic self-projection that a first-person narrator like Humbert can sometimes elicit from the reader.

The first person narrative makes Humbert's spells more enduring than those of his precursor and enhances the drama of the break of these spells. Having already started his work on *Lolita*, in February 1951 Nabokov wrote "The Vane Sisters," a short story in which he perfected his use of the kind of first-person narrator who does not know that he expresses much more than he means to say.[3] To some extent, "The Vane Sisters," is a "firing practice" (*G*, 208) for *Lolita*—perhaps a more conscious preparation for it than "Recruiting" is for *Pnin* (see Chapter 2, above).

The structural principle of *Lolita* elaborates on that of "The Vane Sisters" and of Nabokov's 1932 novel *Despair*: the first-person narrator uses (not quite unsuccessfully) an arsenal of rhetoric in order to im-pose his attitudes on the reader, yet the events described ultimately demand a totally different interpretation of his experience.[4] Like Her-mann of *Despair*, and unlike the sour narrator of "The Vane Sisters" or the villainous one of "The Dashing Fellow" (1930), Humbert claims to be an artist of the quasi–Oscar Wilde type, one who wishes to turn his life into a work of art and therefore solipsistically manipulates the people around him as if they were "methods of composition."[5] The implied author of the novel, however, dissociates himself from Hum-bert, asserts his power over the events of the fictional world, and

[3]The narrator of the story (a French professor on an American college campus), having disapproved of the late Cynthia Vane's probing of the hereafter, is not aware that she and her sister, also dead, haunt the imagery of his text and assert their presence by an acrostic in the last paragraph.

[4]For a discussion of most of his devices, see Nomi Tamir-Ghez, "The Art of Per-suasion in Nabokov's *Lolita*," in Roth, *Critical Essays*, pp. 157–76.

[5]"The Vane Sisters" contains many allusions to Wilde; see Isobel Murray, " 'Plagi-atisme,' Nabokov's 'The Vane Sisters,' and *The Picture of Dorian Gray*," *Durham Uni-versity Journal*, 70 (December 1977), 69–72.

adjusts these events according to his own rather than Humbert's system of values.[6]

II

The cathartic effect of Lolita derives from its promotion of our temporary sympathy for Humbert and inattentiveness to Dolly Haze and then in its making us modify our attitudes. Humbert, of course, spares no effort to impose his sense of "norm" upon the reader. He wants ecstasy, an ingredient of Nabokov's "aesthetic bliss," to be the norm not just in his contact with art but also in his life. The novel-reading audience is well conditioned to sympathize with this desire, but it is not conditioned to sympathize with what Humbert regards as the source of his ecstasy: pedophilia. Eventually, however, the audience is entrapped: it begins to derive a pleasure from the account of the pursuit of ecstasy and to ignore the price of this pursuit, the suffering that Humbert causes to others. This is precisely the effect Humbert wishes to produce on the "Gentlewomen of the Jury" to whom he addresses his confession (until, aware of his approaching death, he no longer cares for self-vindication).[7] His narrative strives to turn the jury's attention into an aesthetic contemplation and then to subject the latter to the rules of visual perspective: the greater the distance, the less distinct the features of the represented scene.

Humbert attempts to present his obsession with little girls as a wide spread and essentially normal phenomenon impeded only by an arbitrary social convention; indeed, who can nowadays draw a line between the eccentric and the insane? Among the initiated, according to Humbert, a sexual preference like his is common enough to merit a name. He supplies the name, "nympholepsy," which is much more flattering than the clinical "pedophilia." His ultimate remorse springs from having ruined Dolly Haze's life; the obsession itself he rather consistently describes as tormenting yet incomparably beautiful, a curse that is also a gift and that singles him out from ordinary mortals.

[6]Following Wayne Booth, The Rhetoric of Fiction (Chicago, 1961), p. 151, I use the concept of the implied author as distinct from the historical author. Many of the techniques through which the implied author asserts his power over Humbert's story are pointed out in Alfred Appel's notes in The Annotated Lolita (L).

[7]For an analysis of Humbert's motives for writing his narrative, see Grabes, Fictitious Biographies; pp. 31–35.

Humbert describes his passion in a way reminiscent of Cincinnatus's metaphysical probings in *Invitation to a Beheading:* he has "caught glimpses of an incomparably more poignant bliss" than the "routine rhythm which shakes the world" (*L,* 20). His difference from Cincinnatus is that he has substituted the violation of a sexual taboo for the breaking of a metaphysical ban. This is Humbert's error, not his crime. His crime consists in an attempt to live by his obsessive fantasies as if they were law, thus turning the object of his passion into his victim and sacrificing whoever may stand in his way. Yet the fact that Humbert is a callous predator and not a tormented artist playing fairy godmother is precisely what tends to elude the reader's intelligence during long stretches of the tale.

Only after the account of the strange couple's coast-to-coast "ramble" is well under way do the wolf's teeth begin to show more and more ominously from under "the enchanted hunter's" mask. Before narrating this "ramble" Humbert tries hard to convince the reader that his sexual exploitation of Dolly need not hurt her and that he can perhaps make her happier than she was under her mother's discipline. Even if not persuaded, the reader is made to slip into a sympathetic attitude toward Humbert; sympathy for a fictional hero who embarks on a mission impossible and displays energy and acumen in its pursuit is a pleasure that few readers wish to give up, despite all the scornful treatment that such a pleasure may receive in various aesthetic theories. Our reluctant sympathy for Humbert's quest is as essential to *Lolita* as Ishmael's sympathy for another "lucid madman" is to *Moby Dick.*

The cathartic experience, however, is produced not by Humbert's rhetoric but by the rhetoric of the implied author, who makes Humbert say more than he can consciously register. The narrative of *Lolita,* like that of Jane Austen's *Emma* or Melville's "Benito Cereno," supplies the reader with clues to the presence of subplots yet delays explicit information. The most obvious instance of this technique is the story of Dolly's conspiracy with Quilty. Only in repeated readings do we decipher the signs of this conspiracy, because not until the very end of the novel does Quilty materialize, only to be messily destroyed in the Pavor Manor episode. Less conspicuous yet more relevant to the study of reader entrapment is the story of Dolly's sexual escapade in Camp Q.

It is a conventional privilege of the first-person narrator to withhold from the reader the information that he himself does not possess at a given moment of the represented time; hence, the reader is not informed about Dolly's adventures in the camp until Humbert learns about them. Moreover, Humbert does not explicitly project the belated information upon the key parts of his story. The conventional reticence of the first-person narrator is here endowed with a psychologically realistic meaning: Humbert the memoirist is ill; his condition deteriorates during his stay in prison, and he has not much energy left to expend on analysis. In chapter 26 of Part I, the shortest chapter of the book, he complains of his "daily headache" and of the effort that the writing costs him: "Don't think I can go on. Heart, head—everything" (L, 111). Symptomatically, even the heavy-handed pun on "Quilty" ("*il faut qu'il t'y mène*") in Mona's letter to Dolly escapes Humbert the punster. His only comment—"The letter contained an element of mysterious nastiness that I am too tired today to analyze" (L, 225)—underscores his fatigue. This technique of the uncomprehending focalizer is one of the methods by which Nabokov, like James, Melville, and other great novelists, creates an illusion of depth behind the surface of the narrative, an illusion that the fictional world is living its own life in a background that the laws of visual perspective render indistinct.

The effect of spatial and psychological depth, however, is largely a product of dramatic irony, which rises to the surface in repeated reading. It is only in a repeated reading of the Enchanted Hunters episode that we become aware of the intensely troubled emotional life behind Dolly's brash facade, the inner life that Humbert brushes off as irrelevant and depraved childish nonsense. When he picks her up from the camp after her mother's death (of which she has not yet been informed), she has not come to terms with her "activities" (L, 116) with Charley Holmes in the woods. She tries to laugh the matter off—"Bad, bad, girl. . . . Juvenile delickwent, but frank and fetching" (L, 115), yet it relentlessly haunts her speech:

> "What have you been up to? I insist you tell me."
> "Are you easily shocked?"
> "No. Go on."
> "Let us turn into a secluded lane and I'll tell you."
> "Lo, I must seriously ask you not to play the fool. Well?"
> "Well—I joined in all the activities that were offered."
> "*Ensuite?*"
> "Ansooit, I was taught to live happily and richly with others and to develop a wholesome personality. Be a cake, in fact."
> "Yes. I saw something of the sort in the booklet." . . .

"The Girl Scout's motto," said Lo rhapsodically, "is also mine. I fill my life with worthwhile deeds such as—well, never mind what. My duty is—to be useful. I am a friend to male animals. I obey orders. I am cheerful. . . . I am thrifty and I am absolutely filthy in thought, word and deed." . . .

"*C'est bien tout?*"

"*C'est.* Except for one little thing, something I simply can't tell you without blushing all over." [*L*, 116-17]

In our first reading we take Dolly's conversation in much the same way as Humbert does. He is deaf to her signals in the represented time, and the author makes him too tired and ill to note his own insensitivity at the time of memoir writing. Hence, we are not alerted to the urgency of Dolly's private troubles. Among the things that we lose by this imposed misreading is not only the psychological complexity but also the exquisite comedy of the *double entendre*.

Later the same night Humbert is impatient for Dolly to fall asleep so that he can secretly indulge his craving for her. He does not wish to listen to her. Nor does the reader. Because explicit information about the Charley Holmes affair is delayed by Humbert (the revelation is used in lieu of an account of the erotic scene—"Anybody can imagine those elements of animality": *L*, 136), the reader fails to realize that Dolly is trying to recover her sense of "norm" by casting Humbert in the role of a fellow conspirator who has sufficient authority to reassure her that sex is, indeed, a normal part of a tough youngster's "furtive world" (*L*, 135). Another reason we fail at first to understand Dolly's signals and doubts is that we still allow Humbert to infect us with his impatience and (let us be frank) his anticipation of an erotic scene:

I had almost to carry her into our room. There, she sat down on the edge of the bed, swaying a little, speaking in dove-dull long-drawn tones.

"If I tell you—if I tell you, will you promise [sleepy, so sleepy—head lolling, eyes going out], promise you won't make complaints?"

"Later, Lo. Now go to bed. I'll leave you here, and you go to bed. Give you ten minutes."

"Oh, I've been such a disgusting girl," she went on, shaking her hair, removing with slow fingers a velvet hair ribbon. "Lemme tell you—"

"Tomorrow, Lo. Go to bed, go to bed—for goodness sake, to bed."

I pocketed the key and walked downstairs. [*L*, 124-25]

Repeated reading reveals that Dolly's troubled inner life, although not conventionally pure, is by no means vulgar or callous. It is amazing, though, how often the effect of the first reading persists and how many critics never change their attitude to Dolly as an "exasperating brat" (L, 150), an attitude that they share with Charlotte Haze and with Humbert at his worst moments.[8] Humbert does eventually realize that he has underestimated Dolly's mind:

> It struck me . . . that I simply did not know a thing about my darling's mind and that quite possibly, behind the awful juvenile clichés, there was in her a garden and a twilight, and a palace gate—dim and adorable regions which happened to be lucidly and absolutely forbidden to me . . . for I often noticed that living as we did, she and I, in a world of total evil, we would become strangely embarrassed whenever I tried to discuss something she and an old friend, she and a parent, she and a real healthy sweetheart, I and Annabel . . . might have discussed—an abstract idea, a painting, stippled Hopkins or shorn Baudelaire, God or Shakespeare, anything of a genuine kind. Good will! She would mail her vulnerability in trite brashness and boredom, whereas I, using for my desperately detached comments an artificial tone of voice that set my own last teeth on edge, provoked my audience to such outbursts of rudeness as made any further conversation impossible, oh my poor, bruised child. [L, 286]

As is usual in Nabokov, immorality is incompatible with satisfactory metaphysics or aesthetics, "God or Shakespeare." Humbert's belated insight sheds a new light on Dolly's demonstrative indifference to the landscape and her love for advertised goods and billboard offers ("She it was to whom ads were dedicated: the ideal consumer": L, 150), with which also she eventually gets bored; all things are soiled for her by Humbert's anti-Midas touch. We can now begin to see a complexity in Dolly's character which, owing to erotic anticipation or to the more respectable "desire for the text," we have not noticed before. We can begin to see the "garden" and the "twilight" and the "palace gate," though whatever lies beyond the gate remains off limits for us. The change in our view of her character reveals how easily we can be tricked into an attitude similar to Humbert's "habit and method to ignore Lolita's states of mind" (L, 289) while ministering to his comforts. Indeed, Humbert's charges against the Ladies and Gentlemen of the Jury—including those implied in the allusion to Baude-

---

[8]For much-needed criticism of such misreadings, see Gladys M. Clifton, "Humbert Humbert and the Limits of Artistic License," in Rivers and Nicol, Fifth Arc, pp. 162–65. Symptomatically, however, even Clifton refers to Dolly as "Lolita"—the name used only by Humbert, with little or no sanction on Dolly's part.

laire's sarcastic fraternization with the *hypocrite lecteur* ("Reader!
Bruder!": *L,* 264)[9]—are not undeserved: in our previous underestima-
tion of the character's complexity we are now forced to recognize a
germ of the same tendency that reduces people to "solipsized" objects
(*L,* 62) in the novel's world.

III

The novel's cathartic reader entrapment, based on the use of
the first-person narrative, is a technique fraught with problems. Exploration of the enchanted hunter's obsession, its seductiveness, the
glamour of the mask, calls for an unregenerated focal character. Yet a
sensitive presentation of the human price that such an obsession exacts
requires a degree of genuine human warmth. Can the same narrative
consciousness supply both the ingredients of the magic potion that the
novel attempts to brew?

Genuinely beautiful emotion permeates the last meeting of Humbert
and Dolly and the memories that crowd in upon his mind when he
drives away from Coalmont. For the first time in his life Humbert
really loves the woman who is no longer a "nymphet" and can therefore generously renounce her. The Coalmont episode thus seems to
produce a therapeutic effect on the protagonist; symptomatically, as it
were, the two very young girls whom he later sees in Pavor Manor
excite nothing but pity and disgust—"so young, so lewd" (*L,* 307).
His lust for Dolly has been replaced by a belated yet genuine compassion and love: "There she was . . . hopelessly worn at seventeen . . .
and I looked and looked at her, and knew as clearly as I know I am to
die, that I loved her more than anything I had ever seen or imagined
on earth, or hoped for anywhere else. . . . What I used to pamper
among the tangled vines of my heart, *mon grand péché radieux,* had
dwindled to its essence: sterile and selfish vice, all *that* I cancelled and
cursed" (*L,* 279–80).

Stridently apostrophizing his Lolita, Humbert claims that he loves
her despite her pregnancy by another man, despite the pollution, the
ravages that may be produced by childbirth: "I would go mad with
tenderness at the mere sight of your dear wan face, at the mere sound
of your raucous young voice" (*L,* 280). His conduct throughout the

[9]See also Appel's note 1 to p. 264 (*L,* 424).

Coalmont episode supports this claim. And yet his new vision of his *"grand péché radieux"* as a "sterile and selfish vice" does not leave a sufficient imprint on the beginning and middle of his narrative. If Humbert is telling his tale after the Coalmont and the Pavor Manor episodes, a complete cure of pedophilia should have made it impossible for him to relive his former ecstasies at the time of the writing. "I cannot paint / What then I was," says Wordsworth in "Tintern Abbey" when he tries, and fails, to revive the raptures known by his former self. The fact that throughout more than half the book Humbert does not fail to paint "what then he was" means that despite his protestations he has not yet succeeded in canceling his obsession.

Indeed, though Humbert the narrator punctuates his memoirs with expressions of remorse and disgust with his former self (unlike the penitence of the novel's closing chapters, this penance is somewhat self-indulgent), he time and again plunges into such an impassioned account of his erotic pursuits that the reader tends to forget their inappropriateness to their object. [10] The self-flagellation does not signify a cure: Humbert knew remorse at the height of his perverted "romance." His experience in writing the memoir actually reenacts the experience of the days when he had Dolly instead of "only words to play with" (*L,* 34) and when he oscillated between sexual urges, tender repentance, and renewed sexual urges that would call for more repentance upon being satisfied:

> I recall certain moments, let us call them icebergs in paradise, when after having had my fill of her—after fabulous, insane exertions that left me limp and azure barred—I would gather her in my arms with, at last, a mute moan of human tenderness . . .—and the tenderness would deepen to shame and despair, and I would lull and rock my lone light Lolita in my marble arms, and moan in her warm hair, and caress her at random and mutely ask her blessing, and at the peak of this human agonized selfless tenderness (with my soul actually hanging around her naked body and ready to repent), all at once, ironically, horribly, lust would swell again—and "oh, *no,*" Lolita would say with a sigh to heaven, and the next moment the tenderness and the azure—all would be shattered. [*L,* 287]

If Humbert were, indeed, cured of his obsession, the tenderness of his remorseful memories of Dolly ("my poor, bruised child": *L,* 286)

---

[10]Cf. Edmund White, "Nabokov: Beyond Parody," in Gibian and Parker, *Achievements,* p. 13: "One of the most amusing paradoxes of *Lolita* is that the satyr Humbert Humbert becomes the minnesinger of courtly love for the twentieth century."

would color the whole of his retrospective narrative and interfere with his presentations of pedophilia as incomparable bliss. That, however, would make it next to impossible to render the full intensity of the conflict between the ecstasy and the destructiveness of his misdirected quest.

The problem of reconciling Humbert's persistent perversity with the event that purports to have removed it must have been a major challenge for Nabokov. He found his solution in a crafty handling of dates that in effect untells Humbert's tale.

The deceptiveness of Humbert's seemingly straightforward retrospective narrative has been noticed only quite recently and has not so far found due appreciation in the critical community. In her 1979 article "Time in *Lolita*," an essay that should have exerted greater influence on Nabokov studies than it seems to have done, Christina Tekiner puts together certain significant facts.

Humbert is supposed to die immediately after completing his manuscript: his use of initials instead of names on the last page suggests haste, an awareness that his time is running out. In the John Ray foreword the date of Humbert's death is given as November 16, 1952. On the penultimate page of his memoirs (supposedly written on that day), Humbert notes that he began his literary labor fifty six days before. This means that he must have started writing the memoir on September 21 or 22. Yet September 22 is the day he received Dolly's letter from Coalmont and, according to the subsequent narrative, immediately set off on his frantic drive to meet Dolly, give her her *"trousseau"* (L, 280), and settle his account with Quilty; hence, he could not have had time to write on this or the following few days. Tekiner therefore concludes (a) that the meeting with Dolly Schiller and the murder of Quilty never happened; (b) that on receiving the letter, Humbert went to a psychiatric clinic and started writing his manuscript; (c) that the account of the final encounter with Dolly and the revenge on the rival were invented by Humbert in prison; and (d) that Humbert was on trial not for the murder of Quilty (indeed, John Ray's foreword never mentions a murder) but for statutory rape and carrying a minor across state lines. Tekiner's main conclusion is that just as earlier in the novel Humbert transformed Dolly Haze into a "solipsized" (L, 62) Lolita, so in the last nine chapters he loves not the real Dolly Schiller but a woman who is, still, his own creation.[11]

---

[11] See Christina Tekiner, "Time in *Lolita*," *Modern Fiction Studies*, 25 (1979), 463–69.

Before examining the issue further, we must note that Nabokov's screenplay for *Lolita* (which Stanley Kubrick eventually rejected in favor of one more appropriate to Hollywood needs) does not support Tekiner's reading: it presents Humbert's ride to meet the pregnant Dolly Schiller and his murder of Quilty (the episode with which both Nabokov's screenplay and Kubrick's movie start) as taking place in Humbert's "reality" rather than in his imagination. But the screenplay, written about five years after the publication of the novel, is a totally new work. It contains a number of scenes that Nabokov had rejected while working on the novel, presents the material in a different sequence, and is timed in a new way: for instance, Humbert comes to America after World War II and not on the eve of the war, as in the novel.

The screenplay, therefore, cannot be used to settle moot points in the novel.[12] A comparison of the different editions of the novel, however, proves beyond a doubt that the logical impossibility of its denouement (the contradiction in dates) is a deliberate device. In the faulty 1958 edition Humbert receives Dolly's letter "early" in September 1952. Subsequently, Nabokov replaces the word "early" with "late."[13] In his 1967 Russian translation Nabokov specifies the date—September 22, 1952—in the description of Humbert's going to the mailbox,[14] whereas in the English original he mentions it three pages later (*L*, 269). This minor change is obviously calculated to emphasize that there is no span left between the receipt of the letter and the

---

[12]Nevertheless, I shall offer my explanation of why Nabokov should begin the screenplay with Quilty's murder. The viewer must, right from the start, be prevented from sympathizing with the character, who would be played by a handsome actor (whether or not Nabokov knew it would be Peter Sellers). In Kubrick's movie, sympathy for Humbert comes all the easier because his beloved looks eighteen rather than twelve years old. It is therefore appropriate for the murder scene to be as long as it is in the film; Nabokov had thought that it "should not last more than one minute." It is also interesting that in Nabokov's screenplay (from which Kubrick again deviated) the shooting takes place in "a silent shadowy sequence" (*LS*, 2) with strong visual images but, it seems, with the sound turned off. There is something dreamlike about it— perhaps an afterglow of the surrealism that colors this episode in the novel. In the original screenplay the viewer's potential sympathy for Quilty is also undermined by a shot of the "drug addict's implementa," from which the camera withdraws "with a shudder" (*LS*, 1). Yet for Nabokov murder is always the most terrible of crimes, no matter who its victim is.

[13]See Appel's note 5 to p. 266 (*L*, 426).

[14]See the Russian version of *Lolita* (Ann Arbor, Mich., 1967), p. 245. Retranslated to English, the passage would read not "that particular morning, late in September 1952" (*L*, 266) but "that morning, September 22, 1952."

writing of the memoir. The trips to Coalmont and Pavor Manor were never made by Humbert; the account of these trips is a story-within-a-story, an inset imagined not only by Nabokov but also by Humbert. Humbert, moreover, does not seem to begin writing his memoirs with the Coalmont episode already in mind; he appears to invent or, rather, construct this episode *at the time of writing it.* He is completely unaware of having crossed the line between "reality" and illusion. Whereas Alexander Nolan in Borges's "Theme of the Traitor and the Hero" plants clues by which posterity may unravel his deceptions, Humbert fails to remove such clues from his narrative.

What is the purpose of these clues? It is certainly not limited to canceling the story by exposing the cognitive unreliability of the narrator. In *Lolita* the reader's awareness of the narrator's unreliability and of the fictional nature of the story is much less important than in *Pnin.* In repeated readings Humbert's unreliability of course makes us more skeptical of, for instance, his self-image as an irresistible specimen of Hollywood manhood, yet as suggested above it is mainly in order to remove the self-contradiction of the narrative stance that Nabokov allows us to diagnose the logical impossibility of the novel's denouement: if the therapeutic Coalmont episode, which evokes a profound sympathy for both Dolly and Humbert (in contrast to the "impartial sympathy" recommended by his lawyer: *L,* 59), did not really take place before Humbert began writing his story, then in the bulk of the narrative the distance between Humbert the erring focal character and Humbert the penitent narrating voice does not have to be as great as it is in, say, Dickens's *Great Expectations.*[15] Suggestively, when after his arrest Humbert receives a consignment of books from the prison library, he seems to dismiss both the Bible and a set of Dickens in preference to a *"Children's Encyclopedia* (with some nice photographs of sunshine-haired Girl Scouts in shorts)" (*L,* 33) and other items, including *Who's Who in the Limelight.*[16]

---

[15]Following Genette, *Narrative Discourse,* pp. 186–89, I use "voice" to mean a person who is supposed to be performing the narrative act: e.g., the mature Pip of *Great Expectations* or the third-person narrator in Nabokov's *Mary.* The "focus" is the character who provides the center of vision: e.g., the erring young Pip of *Great Expectations* or Ganin in the bulk of *Mary.*

[16]Tekiner ("Time in *Lolita,*" 466–67) notes that it is with the help of this *Who's Who* that Humbert discovers Dolly's relationship with the playwright Quilty. To cover her tracks, Dolly had made him believe that Quilty was a woman, but *Who's Who* reveals that he is a man.

IV

The logical impossibility of the denouement also functions as part of the novel's rhetoric of reader entrapment. This trap consists, however, not in encouraging a lack of attention to narrative clues but, conversely, in producing a too diligent imaginative collaboration with them. If Humbert sometimes tells more than he knows, he often also deliberately tells less. His so-called sexual frankness is accompanied by a crafty obliqueness that make the reader responsible for constructing or distorting the erotic scenes. Thus, for a long time most readers thought that in the famous couch episode Humbert has his lengthy orgasm while Dolly is sitting on his lap (see *L*, 59–63); not until the 1981 conference of the American Association of Teachers of Slavic and East European Languages did Alex E. Alexander make it clear that she is supposed to be lying on the couch with her feet in Humbert's lap. Likewise, in the Hourglass Lake episode one has to concentrate on picturing the scene to oneself in order to notice that Charlotte sits up topless (these are the modest late 1940s) expecting to arouse in Humbert (who has just reluctantly given up his plan to drown her) emotions of a totally different nature from those that the reader is invited to infer:

> We sat down on our towels in the thirsty sun. She looked around, loosened her bra, and turned over on her stomach to give her back a chance to be feasted upon. She said she loved me. She sighed deeply. She extended one arm and groped in the pocket of her robe for her cigarettes. She sat up and smoked. She examined her right shoulder. She kissed me heavily with open smoky mouth. Suddenly, down the sand bank behind us, from under the bushes and pines, a stone rolled, then another.
> "Those disgusting prying kids," said Charlotte, holding up her big bra to her breast and turning prone again. [*L*, 90]

Oblique sexual reference gains importance after the episode of Humbert's first night with Dolly in the Enchanted Hunters hotel. At this point, as is well known, the erotic escalation of the surface narrative is discontinued; however, the escalation continues behind the screen, in the spatial background whose presence is suggested by hints and eloquently reticent remarks scattered throughout the novel. Humbert notes that at first Dolly regards everything except kisses on the mouth and the stark sex act either as "romantic slosh" or as something abnormal (*L*, 135). It takes him some time and some blackmail to coax her into more complex exercises, but by the time they settle down in Beardsley their nights contain "things that the most jaded *voyeur* would have paid a small fortune to watch" (*L*, 182). In the end Humbert starts giving Dolly money to make her agree to oral sex and, on one occasion, to under-the-desk contact in her classroom.

Humbert's hunger, a metaphysical "itch of being" (*GI*, xiii) mistaken for an obsessive pursuit of an eidolon, cannot be appeased by the possession of his "nymphet's" body. In a sense it is fortunate for Dolly that, in his wish to go beyond the surface, Humbert thinks not about her heart (of which he despairs) or her mind (which he holds in low esteem) or her soul (in which he does not believe) but, weirdly in tune with Edgar Allan Poe, of her inner organs: "My only grudge against nature was that I could not turn my Lolita inside out and apply voracious lips to her young matrix, . . . lungs, her comely twin kidneys" (*L*, 167).

Whether or not this remark suggests a touch of necrophilia, it definitely implies the possibility of violence. Violence also seems to escalate behind the curtain of the narrative. From between the lines it emerges that Dolly's resistance to Humbert is at times very active: "Whose cat has scratched poor you?" inquires a lady of Humbert at a hotel table d'hôte (*L*, 166). At first he does not want to hurt her physically, but starting with the Beardsley period the element of violence in their conflicts steadily grows (see *L*, 207, 217, 229), so that references to Sade and his Justine acquire a menacing ring.[17] Then a gun is introduced and likewise begins to "grow"—as another revolver does in *The Gift* (cf. *G*, 57): it is transferred from a box to a pocket so that Humbert may be ready "to take advantage of the spell of insanity" (*L*, 231) that he anticipates, not without pleasure. Upon placing Dolly in a hospital in Elphinstone, Humbert wonders whether he should "mention " that his fifteen-year-old daughter had had a minor accident while climbing an awkward fence with her boy friend" (*L*, 242), making the reader wonder whether the loss of virginity is the only thing that Humbert wishes to explain away. In Elphinstone, moreover,

---

[17]See Appel's note on allusion to Sade (*L*, 429–30). Unknowingly, Dolly also makes an allusion to Justine, who was killed by lightning: "I am not a lady and do not like lightning" (*L*, 222) she says during a storm. This is a reference to Quilty's play *The Lady Who Loved Lightning;* Humbert does not realize that Dolly is upset about missing an appointment with Quilty rather than by the rage of the elements.

Dolly wants to "climb Red Rock from which a mature screen star had recently jumped to her after a drunken row with her gigolo" (*L*, 212). Ominously, the name of the place is a translation of the "Roches Roses," the setting of young Humbert's tryst with his Annabel Leigh, who died of typhus shortly afterward. At one point Dolly stops the car at the last minute on the brink of a precipice (*L*, 230–31), and it is on the verge of another precipice, a "friendly abyss" (*L*, 309) that Humbert pauses, after Dolly's disappearance, to mourn the absence of her voice from the imaginary concord of children's voices.

Is the reader expected to infer from these images that despite his assurances to the contrary, Humbert might after all have killed Dolly, or that she might have suffered an accident or committed suicide in a desperate attempt to escape from him? Both the temptation to offer such a detective-story solution of the novel's missing-person case (*Dolores Disparue*) and the resistance to this temptation seem to be equally appropriate responses to *Lolita*. This paradox develops the complex demand made on the reader's response in Nabokov's short story "Signs and Symbols," written in 1948—less than two years before he started work on *Lolita*. The son of the elderly couple whose day is described in this story is kept in a mental hospital because he suffers from "referential mania." Everything in the world around him seems to be "a veiled reference to his personality and existence": "Phenomenal nature shadows him wherever he goes. Clouds in the starring sky transmit to one another, by means of slow signs, incredibly detailed information regarding him. His inmost thoughts are discussed at nightfall, in manual alphabet, by darkly gesticulating trees. Pebbles or stains of sun flecks form patterns representing in some awful way messages that he must intercept. Everything is a cipher and of everything he is the theme" (*ND*, 64–65).

As William Carroll has observed, it is to a character in fiction rather than to a "real person" that everything around him refers.[18] Therefore, if the reader regards the half-dead starling that has fallen out of its nest or the underground train that loses its life current at the beginning of the story as indirect evidence of the young man's ultimate death, he gets trapped in that character's own referential mania.[19] It is true that

---

[18]See William Carroll, "Nabokov's Signs and Symbols," in Proffer, *Book of Things*, pp. 208–10.
[19]For this observation I am indebted to Paul J. Rosenzweig, "The Importance of

a novel's events do not always depend on causality: despite the authority of Novalis, character need not always be fate. Plot developments are not always products of plausibility or consequences of previous actions. They may also be brought about by the tendency of metaphors to turn into physical facts;[20] and one cannot but agree with Jorge Luis Borges that words and images have the power to attract, as if by sympathetic magic, words and images like them.[21] This principle of composition, however, can retain its "magic" only so long as it does not turn into a convention. The recurrent imagery of death need not automatically lead the reader to interpret the open ending of the story as implying the hero's suicide; the escalation of violence and the reference to Red Rocks in *Lolita* need not automatically suggest the violent death of Dolly Haze, even though the reader's cooperative imagination has been activized by Humbert's game of *sous entendre* and even though the denouement offered by Humbert turns out to be logically impossible.

And yet, through persistent *sous entendre* Nabokov does stimulate the reader's cooperative imagination; through the game of cross-reference he does provide this imagination with definite subject matter.[22] And he does leave clues to the fact that Humbert never met Dolly in Coalmont. Moreover, at the end of his imaginary account of the Coalmont episode there is a hint of the possibility of what Borges would have called "forking paths." It is as if for a moment Humbert's imagination were toying with the idea of his somehow making use of his gun after Dolly refuses to give him any hope that she may return to him, but then he immediately realizes that such an ending of the most beautiful scene in his whole memoir would be inappropriate:

"No," she said smiling, "no."
"It would have made all the difference," said Humbert Humbert.

Reader Response in Nabokov's 'Signs and Symbols,' " *Essays in Literature,* 7 (1980), 256–57. A similar point was more recently made in Richter, "Narrative Entrapment," 427–30. A different approach is suggested in John Hagopian, "Decoding Nabokov's 'Signs and Symbols,' " *Studies in Short Fiction,* Spring 1981, 115–19.

[20]A novel structured almost entirely on this principle is *Mezhdu sobakoi i volkom* (Between dog and wolf) by Sasha Sokolov (Ann Arbor, Mich., 1980).

[21]See Jorge Luis Borges, "Narrative Art and Magic," *Triquarterly,* 25 (Fall 1972), 209–15.

[22]Cf. the discussion of techniques for activizing the imagination of the audience in E. H. Gombrich, *Art and Illusion: A Study in the Psychology of Pictorial Representation* (London, 1962), p. 174.

Then I pulled out my automatic—*I mean,* this is the kind of fool thing
a reader might suppose I did. It never even occurred to me to do it.
"Good by-aye!" she chanted, my American sweet immortal dead love;
for she is dead and immortal if you are reading this. *I mean,* such is the
formal agreement with the so-called authorities. [*L,* 282; my italics]

The episode is usually interpreted as making fun of the reader who,
under the influence of Mérimée's *Carmen* (to which an allusion is made
several lines before), expects Humbert to kill his unfaithful love. This
interpretation is certainly correct; however, the passage contains suggestions that Humbert may have "pulled out [his] automatic" on another occasion that is not recorded in the novel. "The intimate
revelations of young men," says Nick Carraway in Fitzgerald's *Great
Gatsby* (Humbert is not so young, but it does not matter), "are usually
plagiaristic and marred by obvious suppressions."[23] The phrase "I
mean," with its possible connotations of insecurity after the references
to the gun and to Dolly's death, can be read as Humbert's attempt to
extricate himself from an embarrassment produced by two slips of his
("automatic"?) pen. At the same time, the pathos of the interview and
the credibility of Humbert's conduct throughout the episode almost
completely neutralize such ominous notes.

In other words, the novel leaves a margin for an alternative denouement, yet it both invites and repels our imaginative contribution to its
tourbook map of forking highways, both provokes and discourages
our usurpation of the role of "Detective Trapp" (see *L,* 239-40). In still
other words, the possibility of Dolly's violent death hovers between the
lines of the story and, even though strenuously denied in Humbert's
comments, becomes one of the things "that the finder cannot unsee
once it has been seen" (*SM,* 310). At the same time, no such death is
allowed into the text; it remains a symbolically appropriate disembodied notion for which the reader is invited to assume full responsibility.
If the invitation were to be accepted, Dolly would, for all practical
purposes, be "killed" by the reader.

V

Although violent death is not Dolly's fate in the text of *Lolita,*
the reader knows that "in reality" violence and murder are very likely

[23]F. Scott Fitzgerald, *The Great Gatsby* (Harmondsworth, 1986), p. 7.

in cases of child molesting—so likely that neither the novelist nor the reader need bother to invent them. Recalling Humbert's "Imagine me; I shall not exist if you do not imagine me" (*L*, 131), the reader and the novelist do not want to imagine a violent end to Dolly's life, since (in the words of *Invitation*) by evoking it they would "grant it existence." If we do not insist on following the detective clues that would incriminate Humbert and overrule the protestations of this "dreadful inventor" (*P*, 185), it is because we want to grant Dolly at least some poetic justice before she makes her exit from the novel's world. So does Nabokov, or why else would he camouflage the impossibility of the Coalmont episode so carefully that it has taken his audience (and then only part of his audience) two decades to detect it?

There is an element of wish fulfillment in our acceptance of the Coalmont episode as a suitable denouement of *Lolita*, just as there is a controlled element of wish fulfillment in the endings of the best novels in history. The relationship between this episode and the previous parts of Humbert's story is oneiric rather than logical. At this point Humbert's life is almost a completed volume—a realization, as it were, of Schopenhauer's metaphor of the book:

> Life and dreams are leaves of one and the same book. The systematic reading is real life, but when the actual reading hour (the day) has come to an end, and we have the period of recreation, we often continue idly to thumb over the leaves, and turn to a page here and there without method or connexion. We sometimes turn up a page we have already read, at others one still unknown to us, but always from the same book. Such an isolated page is, of course, not connected with a consistent reading and study of the book, yet it is not so very inferior thereto, if we note that the whole of the consistent perusal begins and ends also on the spur of the moment, and can therefore be regarded merely as a larger single page.[24]

At the sunset of his life, a life begun by Nabokov "on the spur of the moment," Humbert indulges in a dream and "turns up a page" that contains the tenderness and self-sacrifice "still unknown" to him. The love and the tenderness (and the murder) are "from the same book," even if the psychological realism of the narration demands that they should be invented rather than experienced by Humbert. At the time of writing his memoir Humbert is too sick to read the book of life

[24]Schopenhauer, *The World as Will and Representation*, 1:18.

consistently; its very pages are being turned for him, as it were, by Dolly's classmate Aubrey McFate,[25] the imp of pseudo randomness, of (to adapt "The Vane Sisters") the choice that mimics chance. Humbert's madness is much less lucid at the end of the novel than at the beginning: he is genuinely unable to distinguish his actual experience from fantasy, genuinely unable to realize that (as in *Invitation* or Joyce's *Ulysses*) the book itself has started to dream (cf. *LL,* 350).

The workings of the wish-fulfilling imagination that threatens to disconnect Humbert's inner life from the perception of outward events are already apparent in the account of September 22, 1952, the day of the momentous visit to the mailbox, yet it is not clear exactly when Humbert's wish-fulfilling imagination begins to converge with the dream of the book itself. It would be anti-intuitive to believe—as Tekiner seems to do—that Humbert, having received Dolly's plea for help, would not rush to meet her; that he would, instead, retire to write his memoir and daydream about a brief reunion. There are two ways to restore verisimilitude: (a) Humbert may have been arrested on the same day, almost immediately after reading Dolly's letter, and placed in a psychiatric ward "for observation" (*L,* p. 310) prior to being scheduled for trial; or (b) he may never have received any letter from his *Dolores Disparue,* just as he seems never to have gone to Coalmont or Pavor Manor. As in *Pnin,* the alternatives form a duality rather than an ambiguity: like humdrum "real life" and wish-fulfilling dreams, they coexist and complement each other.

There is in fact a measure of vagueness concerning the matter of the mail. When Humbert takes his letters out of the mailbox on September 22, he has the impression that one of them is from his current mistress's mother. The other letter is from the Ramsdale lawyer John Farlow, who tells Humbert about his new marriage and concludes with a conglomeration of news:

> Since he was "building a family" as he put it, he would have no time henceforth for my affairs which he termed "very strange and very aggravating." Busybodies—a whole committee of them, it appeared—had informed him that the whereabouts of little Dolly Haze were unknown, and that I was living with a notorious divorcee in California. His father-in-law was a count, and exceedingly wealthy. The people who had been renting the Haze house for some years now wished to buy it. He sug-

[25]See Appel's note 3 to p. 54 (*L,* 360–61).

gested that I better produce Dolly quick. He had broken his leg. He enclosed a snapshot of himself and a brunette in white wool beaming at each other among the snows of Chile. [*L*, 268]

The scraps of information about Farlow's affairs serve as conjuror's patter that almost succeeds in diverting the reader's attention from the threat of a police investigation if Dolly's whereabouts remain unknown. This patter is followed by a brief prelude to the text of "Dolly's letter." Symptomatically, Humbert never mentions opening this letter, as he does in the case of Farlow's epistle:

I remember letting myself into my flat and starting to say: Well, at least we shall now track them down—when the other letter began talking to me in a small matter-of-fact voice:

Dear Dad:
How's everything? I'm married. I'm going to have a baby [*L*, 268]

The letter thus seems to be provided by Humbert's "Proustianized and Procrusteanized" fancy (*L*, 266), which is assigned the task of "tracking them down." The section opens with Humbert's remark on "harlequin light that fell through the glass upon an alien handwriting."[26] This light had often twisted the handwriting of other people "into a semblance of Lolita's script causing [him] almost to collapse as [he] leant against an adjacent urn, almost [his] own" (*L*, 265). On previous occasions the illusion was promptly dispelled, yet on the morning of September 22 it takes complete hold on Humbert's imagination because it is brought on not only by his longing for Dolly but also by his fear of legal trouble. The story imagined by Humbert then begins not with the drive to Coalmont but earlier, with the substitution of an imaginary letter from Dolly for an eclipsed one from Rita's mother.

Humbert's wish to "track them down" runs parallel to the wish (his own, Dolly's, the reader's, the book's) for a return to normality. This wish is largely granted in the Coalmont episode. It is as if to satisfy this choric wish that Dolly Schiller has given up Hollywood, adven-

[26]Cf. Baroness Bredow (*bred* is the Russian for "delirium"), née Tolstoy, in Nabokov's *Look at the Harlequins!* (*LATH*, p. 9): "Trees are harlequins, words are harlequins. So are situations and sums. Put two things together—jokes, images—and you get a triple harlequin. Come on! Play! Invent the world! Invent reality!"

ture, excitement, and middle-class comforts for the normal hardships (at the age of seventeen) of working-class life. She has married a wounded veteran of World War II for whom she probably represents a return to normality; in the Coalmont episode she dresses the bruise of their one-armed neighbor, also a war veteran, while trying to forget her own invisible wounds. Having to appeal to Humbert for financial help, she struggles to maintain the attitude of an estranged daughter who pities her sick and lonely father, is grateful for the money he gives her, regrets having had to deceive him, but is in no position to offer him help. Blocking the reminders, however insistent, of a different relationship that has existed between them, she handles the difficult situation with sympathy and tact.

Dolly's chosen life and conduct are a natural sequel to the traits that one can, in repeated readings (the reader, Humbert's *Bruder,* now turns into a "brooder"), observe in her as a child, despite Humbert's distribution of emphasis. He himself is eventually forced to admit that the brashness and vulgarity of little Dolly Haze have been a mask, a "mail," for her vulnerability. When, after a quarrel, she rushes to kiss her mother's lodger goodbye before leaving for summer camp, he attributes this gift to her imitation of movies and ignores the genuinely affectionate nature of the girl who yearns for the love that her mother is withholding. He is amazed at Dolly's early loss of virginity and ignores the fact that she tries and fails to believe that clandestine sex between children is "normal." For a time he almost persuades her that their quasi-incestuous relationship is not an uncommon phenomenon, yet he cannot suppress her intuition for normality, which eventually makes her rebel against their driving across the country "doing filthy things together and never behaving like ordinary people" (*L,* 160). He enumerates his expenses and the tourbook attractions that he lavishes on Lolita but has to admit to the reader that she would sob "in the night—every night, every night—the moment [he] feigned sleep" (*L,* 178).

Upon leaving Coalmont, Humbert is shown recollecting scenes from his past life with Lolita, and these flashbacks are, structurally speaking, a disguised instance of the "sources" technique that is explicit in the last chapter of *Pnin.* Indeed, they contain most of the motifs of which the Coalmont incident has been spun: Lolita's face with its expression of "helplessness so perfect that it seemed to grade into one of rather comfortable inanity" (*L,* 285); and Humbert's surges of self-denying, remorseful, almost parental tenderness, which made him wish to fall "at her dear feet and dissolv[e] in human tears, and sacrific[e] [his] jealousy to whatever pleasure Lolita might hope to derive from mixing with dirty and dangerous children in an outside world that was real to her" (*L*, 286). Here too are his memories of her fear of loneliness and death ("what's so dreadful about dying is that you are completely on your own": *L*, 286), which makes her suicide unlikely; of her pain on observing the normally affectionate relationship of Avis Byrd and her "wonderful fat pink dad" (*L*, 288); and of her romanesque fantasies about her dead mother—one wonders with what ennobling features she might have restrospectively endowed the father figure ineptly impersonated by Humbert. Even if we do not register these connections consciously, they largely account for the aesthetic satisfaction provided by the ending of the novel. The new insights into Dolly's character are, in fact, discoveries of the multiple links between the novel's images and motifs. The pleasure yielded by such discoveries has an ethical dimension, since it coincides with the redress of an injustice done to a brash yet peculiarly bright and gently courageous girl, an Alice who outgrows her Wonderland. The Coalmont episode is a melodramatic apotheosis in which Humbert gives money and the reader gives credit where the credit has been overdue.

This may of course be romanticizing Dolly, just as Dolly romanticizes her memories of Charlotte. Yet if one is to take responsibility for the coproduction of her story, one may just as well choose the most satisfactory script.

In the end Humbert comes to share Dolly's desire for a return to normality—thus a bereaved person develops the features of a lost loved one. The reader's habitual impulse to exonerate the "I" of a confessional narrative can now be indulged almost with impunity. The respite ends, however, in the scene of Quilty's murder. For all the symbolism of the episode—Humbert is destroying his double, the darker side of himself—its details do not allow one to forget that it depicts a murder. As in *Mary*, the moral and aesthetic significance of the episode conflict: Humbert, who imagines the murder, is after all but an artist *manqué*. In addition to his other, more important faults, he is a pseudo-artist who, like Luzhin in *The Defense*, uses imagination as a substitute for life rather than as a part of it.

The alternative possibility, that Humbert actually receives Dolly's letter and is arrested immediately afterward is suggested by John Ray's reference to the death of Mrs. Richard F. Schiller on Christmas Day 1952 in Gray Star, Alaska. This reference confirms the news of Dolly's marriage, pregnancy, and plans to go to Alaska as reported in her letter. In other words, if the impression that Dolly's letter is a product of Humbert's wish-fulfilling imagination (and that we do not know what actually happened to her) is there to remind us of the possibly horrible fate that victims of child molestation do not always escape, the confirmation of her marriage and move to Alaska sanctions an outwardly less cruel finale: she may, indeed, have effected her return to normal life in exactly the way Humbert imagines her to have done. Dolly's move to Alaska and death in childbirth are supported by John Ray's evidence because they are integral parts of the symbolism with which Nabokov (and Aubrey McFate) infuse the story of Humbert.

VI

In his "Philosophy of Composition" Poe chooses the death of a beautiful woman as the most fruitful subject for poetry. The beautiful woman in question is the Lenore of "The Raven." "Lenore" is, likewise, one of the names with which Humbert addresses Dolly (see L, 209), though the allusion is to Gottfried August Bürger's ballad rather than to Poe's poem.[27] Moreover, in the penultimate paragraph, Humbert writes: "The following decision I make with all the legal impact and support of a signed testament: I wish this memoir to be published only when Lolita is no longer alive," thus preparing us for the elegiac tone of the famous last two sentences with their "aurochs and angels" (L, 310–11). This is a proper climax for the intertextual mold into which Humbert has been pouring his experience, a mold in which Poe's "Cask of Amontillado" and "William Wilson" accommodate the Humbert-Quilty relationship, whereas "Annabel Lee" and "Ligea" are used as direct and oblique precedents for Humbert's relationships with Annabel Leigh and Dolly Haze.[28]

But, Dolly does not die for the sake of being immortalized in gushes of "romantic slosh." What, then, is the real function of her death in childbirth?

---

[27]See Appel's note 5 to p. 209 (L, 400).

[28]For Humbert's allusions to Poe, see Appel's note 2 to p. 11 (L, 330–33), which also cites earlier commentaries. Other interesting observations on the subject have been made in Lucy Maddox, *Nabokov's Novels in English* (Athens, Ga., 1983), pp. 74–75; and in Tamir-Ghez, "The Art of Persuasion in Nabokov's *Lolita*," pp. 170–71.

The epilogue-style information about Mrs. Schiller's death in Gray Star reestablishes Dolly's image in its proper dimensions: she is not Poe's nebulous *femme fatale* but a very real abused child. This does not diminish her stature, however: the fate of one "waif" (*L*, 289) is tragic enough to lend her the grandeur of the Outcast of the Universe, a figure of mythic proportions into which Hawthorne transformed his somewhat sordid middle-class Londoner by the name of Wakefield: "Amid the seeming confusion of our mysterious world, individuals are so nicely adjusted to a system, and systems to one another and to a whole, that, by stepping aside for a moment, a man exposes himself to a fearful risk of losing his place forever. Like Wakefield, he may become, as it were, the Outcast of the Universe."[29]

Humbert has led Dolly too far astray to allow her a safe return to normality. The murder of Quilty objectifies a symbolic murder of Dolly. There is, of course, no necessary causal link between Humbert's molestation of her and her death in childbirth in Alaska about two years later. The later event is not the consequence of the earlier one but

---

[29]Hawthorne, "Wakefield," in *Complete Novels and Selected Tales*, p. 926. I have no evidence that Nabokov had read Hawthorne prior to writing *Lolita*, though the changes made in preparing the manuscript of *Laughter in the Dark* (see Chapter 7 above) suggest that he is likely to have done so. Only once in a 1966 interview, did Nabokov refer to Hawthorne, whom he called "a splendid writer" (*SO*, 64); since he paid few compliments to other writers, this remark is not to be dismissed lightly. My essay "Nabokov and the Hawthorne Tradition" points out that upon Nabokov's arrival in America, certain techniques that he had always shared with Hawthorne developed with increased energy—as if catalyzed by a congenial tradition. Nabokov was certainly familiar with Melville by 1947: *Bend Sinister* quotes extracts from *Moby Dick* (see Appel's introduction: *L*, xlviii); and "Pierre Point in Melville Sound," in chapter 9, pt. 1, of *Lolita* (*L*, 35) is an allusion to bk. 9 of Melville's *Pierre* (I am grateful to Charles Feidelson for calling my attention to it). But the fact that Nabokov makes more allusions to Melville than to Hawthorne need not mean that Melville's literary method was closer to his own; on the contrary, his admiration for Melville is free from that touch of uneasiness which may have been produced by a reluctance to recognize a tempermental kinship between Hawthorne and himself. Nabokov shares with both writers a sense that "some certain significance lurks in all things, else all things are little worth, and the round world itself but an empty cipher, except to sell by the cartload, as they do hills about Boston, to fill up some morass in the Milky Way" (Herman Melville, *Moby Dick*, ed. Harold Beaver, [Harmondsworth, 1976], p. 540). For Melville, however, this significance was less dependent on subjective individual perception; hence the courage with which he pursued it, leaving the safe lee shore behind. For Hawthorne and Nabokov, the search for significance was more closely associated with the journey into the individual "self"; hence the element of diffidence that dampened their daring. Yet if what Hawthorne feared to encounter on a "voyage in" was Baudelairean evil (see Feidelson, *Symbolism and American Literature*, pp. 15–16), what Nabokov feared was overwhelming and unappeasable pain.

an emblem of the consequence: Dolly's death stands for the irreparability of the wrong that she has suffered.[30] In Nabokov's early work a woman's death in childbirth is associated with her displacement and waste. The displacement that falls to the lot of Nelly Zilanov in *Glory* or the unnamed heroine of "The Russian Beauty" is political exile; the displacement of Dolly Schiller is her loss of a natural place in her generation.

Humbert realizes the tragedy of this displacement when, soon after her disappearance, he halts on top of the suggestive "friendly abyss" and listens to a "melodious unity of sounds rising like vapor from a small mining town" below: "And soon I realized that all these sounds were of one nature, that no other sounds but these came from the streets of the transparent town, with the women at home and the men away. Reader! What I heard was but the melody of children at play, nothing but that . . . and then I knew that the hopelessly poignant thing was not Lolita's absence from my side, but the absence of her voice from that concord" (*L*, 309–10). By pointing out the relationship between the word *concord* as "musical harmony" and as a synonym of "spectrum" with the French *concours*, Robert J. Levine has shown how intercourse with a "nymphet"—which for Humbert is an *hors-concours* (incomparable) sexual experience—results in depriving a real little girl of her childhood and thereby in pushing Humbert's "ultraviolet darling" outside the spectrum, away from her place in the harmonious system, the concord.[31] Dolly Haze cannot regain her place in the system. Her departure from it is tragic not because it leaves a gap but because, again to adapt Hawthorne's "Wakefield," the gap closes behind her all too soon.[32]

---

[30]Diana Butler, "Lolita Lepidoptera," in Roth, pp. 59–74, claims that the most important passion recorded in *Lolita* is Nabokov's passion for butterflies. Butler goes on to make a statement frequently echoed in Nabokov criticism: "Nabokov tells us that the object of a passion is unimportant, but that the nature of passion is constant" (p. 69). This is not true. In Nabokov's novels, and in *Lolita* in particular, the object of passion is crucially important when it is a human being possessed otherwise than in the lover's imagination. And the nature of passion is not constant: the "itch of being" (*Gl*, p. xiii) felt by the self-sacrificing knight-errant in *Glory* is not the same as the urge of the solipsistic "enchanted hunter" whose hands "have hurt too much too many bodies" (*L*, 276). What Nabokov tells us is that a quest, even if misdirected, may be beautiful only when its inevitable cost is paid by self-sacrifice, not by the victimization of others.

[31]Robert J. Levine, " 'My Ultraviolet Darling': The Loss of Lolita's Childhood," *Modern Fiction Studies*, 25 (1979), 471–79.

[32]See Hawthorne, *Complete Novels and Selected Tales*, p. 923.

Thus Dolly's death is the emblem of the irreversible isolation that she always feared: "What's so dreadful about dying is that you are completely on your own" (*L*, 286). However, it must be borne in mind that in Nabokov the recurrent conception of death is also that of a merger, a merger of the body with the surroundings and of the limited human consciousness with the "infinite consciousness" in which the boundaries of identity dissolve. Nabokov's healthy characters—like Pnin, whose heart attack in the Whitchurch park is a surmountable weakness of the body alone—abhor the threat of a merger. Before her first night with Humbert, Dolly likewise expresses a comic resentment of the idea by willfully misquoting what must have been the text of her Camp Q brochure: "We loved the sings around the fire in the big stone fireplace or under the darned stars, where every girl merged her own spirit of happiness with the voice of the group" (*L*, 116).

Merger—loss of identity, loss of discreteness—is death. "The cranium," Nabokov writes in *Pnin*, "is a space traveler's helmet. Stay inside or you perish. Death is divestment, death is communion. It may be wonderful to mix with the landscape, but to do so is the end of the tender ego" (*P*, 20). Normal life is not a merger but a harmony of individuals, with the borderlines between them defined. It is from this harmony that Dolly is pushed into an eventual merger—with the book that bears the name given her by Humbert. Like Vasiliy Shishkov in Nabokov's eponymous prewar story, she dies, so to say, into the book.

Yet why in Alaska? Because "nymphets do not occur in polar regions" (*L*, 35)? But Dolly is no longer a "nymphet." Rather, it is because Alaska had a personal significance for Nabokov and his generation. It once belonged to Russia, and Alexander II parted with it as placidly as, after the revolution, the new regime parted with or destroyed the intellectual elite of its country. To adapt once again the language of *The Gift*, Russia pined for both when she came to her senses too late. In *Pnin*, Nabokov pays his tribute to the exiled Russian "intelligentsia." It is also not accidental that among the historical episodes he would like to have filmed, Nabokov mentions the *Lolita*-related scenes of "Poe's wedding" and "Lewis Carroll's picnics" and, immediately afterward, "The Russians leaving Alaska, delighted with the deal. Shot of a seal applauding" (*SO*, 61).[33] Alaska is an emblem

---

[33]Immediately preceding these imaginary shots in the list is "Herman Melville at breakfast, feeding a sardine to his cat" (*SO*, 61). The image is similar to that of a

of the motif of displacement, the common denominator of *Lolita* and Nabokov's stories of émigré life. The use of this emblem expresses a belief that one infinity is no smaller than another: the story of one girl's life is not trivial, even though it comes on the heels of historical cataclysms that caused the suffering of millions.

In *Poems and Problems* Nabokov notes that the first strophe of his 1959 Russian-language poem *"Kakoe sdelal ya durnoye delo"* (What is the evil deed) "imitates the beginning of Boris Pasternak's poem in which he points out that his [*Doctor Zhivago*] 'made the whole world shed tears over the beauty of [his] native land.' " In a literal English translation, Nabokov's stanza runs as follows:

> What is the evil deed I have committed?
> Seducer, criminal—is this the word
> for me who set the entire world a-dreaming
> of my poor little girl?
>
> [*PP*, 147]

The less comprehending members of the Russian émigré community were enraged by the substitution of a depraved little American for their long-suffering fatherland, yet Nabokov was far from betraying or forgetting his "roots."[34] He was just as far, however, from allowing that the fate of one girl should be eclipsed by the mass horrors of the revolution or war (symbolically, Humbert spends the World War II period shuttling in and out of psychiatric sanatoria). Even Humbert knows that if it can be proved to him "that in the infinite run it does not matter a jot that a North American girl-child named Dolores Haze had been deprived of her childhood by a maniac," then "life is a joke" (*L*, 285). (This may be one reason for Nabokov's impatience with Hemingway's novels about Spain; see *SO*, 80.) The indignant émigré critics, trained to think "on a larger scale," might find themselves

---

tearful Ivonna Ivanovna carrying a saucer of milk for a cat after Fyodor's father's departure on his last expedition (in *The Gift*); and to that of Pnin feeding his dog after learning that he is soon to lose his job at Waindell (there is no reason "a human's misfortune should interfere with a canine's pleasures": *P*, 171).

[34]The last stanza of the poem runs: "Amusing, though, that at the last indention, / despite proofreader's and my age's ban, / a Russian branch's shadow shall be playing / upon the marble of my hand" (*PP*, 147). In Nabokov's "Recruiting" the quivering shade of a linden branch seems to "erase" whatever it falls upon. It is the shade of a Russian branch that erases the coldly and somewhat funereally congealed hand that has constructed the world of *Lolita*.

having come full circle to the slogan of postrevolutionary Russia: "Chips fly when trees are cut."

The metaphysical background of *Lolita* is, as usual in Nabokov, inseparable from its ethical principle. Both proclaim that the destruction of a single life, or of a single childhood, is a crime of cosmic dimension. It does not eclipse the well-known mass crimes; rather, those infinite crimes emerge as one infinity multiplied by any number that extends endlessly beyond the threshold of consciousness. In the receding distance the individual worlds of the victims merge irreversibly, only seldom allowing our imagination to retrieve for a brief while the discrete identities of some. In Nabokov's novels the gradual evocation of the characters and their ultimate dissolution reenact the working of humanistic imagination when it wishes to pay a well-meaning yet inescapably, avowedly inadequate tribute to the shades that it conjures up from the mass grave of history. That is the intrinsic ethical dimension of his self-conscious art.

12

Conclusion

"By all means place the 'how' above the 'what,' " is Nabokov's advice to critics, "but do not let it be confused with the 'so what' " (*SO*, 66). If the "how" stands for the local felicities of good writing, then the "so what" refers to their integration into a work's general design. But if the "how" stands for the general design, then the "so what" must be the mystery of the literary structure, the moral aspect of the relationship between the content and the form. Nabokov does not merely pay lip service to morality when he makes Humbert "quote" the following couplet of a nonexistent "old poet":

> The moral sense in mortals is the duty
> We have to pay on mortal sense of beauty.
> [*L*, 285]

"The mortal sense of beauty" is a euphemism for carnal pleasure, the pleasure of the senses that must be held in check by one's moral alertness. Yet in the case of aesthetic enjoyment divorced from the gratification of more basic needs, the "moral sense" is not a tax to be paid but a vital dimension of the experience. To put it metaphorically, the "aesthetic bliss" and the "moral sense" are Siamese twins: the disease of one menaces the life of the other. It is noteworthy that *Nabokov's Dozen*, which is largely a programmatic collection of short stories, includes a fragment called "Scenes from the Life of a Double Monster" (written approximately three years after *Lolita*), which realizes, as it were, the metaphor of the Siamese twins.

Such a statement amounts, of course, to treading on thin ice; it is time to recollect the ice of the puddles where Nabokov's toy trains sank near the Hotel Oranien (see *SM*, 27). "Ask yourself if the symbol you have detected is not your own footprint. Ignore allegories," says Nabokov in the interview quoted above (*SO*, 66). And yet in *Bend*

Sinister the puddle that forms a gateway between contiguous worlds does have the shape of someone or other's footprint. Time and again one is tempted to start playing Nabokov's cryptographic games, if only to reduce the "high seriousness" that creeps into any conversation on aesthetics-*cum*-morality.

This is because the conversation must continue. Throughout his career Nabokov sought an integral unity of virtuoso technique and humanistic content; this search is also the major recurrent theme in his novels. His fiction is a city of many gates. There are avenues leading to the center from any gate, though there are also numerous discoveries to make and blind alleys to stray into on the way. The segments of the city, each an architectonic feat in its own right, offer a grateful context for one another, but this context—as well as some caryatids and bridges—must be constructed (building can be edifying) by the wanderer's own imagination. The aesthetic in Nabokov is inseparable from the ethical: both author and reader must take responsibility for the worlds that they "invent."

The aesthetic is, at the same time, the anaesthetic because, among other things, it silences the suffering and the desires of the consumer world. And it is not mere wordplay to claim that in Nabokov the aesthetic is also closely linked with the synaesthetic: synaesthesia—the blending of the senses which he experienced most concretely as *audition colorée* and attempted to convey through the tremulous images that make up the landscapes and portraits in his fiction—is a promise of transcendent reality waiting just beyond the bend. In the utopia erected by Nabokov in collaboration with the reader, moments of aesthetic bliss are among the repetitions of that promise.

Bibliography of Works Cited

Alter, Robert. *Fielding and the Nature of the Novel*. Cambridge, Mass.: Harvard University Press, 1968.

——. *"Invitation to a Beheading:* Nabokov and the Art of Politics." In Appel and Newman, *Nabokov,* pp. 41–59.

——. "Nabokov's Game of Worlds." In *Partial Magic.* Berkeley: University of California Press, 1975, pp. 180–217.

Appel, Alfred, Jr. *Nabokov's Dark Cinema.* New York: Oxford University Press, 1974.

——. "Nabokov's Puppet Show." In Jerome Charyn, ed., *The Single Voice,* pp. 87–93. London: Collier Macmillan, 1969.

Appel, Alfred, Jr., and Charles Newman, eds. *Nabokov: Criticism, Reminiscences, Translations, and Tributes.* London: Weidenfeld & Nicolson, 1971.

Bachelard, Gaston. *The Poetics of Space,* trans. Maria Jolas. Boston: Beacon Press, 1969.

Bader, Julia. *Crystal Land: Artifice in Nabokov's English Novels.* Berkeley: University of California Press, 1972.

Baer, Joachim T., and Norman W. Ingham, eds. *Mnemozina: Studia literaria russica in honorem Vsevolod Setchkarev.* Munich: Wilhelm Fink, 1974.

Bakhtin, Mikhail. *Problems of Dostoevsky's Poetics,* ed. and trans. Caryl Emerson. Minneapolis: University of Minnesota Press, 1984.

Bal, Mieke. "Mise en abyme et iconicité." *Littérature,* 29 (1978), 116–28.

Barabtarlo, Gene. "Pushkin Embedded." *Vladimir Nabokov Research Newsletter,* 8 (1982), 28–31.

Bensick, Carol. "His Folly, Her Weakness: Demystified Adultery in *The Scarlet Letter."* In Michael Colacurcio, ed., *New Essays on The Scarlet Letter,* pp. 137–59. Cambridge: Cambridge University Press, 1985.

Bergson, Henri. "Laughter." In *Comedy,* pp. 61–190. Garden City, N. Y.: Doubleday Anchor Books, 1956.

——. *Matter and Memory,* trans. Nancy Margaret Paul and W. Scott Palmer. London: Allen & Unwin, 1929.

Bienstock, Beverly Gray. "Focus Pocus: Film Imagery in *Bend Sinister."* In Rivers and Nicol, *Fifth Arc,* pp. 125–38.

Bloom, Harold. *The Anxiety of Influence: A Theory of Poetry.* New York: Oxford University Press, 1973.

Boegman, Margaret Byrd. "*Invitation to a Beheading* and the Many Shades of Kafka." In Rivers and Nicol, *Fifth Arc,* pp. 105–16.

Booth, Wayne. *The Rhetoric of Fiction.* Chicago: University of Chicago Press, 1961.

Borges, Jorge Luis. *Labyrinths.* New York: New Directions, 1964.

——. "Narrative Art and Magic." *Triquarterly,* 25 (Fall 1972), 209–15.

Boyd, Brian. *Nabokov's "Ada": The Place of Consciousness.* Ann Arbor, Mich.: Ardis, 1985.

Butler, Diana. "Lolita Lepidoptera." In Roth, *Critical Essays,* pp. 59–74. Reprinted from *New World Writing,* 16 (1960), 58–84.

Carroll, William. "Nabokov's Signs and Symbols." In Proffer, *Book of Things,* pp. 203–17.

Cavell, Stanley. *Pursuits of Happiness: The Hollywood Comedy of Remarriage.* Cambridge, Mass: Harvard University Press, 1981.

——. *The Senses of "Walden."* San Francisco: North Point Press, 1981.

Chekhov. *See* Tchehov, A. P.

Clifton, Gladys M. "Humbert Humbert and the Limits of Artistic License." In Rivers and Nicol, *Fifth Arc,* pp. 153–70.

Couturier, Maurice. *Nabokov.* Lausanne: L'Age d'Homme, 1979.

Cowart, David. "Art and Exile: Nabokov's *Pnin.*" *Studies in American Fiction,* 10 (1982), 197–207.

Dällenbach, Lucien. *Le récit spéculaire: Essay sur le mise in abyme.* Paris: Seuil, 1977.

Davydov, Sergei. "*The Gift:* Nabokov's Aesthetic Exorcism of Chernyshevskii." *Canadian-American Slavic Studies,* 19 (1985), 357–74.

——. *Teksty-Matreshki Vladimira Nabokova.* Munich: Otto Sagner, 1982.

De Jonge, Alex. "Nabokov's Uses of Pattern." In Quennell, *Nabokov: A Tribute,* pp. 59–72.

Dembo, L. S., ed. *Nabokov: The Man and His Work.* Madison: University of Wisconsin Press, 1967. Reprinted from *Wisconsin Studies in Contemporary Literature,* 8, no. 2 (1967), special issue devoted to Vladimir Nabokov.

Dickens, Charles. *Hard Times,* ed. David Craig. Harmondsworth: Penguin Books, 1978.

Dillard, Richard. "Not Text but Texture: The Novels of Vladimir Nabokov." In R. H. W. Dillard, George Garrett, and John Rees Moore, eds., *The Sounder Few: Essays from the Hollins Critic,* pp. 139–71. Athens: University of Georgia Press, 1971.

Ejkhenbaum, Boris. "Kak sdelana 'Shinel'' Gogolia" (How Gogol's "The Overcoat" Is Made) and "Illiuziya Skaza" (The "Skaz" illusion). In Jurij Striedter, comp., *Texte der Russischen Formalisten,* 1:122–58, 160–66. Munich: Wilhelm Fink, 1969.

Eliade, Mircea. *The Sacred and the Profane*. New York: Harcourt Brace & World, 1959.

Emerson, Ralph Waldo. *The Complete Works*. New York: AMS Press, 1968.

Feidelson, Charles. *Symbolism and American Literature*. Chicago: University of Chicago Press, 1953.

Field, Andrew. *Nabokov: His Life in Art*. Boston: Little, Brown, 1967.

Filonov Gove, Antonina. "Multilingualism and Ranges of Tone in Nabokov's *Bend Sinister.*" *Slavic Review*, 32 (1973), 79–90.

Fitzgerald, F. Scott. *The Great Gatsby*. Harmondsworth: Penguin Books, 1986.

Fontanier, Pierre. *Les figures du discours*. Paris: Flammarion, 1977.

Foster, Ludmila A. "Nabokov's Gnostic Turpitude: The Surrealistic Vision of Reality in *Priglashenie na kazn'.*" In Baer and Ingham, *Mnemozina*, pp. 117–29.

Fowler, Douglas. *Reading Nabokov*. Ithaca: Cornell University Press, 1974.

Garrett-Goodyear, J. H. " 'The Rapture of Endless Approximation': The Role of the Narrator in *Pnin*," *Journal of Narrative Technique*, 16 (1986), 192–203.

Genette, Gérard. *Narrative Discourse: An Essay in Method*, trans. Jane E. Lewin. Ithaca: Cornell University Press, 1980.

Gibian, George, and Stephen Jan Parker, eds. *The Achievements of Vladimir Nabokov*. Ithaca: Cornell University Center for International Studies, 1984.

Gide, André. *Journal 1889–1939*. Paris: Gallimard, 1948.

Gombrich, E. H. *Art and Illusion: A Study in the Psychology of Pictorial Representation*. London: Phaidon Press, 1962.

Grabes, Herbert. *Fictitious Biographies: Vladimir Nabokov's English Novels*, trans. Pamela Gliniars and Herbert Grabes. The Hague: Mouton, 1977.

Grams, Paul. "*Pnin*: The Biographer as Meddler." In Proffer, *Book of Things*, pp. 193–202.

Grayson, Jane. *Nabokov's Translated: A Comparison of Nabokov's Russian and English Prose*. Oxford University Press, 1977.

Haardt, Robert. *Gnosis: Character and Testimony*, trans. J. F. Hendry. Leiden: E. J. Brill, 1971.

Hagopian, John V. "Decoding Nabokov's 'Signs and Symbols.' " *Studies in Short Fiction*, Spring 1981, 115–19.

Hardy, Thomas. *Tess of the d'Urbervilles*. Harmondsworth: Penguin Books, 1982.

Hawthorne, Nathaniel. *The Complete Novels and Selected Tales of Nathaniel Hawthorne*, ed. Normal Holmes Pearson. New York: Random House, 1937.

Hirsch, E. D. *Validity in Interpretation*. New Haven, Conn.: Yale University Press, 1967.

Hofstadter, Douglas R. *Gödel, Escher, Bach: An Eternal Golden Braid*. Harmondsworth: Penguin Books, 1980.

Hyde, G. M. *Vladimir Nabokov: America's Russian Novelist.* London: Marion Boyars, 1977.

Hyman, Stanley Edgar. "The Handle: *Invitation to a Beheading* and *Bend Sinister.*" In Appel and Newman, *Nabokov*, pp. 60–71.

Iser, Wolfgang. *The Act of Reading: A Theory of Aesthetic Response.* Baltimore, Md.: Johns Hopkins University Press, 1978.

Johnson, Donald Barton. "Eyeing Nabokov's *Eye.*" *Canadian-American Slavic Studies*, 19 (1985), 328–50.

——. "Nabokov as a Man-of-Letters: The Alphabetic Motif in His Work." *Modern Fiction Studies*, 25 (1979), 397–412.

——. *Worlds in Regression: Some Novels of Vladimir Nabokov.* Ann Arbor, Mich.: Ardis, 1985.

Karlinsky, Simon. "Vladimir Nabokov's Novel *Dar* as a Work of Literary Criticism: A Structural Analysis." *Slavic and East European Journal*, 7 (1963), 284–90.

——, ed. *The Nabokov-Wilson Letters, 1940–1971.* New York: Harper Colophon Books, 1980.

Khodasevich, Vladislav. "On Sirin." In Appel and Newman, *Nabokov*, pp. 96–101.

Lee, Lawrence L. *Vladimir Nabokov.* Boston: Twayne, 1976.

Levine, Robert J. " 'My Ultraviolet Darling': The Loss of Lolita's Childhood." *Modern Fiction Studies*, 25 (1979), 471–79.

Lokrantz, Jessie Thomas. *The Underside of the Weave: Some Stylistic Devices Used by Vladimir Nabokov.* Uppsala: Acta Universitatis Uppsaliensis, 1973.

Maddox, Lucy. *Nabokov's Novels in English.* Athens: University of Georgia Press, 1983.

Mandelstam, Osip. *The Prose of Osip Mandelstam*, trans. Clarence Brown. Princeton, N.J.: Princeton University Press, 1967.

Mason, Bobbie Ann. *Nabokov's Garden: A Guide to "Ada."* Ann Arbor, Mich.: Ardis, 1974.

Melville, Herman. *Moby Dick*, ed. Harold Beaver. Harmondsworth: Penguin Books, 1976.

Merivale, Patricia. "The Flaunting of Artifice in Vladimir Nabokov and Jorge Luis Borges." In Dembo, *Nabokov*, pp. 209–24.

Meyer, Priscilla. "Nabokov's *Lolita* and Pushkin's *Onegin*: McAdam, McEve, and McFate." In Gibian and Parker, *Achievements*, 179–211.

Miller, Perry. *The Raven and the Whale: The War of Words and Wits in the Era of Poe and Melville.* New York: Harcourt, Brace & World, 1956.

Moody, Fred. "At *Pnin's* Center." *Russian Literature Triquarterly*, 14 (1976), 70–83.

——. "Nabokov's Gambit." *Russian Literature Triquarterly*, 14 (1976), 67–70.

Morton, Donald. *Vladimir Nabokov.* New York: Frederick Ungar, 1974.

Moynahan, Julian. "A Russian Preface for Nabokov's *Beheading.*" *Novel*, 1, (1967), 12–18.

——. *Vladimir Nabokov.* Minneapolis: University of Minnesota Press, 1971.

Murray, Isobel. " 'Plagiatisme,' Nabokov's 'The Vane Sisters,' and *The Picture of Dorian Gray.*" *Durham University Journal*, 70 (December 1977), 69–72.

Nabokov, Vladimir. *Lolita* (Russian translation). Ann Arbor, Mich.: Ardis, 1967.

Nicol, Charles. "The Mirrors of Sebastian Knight." In Dembo, *Nabokov*, pp. 85–94.

——. "Pnin's History." In Roth, *Critical Essays*, pp. 93–105.

O'Connor, Catherine Tiernan. "Nabokov's *The Real Life of Sebastian Knight:* In Pursuit of a Biography." In Baer and Ingham, *Mnemozina*, pp. 281–93.

Packman, David. *Vladimir Nabokov: The Structure of Literary Desire.* Columbia: University of Missouri Press, 1982.

Parker, Stephen Jan. "Nabokov Studies: The State of the Art." In Gibian and Parker, *Achievements*, pp. 81–97.

Patteson, Richard F. "Nabokov's *Bend Sinister:* The Narrator as God." *Studies in American Fiction*, 5 (1977), 241–53.

Peterson, Dale E. "Nabokov's *Invitation:* Literature as Execution." *PMLA*, 96 (1981), 824–36.

Petty, Chapel Louise. "A Comparison of Hawthorne's 'Wakefield' and 'The Leonardo': Narrative Commentary and the Struggle of the Literary Artist." *Modern Fiction Studies*, 25 (1979), 499–507.

Pifer, Ellen. *Nabokov and the Novel.* Cambridge, Mass.: Harvard University Press, 1980.

Proffer, Carl R. "From *Otchaianie* to *Despair.*" *Slavic Review*, 27 (1968), 258–67.

——. "A New Deck for Nabokov's Knaves." In Appel and Newman, *Nabokov*, pp. 293–309.

——. *The Simile and Gogol's "Dead Souls."* The Hague: Mouton, 1967.

——, ed. *A Book of Things about Vladimir Nabokov.* Ann Arbor, Mich.: Ardis, 1974.

Purdy, Strother B. "Solus Rex: Nabokov and the Chess Novel." *Modern Fiction Studies*, 14 (Winter 1968–69), 379–95.

Quennell, Peter, ed. *Vladimir Nabokov: A Tribute.* New York: William Morrow, 1980.

Rampton, David. *Vladimir Nabokov: A Critical Study of the Novels.* London: Cambridge University Press, 1984.

Richter, David H. "Narrative Entrapment in *Pnin* and 'Signs and Symbols.' " *Papers on Language and Literature*, 20 (1984), 418–30.

Rimmon, Shlomith. *The Concept of Ambiguity—The Example of James.* Chicago: University of Chicago Press, 1977.

———. "Problems of Voice in Nabokov's *The Real Life of Sebastian Knight.*" In Roth, *Critical Essays,* pp. 109–29. Reprinted from *PTL (A Journal for Descriptive Poetics and Theory of Literature),* 1 (1976), 489–512.

Rivers, J. E., and Charles Nicol, eds. *Nabokov's Fifth Arc: Nabokov and Others on His Life's Work.* Austin: University of Texas Press, 1982.

Rosenfield, Claire. "*Despair* and the Lust for Immorality." In Dembo, *Nabokov,* pp. 66–84.

Rosenzweig, Paul J. "The Importance of Reader Response in Nabokov's 'Signs and Symbols.' " *Essays in Literature,* 7 (1980), 255–60.

Ross, Charles S., "Nabokov's Mistress-Muse Metaphor: Some Recent Books." *Modern Fiction Studies,* 25 (1979), 514–24.

Roth, Phyllis A., ed. *Critical Essays on Vladimir Nabokov.* Boston: G. K. Hall, 1984.

Rowe, W. W. *Nabokov and Others: Patterns in Russian Literature.* Ann Arbor, Mich.: Ardis, 1979.

———. *Nabokov's Spectral Dimension.* Ann Arbor, Mich.: Ardis, 1981.

Salehar, Anna Maria. "Nabokov's *Gift:* An Apprenticeship in Creativity." In Proffer, *Book of Things,* pp. 70–83.

Sartre, Jean-Paul. *Literary and Philosophical Essays,* trans. Annette Michelson. New York: Collier Books, 1962.

Schaeffer, Susan F. "*Bend Sinister* and the Novelist as Anthropomorphic Deity." *Centennial Review,* 17 (1973), 115–51.

Schopenhauer, Arthur. *The World as Will and Representation,* trans. E. F. J. Payne. New York: Dover, 1969.

Shapiro, Gavriel. "Russkie literaturnye alliuzii v romane Nabokova *Priglashenie na kazn'.*" *Russian Literature,* 9 (1981), 369–78.

Sheidlower, David I. "Reading between the Lines and the Squares." *Modern Fiction Studies,* 25 (1979), 413–25.

Sokolov, Sasha. *Mezhdu sobakoi i volkom* (Between dog and wolf). Ann Arbor, Mich.: Ardis, 1980.

Stegner, Page. *Escape into Aesthetics: The Art of Vladimir Nabokov.* New York: Dial Press, 1966.

Struve, Gleb. "Notes on Nabokov as a Russian Writer." In Dembo, *Nabokov,* pp. 45–46.

Stuart, Dabney. *Nabokov: The Dimensions of Parody.* Baton Rouge: Louisiana State University Press, 1978.

Suagee, Stephen. "An Artist's Memory Beats All Other Kinds: An Essay on *Despair.*" In Proffer, *Book of Things,* pp. 54–62.

Tamir-Ghez, Nomi. "The Art of Persuasion in Nabokov's *Lolita.*" In Roth, *Critical Essays,* pp. 157–76. Reprinted from *Poetics Today,* 1 (1979), 65–83.

Tchehov, A. P. *The Cherry Orchard and Other Plays,* trans. Constance Garnett. London: Chatto & Windus, 1965.

Tekiner, Christina. "Time in *Lolita*." *Modern Fiction Studies*, 25 (1979), 463–69.

Thoreau, Henry David. *Walden, or Life in the Woods*. New York: Rinehart, 1950.

Toker, Leona. "Between Allusion and Coincidence: Nabokov, Dickens, and Others." *HSLA (Hebrew University Studies in Literature and the Arts)*, 12 (1984), 175–98.

———. "Nabokov and the Hawthorne Tradition." *Scripta Hierosolymitana*, 32 (1987), 323–49.

———. "A Nabokovian Character in Conrad's *Nostromo*." *Revue de littérature comparée*, no. 1 (1985), 15–29.

———. "Self-Conscious Paralepsis in Vladimir Nabokov's 'Recruiting' and *Pnin*." *Poetics Today*, 7 (1986), 459–69.

Updike, John. "Grandmaster Nabokov." In *Assorted Prose*, pp. 318–27. New York: Alfred A. Knopf, 1965.

Varshavskii, V. Review of *Podvig*. *Tchisla*, 7–8 (1933), 266–67.

White, Edmund. "Nabokov: Beyond Parody." In Gibian and Parker, *Achievements*, pp. 5–27.

Index

239

Library of Congress Cataloging-in-Publication Data

Toker, Leona.
  Nabokov: the mystery of literary structures.

  Bibliography: p.
  Includes index.
  1. Nabokov, Vladimir Vladimirovich, 1899–1977—Criticism and interpreta-
tion. I. Title.
PG3476.N3Z895   1989   813'.54   88–47927
ISBN 0–8014–2211–6 (alk. paper)